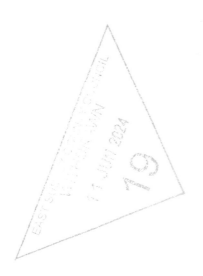

Cross Channel and Short Sea Ferries

An Illustrated History

Cross Channel and Short Sea Ferries

An Illustrated History

Ambrose Greenway

Seaforth
PUBLISHING

Half title page photo: *Koningin Wilhelmina*, see page 55.
Title page photo: *Canterbury*, see page 120.

Copyright © Ambrose Greenway 2014

First published in Great Britain in 2014 by
Seaforth Publishing,
Pen & Sword Books Ltd,
47 Church Street,
Barnsley S70 2AS

www.seaforthpublishing.com

British Library Cataloguing in Publication Data
A catalogue record for this book is available from the British Library

ISBN 978 1 84832 170 0

Typeset and designed by Ian Hughes, Mousemat Design Limited
Printed and bound in China by 1010 Printing International Ltd

Contents

Preface

There is a natural blurring between cross-channel and short-sea ferries and a further complication arises in that a number of coastal passenger steamers can also be described as ferries for certain sections of their routes.

As there is a limit to how much can be squeezed into one publication, I have had to restrict my choice of subjects to the traditional types of passenger ferry, often referred to as 'classic' vessels, in order to provide world coverage. This has meant excluding both car and train ferries which are separate subjects in themselves. The former have already been well covered but I have made an exception for what I term 'interim' vessels that resembled traditional ferries with normal bow and stern but nevertheless incorporated a full vehicle deck accessed through side doors and ramps.

As far as short-sea vessels are concerned, those operating across the North Sea and the Mediterranean dominate and I have limited my selection to ships which made regular international voyages lasting no more than 24 hours, thus excluding many of the earlier vessels. I have, however, made a few exceptions in order to include a number of interesting ships that made longer voyages such as the Swedish Lloyd ships running between Gothenburg and London, Nippon Yusen Kaisha's *Nagasaki Maru* pair on the Nagasaki–Shanghai route and P&O's *Isis* and *Osiris* which ran between Brindisi and Port Said, a voyage of nearly 1,000 miles taking just under two days, but which in appearance and performance were similar to cross-channel steamers.

Excursion vessels are another stand-alone subject but I have included the Isle Man steamers which in addition to their seasonal holiday traffic also maintained a year-round lifeline to the island and were without doubt the equivalent of cross-channel steamers. I have also regarded worthy of inclusion the Canadian vessels primarily engaged in ferry as opposed to coastal service, such as those linking the cities of Vancouver, Victoria and Seattle and running across the Bay of Fundy. The estuarial ferries linking Buenos Aires with Montevideo across the shallow River Plate estuary are also included as they have not received much coverage hitherto.

I make no claim as to comprehensiveness but I hope that my selection will provide a broad picture of the development of these attractive and hard-working ships which were loved by some and hated by others, especially those who suffered from *mal-de-mer*.

I would like to express my gratitude to all who have provided assistance and photographs, especially Barbara Jones, Anne Cowne and the ever helpful team at Lloyd's Register of Shipping Information Services; Roger Jordan and Bruce Peter; also the excellent websites Miramar Ship Index and Histarmar. Despite my best endeavours, I have been unable to trace the original source of a number of old photographs and if I have infringed anyone's copyright I can only apologise.

Finally, and most of all, I would like thank my long-suffering wife who has been effectively widowed for long stretches at a time by 'that hateful computer'.

AMBROSE GREENWAY MOREBATH JANUARY 2014

Introduction

Cross-channel steamers

The cross-channel steamer is a peculiarly British phenomenon and owes its development first and foremost to the geographical make-up and position of the British Isles. To the west of the mainland lay Ireland, an integral part of the United Kingdom until 1922, with the small Isle of Man positioned in between in the Irish Sea. To the south the Channel Islands lay close to France on the southern side of the English Channel. Connections could only be maintained by sea, initially by sailing ships on an irregular basis, but later by steamships carrying both passengers and mail. In addition to these domestic routes, another network of services developed to the European mainland, just twenty miles away at its nearest point across the Dover Strait. Sea connections to France further west increased to sixty-four miles between Newhaven and Dieppe and to as much as 150 miles between Southampton and St Malo. To the east, the Belgian port of Ostend was just over sixty miles from Dover and, although technically not cross-channel services, those linking the UK to Holland across the southern part of the North Sea were nevertheless served by cross-channel-type steamers.

In parallel with Britain, Holland, Belgium and France developed their own cross-channel fleets. In the Mediterranean, some of the ships serving the Balearic Islands, Corsica, Sardinia and Sicily fell somewhere between cross-channel and short-sea ferries. Across the Atlantic, cross-channel-type services ran in the Bay of Fundy in eastern Canada and from Boston to Nova Scotia, while on the west coast the Canadian Pacific Railway Co's services to Vancouver Island and on the 'Triangle route' linking Vancouver, Victoria and Seattle were run by larger ferries that fell somewhere between cross-channel and short-sea steamers. In South America, the River Plate estuary service between Buenos Aires and Montevideo was serviced by overnight ferries, of which pale blue-hulled vessels of Nicolas Mihanovich became a familiar sight.

On the opposite side of the Southern Hemisphere, the Bass Strait crossing between Melbourne and Tasmania was essentially a cross-channel service, while on the inter-island service across New Zealand's Cook Strait, the olive green-hulled ships of the Union Steamship Co of New Zealand became something of an institution. Further north in Japan, railway services developed across the Tsugaru Strait between the islands of Honshu and Hokkaido and from Shimonoseki at the south-western tip of Honshu to Korea, which was annexed to Japan in 1910 and remained so until 1945.

Short-sea vessels

While cross-channel steamers have often been described as miniature liners, this description is perhaps more appropriately applied to short-sea passenger vessels, which operated on longer routes in the 200–500 mile range, primarily across the North Sea and the Mediterranean. The former linked British east coast ports with Bergen, Olso, Gothenburg, Esbjerg and Rotterdam and the ships deployed developed from small cargo steamers into more substantial vessels, several of which also carried passengers. For many years the services were run by Britain's Thomas Wilson, Sons & Co and the Great Central Railway Co, Norway's Bergen Line and Fred Olsen & Co, Sweden's Thule Line and its successor Swedish Lloyd and Denmark's Det Forenede D/S (United Steamship Co: DFDS). Apart from the latter's paddle steamer *Koldinghus* (1883), all of the ships were screw-driven and did not exceed 14 knots in service, which resulted in passage times of over twenty-four hours, placing them beyond the scope of this work. With few exceptions, it was not until the 1920s that the North Sea services began to receive larger and faster tonnage and in 1925, the DFDS *Parkeston* became the first of her type in the world to be propelled by a diesel engine.

In the Mediterranean, the main services linked France with its North African department of Algeria and protectorate of Tunisia, while Spain ran sea connections to its Balearic Islands in addition to its North African enclaves in Melilla and Ceuta.

The railway connection

Another important factor in the development of both cross-channel and short-sea passenger steamers can be attributed to the changes brought about by the Industrial Revolution in the UK. The use of steam as a motive power had profound implications for transport in general and the development of both railways and steamships was accelerated by the drive and innovation of the Victorian era. In shipyards, the use of iron and later steel helped the UK become the leading shipbuilding nation in the world, a position it would retain, apart from emergency wartime construction in the United States, until overtaken by Japan in the 1960s.

The expansion of the UK railway system was to have a profound influence on the development of cross-channel travel. Once their respective tracks had reached the seaports, the railway companies naturally became interested in the sea connections with other parts of the kingdom and the mainland of Europe. However, they were prevented from running their own ships because the Acts of Parliament that had established them in the first place lacked the necessary powers. As an interim measure, they were forced to do deals with existing steamship operators or alternatively establish or provide finance for new companies. Parliamentary powers to run steamships were obtained from 1853 onwards and after absorbing many of the private steamship companies, the way was clear for the railways to play a major part in the development of cross-channel steamers over the next century.

They did not act alone, however, because several private shipping companies had also been developing cross-channel services across the Irish Sea. These were the old-established Glasgow companies of G & J Burns and the Glasgow & Londonderry Steam Packet Co (later Laird Line) and three Irish concerns: Belfast Steamship Co, City of Dublin Steam Packet Co and City of Cork Steam Packet Co. Services generally ran overnight, but the City of Dublin company was an exception, running both day and night services. In 1850 it obtained the contract for the carriage of the Irish mails between Kingstown (today's Dun Laoghaire) and Holyhead and after this was renewed in 1859, it set about replacing its existing ships with four new paddle steamers that were the largest and finest cross-channel ships of their day in addition to ranking among the fastest ships afloat.

The paddle era

The 90-ton wooden paddle steamer *Rob Roy*, built in 1818, is generally regarded as the first regular cross-channel passenger steamer, running initially between the Clyde and Belfast before she moved south in 1821 for service between Dover and Calais. Two years later, she was bought by the French postal administration and her name changed to *Henri Quatre*. Up to this date, mail was carried in sailing packets operated by the British

Post Office, which received its first paddle packets *Dasher* and *Arrow* in 1821–2. In 1823 the running of the postal packets was transferred to the Admiralty and paddle steamers soon began to replace the sailing ships. Iron replaced wood in construction and when the Admiralty withdrew in 1850, the Post Office entered into mail contracts with private steamship companies. Paddle steamers were well suited to cross-channel service because their shallow draught enabled them to operate from still-undeveloped ports, many of which were too shallow to be used at low tide, but they suffered from a major drawback in that their paddle floats were prone to damage by driftwood or heavy seas and the loss of a paddle wheel effectively put a vessel out of action. More efficient feathering paddle floats were patented by William Stroudley, locomotive superintendent of the London, Brighton & South Coast Railway Co, and first used in that company's *Normandy* and *Brittany* in 1882. The early paddle steamers were generally driven by simple oscillating or diagonal engines but gradually these were superseded by compound machinery. Triple-expansion engines appeared fairly late in the development of the paddle steamer and were only used in a handful of vessels.

The last decade of the nineteenth century marked the peak of paddle steamer development and no further vessels were built for cross-channel service in Europe after the steam turbine had made its appearance in 1903. The final ships were quickly relegated to secondary services and only a few remained in service after the First World War. The last disappeared in 1929, but paddle steamers still retained a presence on the River Plate.

Screw-driven steamers

Screw-driven steamers propelled by compound machinery began to appear in the 1870s, initially on routes on which shallow harbours did not present a problem, such as those linking the Clyde with Ireland and Southampton with the Channel Islands. They were more efficient than paddle steamers because their propellers were positioned far enough below the surface of the water so as to be unaffected by most sea conditions. In 1887, the G & J Burns' 771-grt *Hare* became the first cross-channel steamer to employ the more efficient triple-expansion engine, followed a year later by the Glasgow & Londonderry Steam Packet Co's *Ivy*. The London & South Western Railway Co's *Dora* of 1889 became the first English Channel steamer to be so propelled but was quickly eclipsed by the Great Western Railway Co's twin-screw *Lynx* and her two sisters. These in turn engendered a quick response from the London & South Western Railway Co in 1890, with its three larger and faster *Frederica* trio.

The use of triple-expansion machinery became more extensive as ports were deepened by dredging, permitting entry and exit at all states of the tide and allowing fixed schedules to be maintained. The Newhaven–Dieppe service was unique in that it was jointly owned by the London, Brighton & South Coast Railway Co and the Chemin de Fer de l'Ouest. The shareholding was based on the respective rail distances from Newhaven to London and Dieppe to Paris, which worked out at roughly one third and two thirds and although the ships were jointly owned, they were crewed by their country of origin. The first French-built cross-channel passenger ship, *Seine* of 1891, was in many ways an innovator. Not only was she the first twin-screw passenger vessel on the joint service, but also she introduced a rudimentary cruiser stern, which had been pioneered a year earlier in the l'Ouest railway cargo steamers *Anjou* and *Caen*, built by same Le Havre shipyard. She was also the first of her type to have watertube boilers, although these proved troublesome.

Triple-expansion-driven ships proliferated, most having either one or two three-cylinder engines but twin four-cylinder units, which had an extra low pressure cylinder, appeared in 1896 in City of Dublin Steam Packet Co's 24-knot *Ulster*, which was the first of a quartet that were as advanced in terms of size as speed as the 1860 sisters whose names they repeated. Despite the undoubted merits of reciprocating engines, paddle propulsion continued to be used on the shorter Dover Strait and Stranraer–Larne routes.

Steam turbines

The invention of the steam turbine by Charles Parsons was to have a profound effect on merchant ship propulsion. Not only was it much more efficient than paddle propulsion, which had reached the limit of its development, but also it marked an improvement on the reciprocating engine, although lighter and more economical. The South Eastern & Chatham Railway Co's *The Queen* and the London, Brighton & South Coast Railway Co's *Brighton*, which appeared from Wm Denny & Bros a few months apart in 1903, were only the third and fourth merchant ships in the world to be propelled by the new machinery that comprised three steam turbines each driving to a separate propeller shaft. Their success led to further orders and it is worth noting that the shorter crossings on the Dover Strait (including the crossing to Ostend) and between Stranraer and Larne were alone in switching directly from paddle to turbine without being served by reciprocating-engine vessels. The Belgian *Princesse Elisabeth* of 1905 was the first of these early turbine vessels to have a cruiser stern. On the Irish Sea, the Midland Railway Co stole a march on its competitors by stipulating turbine machinery for two of the four new ships built in separate yards in 1904 for overnight Belfast and seasonal Douglas, Isle of Man, services from its newly-completed port at Heysham. The Isle of Man Steam Packet Co countered with its own turbine steamer, *Viking*, and, further north, G & J Burns replaced its paddle steamer *Adder* on the

The 270-grt *Princess Alice* built in 1843 and acquired the following year by the Admiralty was a postal packet on the Dover-Calais run.

Ardrossan–Belfast daytime service with its only turbine steamer, *Viper*. To the south, the Great Western Railway Co built four turbine ships for its new Fishguard–Rosslare service, while Union Steamship Co of New Zealand's Denny-built *Loongana* of 1905 was the first turbine ferry for overseas use and the first to sail in the Southern Hemisphere.

Reciprocating engines continued to be used in several new ships built for overnight Irish Sea services and quadruple-expansion engines were introduced in 1906 in Belfast Steamship Co's *Graphic* and *Heroic* and Dublin & Glasgow Sailing & Steam Packet Co's *Duke of Montrose*.

By 1911, steam turbines had been adopted by most cross-channel operators – the exceptions were Laird Line, the Irish companies and Holland's Zeeland Line. They had also been used to power ferries built in the UK for New Zealand (*Maori*) and Japan (*Hirafu Maru* and *Tamura Maru*), while Parsons engines also propelled France's first turbine steamer *Charles Roux*, which was built at St Nazaire for Compagnie Générale Transatlantique's North Africa services in 1908 and the Italian-built ferries *Città di Catania* and *Città di Palermo* of 1910.

The next development came in 1912 when, following earlier trials in a converted cargo steamer, Sir Charles Parsons' new geared turbines were installed for the first time in the London & South Western Railway Co's twin-screw *Normannia* and *Hantonia*, built by Fairfield Shipbuilding & Engineering Co for the Southampton–Le Havre overnight service. The slower running, single-reduction engines proved to be smoother and more economical than the earlier direct-drive vessels, but were equally suited to powering high-speed ships such as the London, Brighton & South Coast Railway Co's 25-knot *Paris* of 1913. Only a few more direct-drive turbine ships were built and thenceforward geared turbines became firmly established as the most popular choice of propulsion for ferries.

The First World War

Because of their speed and ability to carry large numbers of passengers, both cross-channel and short-sea ships were to prove invaluable in time of war. This had not escaped the notice of the British Admiralty and during the First World War many ships were quickly requisitioned to transport troops across the English Channel, while others were converted to ambulance carriers for returning wounded soldiers to the UK. Further ships were commissioned for specific naval tasks, such as armed boarding steamers, auxiliary minelayers/minesweepers and even early aircraft carriers.

Hospital ships

One of the inevitable consequences of war is the need to evacuate wounded troops from the battlefield. With much of the action in the First World War taking place in the trenches of northern France and Belgium, cross-channel steamers were the most obvious choice for carrying wounded back to base hospitals in the UK and the following were taken up as ambulance carriers for various periods during the conflict and up to May 1920: Great Western Railway – *St Andrew*, *St David*, *St Patrick*; Great Eastern Railway – *St Denis*, *Copenhagen*; London & North Western Railway – *Anglia*, *Cambria*; London, Brighton & South Coast Railway – *Brighton*, *Dieppe*: Chemin de Fer de l'Etat – *Newhaven*; Belgian government – *Jan Breydel*, *Stad Antwerpen*, *Princesse Elisabeth*, *Pieter de Coninck*, *Ville de Liège*; Canadian Pacific Railway – *St George*; Yarmouth Steamship Co – *Prince George*, *Prince Arthur*. These were fitted out with a mixture of berths and cots and capacities generally ranged from around 150 of the former to twenty or thirty of the latter but these figures were exceeded in a number of vessels, notably *Anglia* 244/25, while *Copenhagen* and *St Denis* each had over 100 cots and *Pieter de Coninck* 320 berths.

Armed boarding steamers

The following steamers were taken up in the first few months of the war and commissioned as armed boarding vessels: Great Eastern Railway – *Amsterdam*, *Louvain**, *Vienna*; London & South Western Railway – *Caesarea*, *Sarnia**; London & North Western Railway – *Anglia*, *Cambria*, *Hibernia* (as HMS *Tara**), *Scotia*; Barrow Steam Navigation Co – *City of Belfast*, *Duchess of Devonshire*; Midland Railway – *Duke of Albany**, *Duke of Clarence*, *Duke of Cornwall*; G & J Burns – *Partridge*, *Woodcock* (as HMS *Woodnut*); Laird

The French-built Newhaven–Dieppe steamer *Newhaven* (1912) was one of several cross channel ships which acted as ambulance carriers.

The Isle of Man S P Co's *Snaefell* (1910) operated as an armed boarding steamer until torpedoed in the Mediterranean in June 1918.

Line – *Hazel, Rowan*; Belfast Steamship Co – *Heroic*; Isle of Man Steam Packet Co – *King Orry, Peel Castle, Snaefell*, The Ramsey*.

Lightly armed, they were used to patrol UK waters and intercept any ship that might attempt to beat the blockade of Germany. Later, in support of the Gallipoli campaign, many were transferred to the Mediterranean, where they were used to board neutral steamers and send them to Mudros for inspection. They also assisted in the evacuation of troops from Suvla and Anzac beaches. The majority were retained for the greater part of the war, but *Anglia* and *Cambria* were converted to hospital carriers in April and August 1915 and *Caesarea* was released that

December. *Anglia* was replaced by *Vienna*, which had been used as an accommodation ship and a Q-ship. During the course of the conflict, five vessels were lost to torpedo attack(*) and *The Ramsey* was sunk by gunfire from the German raider *Meteor* (the former Currie Line passenger ship *Vienna*).

Auxiliary minelayers, minesweepers, and netlayers

At the start of the war, the Royal Navy found itself short of fast minelayers and requisitioned several cross-channel steamers to lay mines around the UK and off the northern coast of Germany. Canadian Pacific Railway Co's newly-completed *Princess Margaret* and her incomplete sister *Princess Irene* were requisitioned and converted to large minelayers with a capacity of 500 mines. After making only two voyages, *Princess Irene* blew up off Sheerness while her third cargo of mines was being primed, causing widespread damage and killing 352 persons. The London, Brighton & South Coast Railway Co's *Paris* (140 mines) was one of the fastest channel steamers and is reputed to have comfortably exceeded 25 knots on one occasion when surprised by three German destroyers. The South Eastern & Chatham Railway Co's *Biarritz* (180 mines) was converted in 1915 for the Gallipoli campaign and was briefly joined between May and November of that year by the Great Western Railway Co's smaller *Gazelle*, which carried just fifty mines for laying in the Dardanelles. *Princess Margaret* was retained by the Admiralty after the war.

Four Great Western Railway Co ships were also used for

The London, Brighton & South Coast Railway Co's fast geared turbine steamer *Paris* (1913) was well-suited to her role as a minelayer. (*Newhaven Historical Society*)

minesweeping purposes; *Roebuck* (as HMS *Roedean*), *Reindeer*, *Lynx* (as HMS *Lynn*) and *Gazelle*. *Roedean* was lost in Scapa Flow on 13 January 1915 after dragging her anchor and *Gazelle* spent six months as a minelayer in 1915.

The Isle of Man Steam Packet Co's paddle steamers *Mona's Isle*, *Prince of Wales* (as HMS *Prince Edward*) and *Queen Victoria* were requisitioned to lay anti-submarine nets and the latter pair was transferred to the Mediterranean in 1915 for the Gallipoli campaign.

Seaplane carriers

When war broke out, the Royal Navy's two experimental aircraft carriers, HMS *Hermes* and HMS *Ark Royal*, were out of commission. To meet the shortfall, the Admiralty quickly requisitioned the South Eastern & Chatham Railway Co's steamers *Empress*, *Riviera* and *Engadine* and converted them at Chatham to rudimentary seaplane carriers (three aircraft) by adding temporary canvas hangars aft. The following year, the temporary hangars were replaced by more substantial constructions and two electric cranes for the launching and recovery of aircraft, which had been increased to four. In 1915–16, the Isle of Man Steam Packet Co's steamers *Ben-My-Chree* (four to six aircraft) and *Viking* (renamed

HMS *Vindex*; seven aircraft) and the Midland Railway's *Manxman* (eight aircraft) were taken up and given more extensive conversions, which included fitting twin masts and temporary wooden ramps forward for launching land planes off trolleys. In 1917 the Admiralty took over two more ships that were still under construction, Huddart Parker's *Nairana* and the Great Eastern Railway Co's *Stockholm*, and completed them as HMS *Nairana* (seven aircraft) and HMS *Pegasus* (nine aircraft) respectively. *Ben-My-Chree* was lost on 11 January 1917 when set on fire by Turkish artillery at Kastelorizo and HMS *Pegasus* was retained by the Admiralty after the war and never saw service with her intended owner.

The inter-war period

The period between the two world wars was a turbulent one. An initial boom quickly turned into a slump followed by a period of industrial unrest. The ramifications of the Wall Street Crash in 1929 led in turn to the greatest financial depression the world

The Great Eastern Railway Co's unfinished *Stockholm* was completed in 1917 as the early aircraft carrier HMS *Pegasus*. The large hangar aft housed seaplanes and land planes could be launched over the bow on a temporary wooden ramp.

had yet seen and just when recovery had become established, the world was once again plunged into war.

The early 1920s were marked by the delivery of the four *Anglia* class ships for the London & North Western Railway's Holyhead–Dun Laoghaire service, which finally managed to wrest the mail contract from the City of Dublin Steam Packet Co. These were the largest traditional British cross-channel steamers yet built and were capable of around 25 knots but still retained counter sterns. In France, the government stepped in the help cash-strapped shipowners and ordered four new 'Gouverneur Général' class ships for Compagnie Générale Transatlantique's North Africa services.

The mid 1920s saw major innovations in design and propulsion. The first involved the practice of enclosing promenade decks to provide better shelter for passengers, initially in the Southern Railway Co's Dover Strait sisters *Isle of Thanet* and *Maid of Kent* and the Newhaven–Dieppe service *Worthing*. Prior to this, the open decks of steamers on the shorter daytime services had been constantly swept by spray in poor weather, making them more or less untenable unless protected by temporary canvas screens. Fully enclosed decks quickly became established for new tonnage and several operators partially or fully plated in the open decks of some of their existing ships during refits.

First motorships

The other great change involved the first use of diesel propulsion in the short-sea passenger sector. Thirteen years after Det Ostasiatiske D/S (East Asiatic Company) had pioneered the deep sea use of diesel propulsion in its *Selandia* in 1912, another Danish shipowner, Det Forenede (United Steamship Company: DFDS), introduced its new motor vessel *Parkeston* onto the Esbjerg–Harwich service. Her success led to the construction of three sister ships and thereafter the company never built another steamship. Four years later the first cross-channel motorship made its debut from Harland & Wolff's Belfast shipyard. Distinctive in shape with a three-island type hull and two squat funnels, the advanced *Ulster Monarch* was the first of a trio of vessels for Belfast Steamship Company's overnight Liverpool service. The City of Cork Steam Packet Company's smaller *Innisfallen* followed in 1930 and together these ships set the pattern for over a dozen subsequent Irish Sea motorships, the last of which was Coast Lines' *Scottish Coast* of 1957.

Motor-driven ferries also made an appearance in the Mediterranean in 1929 in the shape of Italy's three *Caralis* class ships for the Civitavecchia–Sardinia service and Spain's *Infante Don Jaime* pair for the Barcelona–Majorca route. In France, Compagnie Fraissinet's first motor vessel, *Cyrnos*, built under war reparations in Germany in 1929 for the Corsica service, was also notable as the first cross-channel ship to incorporate a curved Maierform stem designed to reduce resistance and improve sea-keeping. This feature was shared by her turbine-driven consort *Ile de Beauté*, which followed from Germany in 1930 and to a less marked extent by the *Isle of Sark*, third of the Southern Railway Co's twin-funnelled turbine trio for the Channel Islands service, which also gained fame as the first vessel to be fitted with gyro-controlled fin stabilisers to reduce rolling.

The majority of new steamers were still driven by geared turbines, including three new 'Dukes' for the Heysham–Belfast service, Swedish Lloyd's elegant sisters *Britannia* and *Suecia* for the Gothenburg–London service and three *Vienna* class sisters for the Harwich–Hook run. On the west coast of Canada, Canadian

Cambria (1921), third of LNWR Holyhead quartet.

Esbjerg (1929), third of DFDS' pioneer North Sea motorships.

National Railway built three *Prince Robert* type ferries in an expensive and ultimately unsuccessful bid to compete with Canadian Pacific Railway's well-established 'Princesses', while the Union Steamship Co of New Zealand opted for turbo-electric machinery to power its inter-island steamer *Rangatira*, no doubt influenced by its principal P&O's success with the liner *Viceroy of India*.

Despite the Depression, which materially affected industrial output, further motor vessels were delivered in the early 1930s including Florio Società Italiana Navigazione's *Città di Napoli* quartet and Bergen Line's *Venus*, which set new standards on the North Sea in a bid to compete with the new Swedish Lloyd ships. In 1934, the Belgian government's distinctively-styled motorship *Prince Baudouin* caused a sensation in maritime circles when she attained over 25 knots on trials, proving that the diesel engine could also be used to power high-speed vessels.

Meanwhile, France's North Africa services were enhanced by fine new turbine steamers such as Compagnie de Navigation Mixte's three new '*El*' class steamers and later Compagnie Générale Transatlantique's striking 10,000-grt sisters *Ville d'Alger* and *Ville d'Oran*, which were the largest and fastest yet built for the trans-Mediterranean routes.

In 1937, Belgian Marine's *Prince Baudouin* was joined on the Ostend route by her fractionally faster sister *Prins Albert* and a third ship was still under construction when German forces overran the Low Countries in 1940, but managed to escape to England on one engine. The increasing popularity of motorships was evidenced by Harland & Wolff's delivery of two pairs of second-generation vessels for Coast Lines' Irish Sea services, while on the North Sea new vessels were completed for Det Forenede, Det Bergenske and Fred Olsen & Co, and Bergenske's *Vega* was built in Italy in exchange for fish exports. On the eve of the outbreak of war in 1939, Zeeland Line received the advanced motorships *Koningin Emma* and *Prinses Beatrix* for its Flushing–Harwich service, making a direct switch from reciprocating-engined ships, which made it the only one of the major cross-channel companies never to have owned a turbine steamer.

Fast Belgian motorship *Prince Baudouin* (1934).

The Second World War

As in the First World War, many ships were quickly taken up for military duties. These were wide-ranging and were considerably more dangerous than in the earlier conflict due to advances in both aerial and submarine warfare. This was borne out by the fact that nearly fifty ships were lost from both cross-channel and short-sea routes.

Troopships

Early in the war, many ships were used for transporting the troops of the British Expeditionary Force to Europe and later many were involved in the epic evacuation from Dunkirk and subsequent withdrawals from north-west France and the Channel Islands. Trooping runs were also made to Iceland and between Aberdeen and Scapa Flow. Following the Normandy invasion, troop movements across the English Channel began again and these accelerated after the Armistice, when both Dover and Harwich became focal points for troop and refugee movements.

Hospital carriers

Initially a dozen British cross-channel ships were taken up as hospital carriers for the repatriation of wounded from the near Continent. Southern Railway's *Isle of Thanet*, *Maid of Kent*, *Brighton*, *Worthing*, *Paris*, *Dinard*, *Isle of Jersey* and *Isle of Guernsey*; Great Western Railway's *St Andrew*, *St David*, *St Patrick* and *St Julien* and British & Irish's *Leinster*. The latter was larger than the others and was fitted with an operating theatre, beds for 383 patients and six flat-bottomed wooden ambulance boats for operating from beaches. Later, a further eight ships were converted in preparation for the Normandy landings: London & North Eastern Railway's *Prague* and *Amsterdam*, London Midland & Scottish Railway's *Duke of Lancaster*, *Duke of Rothesay*, *Duke of Argyll* and British & Irish's *Lady Connaught* and *Longford*. *Dinard*, *Prague*, *St Julien* and *Lady Connaught* were loaned to the US Navy but *St Julien* was damaged by a mine on the second day of the invasion and took no further part.

Despite carrying full hospital ship markings, four vessels were lost to bombing during the course of the war – *Maid of Kent* and *Brighton* at Dieppe in May 1940 and *Paris* off Dunkirk a few days later. *St David* was sunk in darkness (some sources say by a rocket propelled bomb) off Anzio in January 1944 and in the following August, *Amsterdam* was mined off the Cherbourg peninsula while returning with casualties from the Normandy beachhead.

Infantry landing ships

Learning from experience gained from the failed Zeebrugge and Ostend raids during the First World War, the Admiralty identified a need for a new type of vessel to carry out amphibious raids. To this end it requisitioned six of the Belgian government ferries which had escaped to England in 1940 and converted them to small infantry landing ships (LSI [S]) for the carriage of around 250 troops and their equipment. *Prince Charles*, *Prince Leopold*, *Prince Philippe*, *Prins Albert*, *Prinses Astrid* and *Prinses Josephine Charlotte* had their mainmasts removed and promenade decks stripped to allow for the fitting of gravity davits to carry eight flat-bottomed assault landing craft (LCAs), each of which could carry thirty-six men. Defensive anti-aircraft armament comprised a single 12-pounder gun, two 2-pounder pom-poms and six 20-mm Oerlikons. *Prince Philippe* was sunk in collision in the Irish Sea in July 1941, but the others were used in raids on the Lofoten Islands, Bruneval and Dieppe. Later, they took part in the Mediterranean landings – North Africa, Sicily, Italy (Anzio and

HMS *Prince Leopold* (1930) was one of several Belgian cross-channel ships converted to small infantry landing ships carrying eight landing craft. She was torpedoed in the English Channel in July 1944.

S M Zeeland's 1939-built sisters *Koningin Emma* and *Prinses Beatrix** were almost unrecognisable after being rebuilt as medium infantry landing ships, the former as HMS *Queen Emma*.

Salerno) and southern France. *Prins Albert*'s sister. *Prince Baudouin*, was similarly converted late in 1943 and all seven were present at the Normandy landings in June 1944. Later some headed east to the Indian Ocean for the final stages of the war against Japan, placing them among the most widely travelled of all the smaller channel packets.

In addition to the small landing ships, Zeeland's new *Koningin Emma* and *Prinses Beatrix* underwent more extensive conversions in the latter half of 1940 to medium infantry landing ships (LSI [M]) for 460 troops. Their superstructure was stripped down to the weather deck and gravity davits fitted to carry six assault landing craft (LCAs) and two larger tank landing craft (LCTs), which could also carry seventy troops. A raised gun platform was placed on the forecastle in front of a new naval-type bridge and the original funnel was replaced by a long low structure with slanting top immediately abaft a tall signal mast. On completion they were commissioned as HMS *Queen Emma* and HMS *Princess Beatrix* respectively. Their naval service took them from northern Norway to eastern waters and included both the Mediterranean and Normandy landings.

The success of the assault ship concept led to the conversion of more channel steamers in preparation for the landings in North Africa (Operation Torch) and later still more were altered for the Normandy landings, including Zeeland's *Mecklenburg*. They differed from the Belgian ships in that they carried only six landing craft, which were slung outboard from fixed davits attached to the ship's side. They were launched and recovered manually, hence their designation as LSI (H), the H standing for hand-hoist. Troop complements varied from just under 400 in *Isle of Guernsey* to 580 in *Ulster Monarch* and armament consisted mainly of a single 12-pounder AA gun. In addition, two more 550-troop medium landing ships were converted. These were the former Canadian National Line ships *Prince Robert* and *Prince David*, which had been purchased by the Royal Canadian Navy in 1940 and rebuilt as auxiliary cruisers with a naval bridge and the first two funnels trunked into a single broad stack.

Anti-aircraft ships

Two vessels were rebuilt as Royal Navy anti-aircraft ships, emerging with the appearance of small warships. Stripped of their superstructure, they were built up forward and fitted with a high naval-type bridge and two tall tripod masts. Armament comprised six 4-in guns in twin mounts (two forward/one aft), two four-barrel pom-poms, two machine guns and two Oerlikons. The Isle of Man Steam Packet Co's *Tynwald* was altered in Portsmouth

The Isle of Man S P Co's *Tynwald* (1937) underwent a major conversion to an anti-aircraft ship but was torpedoed off Bougie in November 1942.

between July 1940 and October 1941 and her funnel was given a French navy-style cowl top. Belfast Steamship Co's *Ulster Queen* was requisitioned in August 1940 while under repair by Harland & Wolff in Belfast for grounding damage and work was finally completed in July 1941. Her two funnels were replaced by a single larger funnel positioned further aft than that of *Tynwald*. The latter was lost off Bougie during the North Africa landings but *Ulster Queen* served in Russian convoys, the Mediterranean and later eastern waters, by which time her armament had been amended to four 4-in, eight quadruple pom-poms and ten Oerlikons.

Other uses

Other vessels were used for a variety purposes, among which were *Isle of Sark* (radar training ship then AA ship), *Worthing* (Fleet Air Arm target ship HMS *Brigadier*, then LSI), *Vienna* (coastal forces depot ship in the Mediterranean), *London-Istanbul* (minesweeper depot ship *Algoma*, then HMS *Ambitious*), *Batavier IV* (ASW HQ ship *Eastern Isles*, then *Western Isles*), *Princess Marie José* (ASW training *Southern Isles*, then HMS *Nemesis*), *Hantonia*, *Batavier II* (accommodation ships).

Axis-requistioneded ships

Like their British counterparts, French cross-channel steamers were initially used for trooping and evacuation purposes and several of the larger French trans-Mediterranean ships were taken

One of several ships to take part in both world wars, the French-built *Newhaven* (1912) was captured by the Germans and spent some time as the patrol ship *Skorpion*.

up as auxiliary cruisers, assisting in the Norwegian campaign in 1940 and later used to carry France's gold reserves to safety in Casablanca. German forces invading Denmark and Norway seized a number of vessels and Det Bergenske's *Venus* and *Vega* and Fred Olsen's *Black Watch* were later employed as submarine depot ships, while Det Forenede's *Kronprins Olav* became the hospital ship *Frankfurt* in the final stages of the war. The four *Parkeston* class were used as target ships or floating barracks and *A P Bernstorff* as the ambulance carrier *Renate*. Of the five French cross-channel ships seized by the advancing German forces, *Cote d'Azur* and *Cote d'Argent* were used as minelayers, while the three Newhaven service ships undertook a number of different roles. The still incomplete *Londres* was launched and fitted out as the minelayer *Lothringen*, but was also used as a submarine target ship. The Mediterranean ships operated initially under Vichy control but were hampered by a shortage of fuel. Most were transferred to Germany's ally Italy after the occupation of southern France in 1943, but were taken back later that year following Italy's capitulation. Some of the larger vessels were converted to hospital ships and a few smaller vessels to flak ships, while Compagnie Fraissinet's *Ile de Beauté* became a night fighter direction ship until sunk by Allied forces. Those that survived were scuttled by the retreating German forces.

The few American ferries were used as army troop carriers, but *Saint John* was later commissioned as the submarine tender USS *Antaeus* and her sister *Acadia* became America's first full-time hospital ship for the war. In the Pacific, Japan's railway ferries were also used for troop movements and the two largest and newest, *Tenzan Maru* and *Konron Maru* completed in 1943, were both sunk by US forces without ever entering commercial service.

Post-war reconstruction

During the immediate post-war period, UK shipyards were initially busy restoring the ships to their peacetime state. The Union Steamship of New Zealand's turbo-electric *Hinemoa* was the first sizeable new passenger ship to be completed in 1946 and in the same year, the Isle of Man Steam Packet Co took delivery of *King Orry*, lead ship of a series that eventually numbered seven. Several new railway steamers were under construction when the four pre-war railway companies were nationalised in 1948 and their existing ships transferred to the various regions of the new British Transport Commission. The Midland Region's *Cambria* and *Hibernia*, completed in 1949 for the Holyhead–Dun Laoghaire service, were unique as the only conventional UK railway ferries to be diesel driven and the Southern Region's *Brighton* of 1950 was the first to be fitted with lighter tripod masts in place of the previous tall pole masts.

Canadian Pacific Railway replaced its two war losses in 1949 with the elegant turbo-electric *Princess Marguerite* and *Princess Patricia* and these were followed a year later by the side-loading car ferry *Princess of Nanaimo*.

North Sea services had been enhanced by two motor vessels whose construction had been delayed by the war; Det Forenede's streamlined *Kronprins Frederik* and Swedish Lloyd's *Saga*. Det Forenede's similar *Kronprinsesse Ingrid* followed in 1949 and in 1951–2, Fred Olsen replaced its lost *Black Prince* and *Black Watch* with the eye-catching motorships *Blenheim* and *Braemar*, whose hulls were built in Southampton. Swedish Lloyd's beautiful *Patricia*, which was also designed for winter cruising, joined *Saga* on the Gothenburg–London run in 1951.

Most of the continental yards had been severely damaged by the war, except perhaps Belgium's Cockerill yard, which completed the improved *Prince Baudouin*-type packets *Koning Albert* and *Prince Philippe* in 1948. In France, it took some time before the ships scuttled during summer 1944 could be raised and in some cases repaired. These included Compagnie de Navigation Mixte's new *Kairouan*, which had been nearing completion when scuttled, but suffered a further setback when a fire delayed her delivery until 1950. She was the fastest and most powerful short-sea passenger ship ever built, capable of maintaining 26 knots, with her turbines developing a maximum of 28,000 shp. However, excessive fuel consumption precluded too much fast running. New French construction included Compagnie Navigation Mixte's striking engines-aft *El Djezair* (1952) and Compagnie Générale Transatlantique's large *Ville de Marseille* pair. These were the last conventional ships built for France's trans-Mediterranean services as increasing political problems in North Africa led to Tunisia's independence in 1956 and Algeria's six years later.

Italy lost most of its tonnage during the war and it was not until 1952 that services to Sardinia and Sicily began to be replenished by five new motor ferries named after Italian regions and headed by *Calabria*.

No new traditional short-sea ships were built in the United States, but Canadian Vickers produced the side-loading car ferries *Bluenose* and *William Carson* in 1955. These were developments of the garage system employed in some of the earlier Canadian Pacific Railway ferries but incorporated a full car deck while retaining a normal bow and stern.

Japan's need for a regular sea connection with Korea ended with that country's independence after the war and by the time its war-torn shipbuilding industry had begun to recover, no further passenger-only ships were required for the Tsugaru Strait service, which was subsequently served by train ferries.

Final deliveries

From the mid-1950s, deliveries of traditional passenger ships began to decline because operators began to switch their attention to building car ferries to meet the demands arising from increasing car ownership. With one or two exceptions, the majority of newbuildings were destined to be the last of their type built for their respective routes. These ranged from Bergenske's fine turbine-driven *Leda* in 1954 to the Belgian government's motorship *Prinses Paola* of 1966, the last conventional Dover Strait ferry. In between, the three railway-owned 'Dukes' of 1956 and Coast Line's motor vessel *Scottish Coast* of 1957 were the last of their type built for Irish Sea service, *Caesarea* and *Sarnia* (1960–1) the last to serve the Channel Islands and *Avalon* (1963), at 6,584 grt the largest of all the British channel ferries, the final ship for the Harwich–Hook run, although she was also designed with off-season cruising in mind. Some of the final ships were interim ships, such as Det Forenede's beautiful side-loader *England* of 1964, which incorporated a full car deck but retained a normal bow and stern at the express wish of the then chairman. Also falling into this category were two pairs of ferries – one turbine, one diesel – with unusual side-loading arrangements built for Isle of Man Steam Packet Co and Compania Trasmediterránea's four so-called X type (later renamed the 'Albatross' class) led by *Juan March*. The same owner's smaller *Antonio Lazzaro* and *Vicente Puchol* of 1968 were the last ships of their type to be built anywhere.

Last survivors

Although no more traditional ships were built, many of the final generation remained in service for more than twenty years and a number underwent mid-life conversions to car ferries, which involved the fitting of a new vehicle deck accessed through a stern door. Eventually they were rendered obsolete by new vehicle ferries that loaded through bow and/or stern doors and could carry trucks and coaches in addition to greater numbers of cars. These hastened the decline of the traditional rail-transported foot passenger.

At the time of writing, just five of the many hundreds of these attractive little ships built over a 100-year period are still in existence. The former *Duke of Lancaster*, the last surviving example of a traditional UK railway-owned cross-channel steamer, lies quietly rotting as *Duke of Llanerch-y-Mor* in her mud berth near Mostyn, while on the other side of the world the former Spanish ferry *Vicente Puchol* remains laid up in Manila as the cruise ship *7107 Islands Cruise*, victim of a protracted wrangle over import duty.

Two of the vessels are former Baltic ferries. Bore Line's twin-funnelled *Bore* (1960), the last steamship to be built in Sweden, is preserved as a hotel/museum in Turku after having spent a second twenty-one-year career as the cruise ship *Kristina Regina* during which she operated as far afield as the Mediterranean and Red Sea. The sixty-year-old former Svea Line ferry *Birger Jarl* (1953), which from 1979 had operated as *Baltic Star* on one-night cruises from Stockholm to the Åland Islands under the Ånedin Line banner and reverted to her original name in 2002, finally ended her active career in June 2013 and is now a hostel ship in the Swedish capital. This leaves just one vessel still active, the former Compania Trasmediterránea ferry *Juan March* (1966), which underwent a major conversion to a cruise ship in Greece in the early 1990s and still sails in the charter market as the Portuguese-flagged *Ocean Majesty*.

William Denny & Brothers

No ferry book would be complete without mention of the most prolific builder of cross-channel vessels, William Denny & Brothers, which was incorporated at Dumbarton on the River Clyde in 1849. Shipbuilding had been undertaken for some time before this and one of William Denny and Archibald McLachlan's products, the 70-ton *Marjory* of 1814, was the first steamship to operate on the River Thames and the first to cross the English Channel in 1816 following her sale to France. Another Denny product, the 90-ton *Rob Roy* built for Glasgow–Belfast service in 1819, started the first regular service from Dover to Calais in 1821 and later became the French mail packet *Henri Quatre*.

The company gained a reputation for innovation, having introduced progressive measured mile trials, the adoption of mild steel and the application of cellular double bottoms in merchant ships. It also instigated a monetary awards scheme for members of its staff who came up with ideas for improvements. Another shrewd move involved the building of the first commercial experimental testing tank at its Leven shipyard. The 300-ft long, 22-ft wide and 10-ft deep facility was based on the tank built for Dr Froude at his home in Torquay and paid for by the Admiralty from public subscription. Denny used paraffin wax models up to 20 ft long that were drawn along the tank at different speeds by a steam engine. The first test took place in February 1883 and later a 40-in narrow gauge electric railway was built to replace the original steam motive power. The tank was lengthened by around 50 ft in 1924 following a fire.

It was largely due to its testing tank that Denny first got involved with building cross-channel steamers. The Belgian government was seeking tenders for a new paddle steamer for its Ostend–Dover mail service and the specification stipulated a speed of 20.5 knots on a length of 300 ft. At that time 15–16 knots was considered a fair speed but Denny's tank tests showed that hull resistance could be reduced by adopting a wider beam and the firm duly won the contract. The double-ended *Princesse Henriette* made over 21 knots on trials and a second ship, *Princesse Josephine*, followed.

The success of the Belgian ships led to Denny building seven more paddle steamers and ten reciprocating-engined ships for various cross-channel operators but it was an association with Charles Parsons, who had supplied a turbo-generator for the Clyde paddle steamer *Duchess of Hamilton* built by Denny in 1890, which ultimately led to its cross-channel business really taking off. The latter was looking to build a full-sized merchant ship powered by his new steam turbines that he had successfully demonstrated in his high-speed experimental vessel *Turbinia* at

Engadine (1911) – a typical Denny product

Queen Victoria's Diamond Jubilee Naval Review in 1897. As no Clyde shipowner was prepared to risk ordering such a vessel, Parsons, Denny and a Captain Williamson, who would manage the new ship, formed the Turbine Steamers Syndicate to which Denny was the largest contributor. The resulting Clyde excursion steamer *King Edward* was the world's first commercial ship to be driven by steam turbines and her success led to a second ship, *Queen Alexandra*, following a year later. Denny was then instrumental in persuading both the South Eastern & Chatham Railway Companies Joint Management Committee, a newly-formed merger of the London, Chatham & Dover and London & South Eastern Railway companies, and the London, Brighton and South Coast Railway Co to choose turbine propulsion for their new ships, delivering *The Queen* to the former and *Brighton* to latter a few months apart in summer 1903. As a result, all Denny's subsequent cross-channel steamers were turbine propelled and by 1914 it had delivered almost twenty vessels, including ships for New Zealand, Japan and Canada.

In 1911, Denny introduced watertube boilers in the South Eastern & Chatham Railway's *Engadine* and continued to work with Parsons, building under subcontract the first warships to be fitted with his new single-reduction geared turbines – the destroyers HMS *Badger* and HMS *Beaver* – in 1912. The following year it completed the shallow-draught, geared turbine channel steamer *Paris* for the London, Brighton & South Coast Railway Co. Built largely on torpedo boat lines and with a cruiser stern, she was capable of 25 knots and was the fastest commercial ship for her length in the world.

A slump in 1922 resulted in two cancellations, which gave Denny the opportunity to build two more turbine ships for Japan, in this case for Nippon Yusen Kaisha's Nagasaki–Shanghai service.

Denny enjoyed particularly close associations with the railway companies operating Irish Sea services from Stranraer and Holyhead and those responsible for running English Channel services from Dover, Folkestone, Newhaven and Southampton. The *Isle of Thanet* built for the Southern Railway Co in 1925 introduced the fully enclosed promenade deck and in 1939 Denny was responsible for the UK's first purpose-built stern-loading car ferry, the London Midland & Scottish Railway Co's *Princess Victoria*, which was also the first UK railway ship to be propelled by diesel engines.

After the Second World War Denny built a further five conventional turbine-driven channel steamers for the British Transport Commission, ending with *Duke of Rothesay* in 1956, in addition to the single motorship *Innisfallen* for B & I Line. *Duke of*

Rothesay was its last conventional channel ferry to be completed in 1956 but by then the emphasis was shifting towards car ferries. Denny had already built a near-identical replacement for the lost *Princess Victoria* in 1946 and in 1952 delivered the *Lord Warden*, the first British purpose-built car ferry on the Dover Strait. Innovative as ever, it also completed the first UK-built roll-on/roll-off passenger and freight ferry, the Transport Ferry Company's *Bardic Ferry*, in 1957. All was not well, however, with the UK shipbuilding industry which was increasingly beset by industrial action as well as facing increasing competition from Japan. Denny's final cross-channel car ferry, the *Caledonian Princess* for the Stranraer–Larne run, was completed in 1961 and two years later the company went into liquidation.

Notes on ship design

Cross-channel ships generally operated in all weathers, especially where railway connections had to be met, and they were given sufficient reserves of power to make up for any delays. Fog was the only major problem before the days of radar and very occasionally services across the English Channel were suspended, leading to the classic newspaper headline 'Fog in Channel, Continent cut off'. Schedules called for frequent berthing, especially on the shorter routes, and for this reason hulls were usually fitted with prominent rubbing strakes which often extended around the stern. Some ports had to be entered or left astern and the fitting of bow rudders became widespread.

The various channel crossings can be divided into three different categories. The shorter routes of twenty to forty miles, such as those across the Dover Strait and between Stranraer and Larne could be maintained by ships capable of making 21–22 knots. The medium routes of around sixty to seventy miles such as Dover–Ostend, Newhaven-Dieppe and Holyhead–Kingstown (Dun Laoghaire) required higher speeds of up to 24 knots, giving passage times of three to four hours. Finally the longer routes of just over 100 miles usually involved overnight services where speed was less of a concern to avoid arrival at the destination too early in the morning

Over time, different ship designs emerged according to the route served. The day ships on the shorter crossings were generally flush-decked with a high bridge and low superstructure. They offered more public rooms than the overnight ships running from Southampton to Le Havre and St Malo which had largely cabin accommodation. Raised forecastle were a feature of ships operating on the rougher passages such as the Fishguard–Rosslare and later Weymouth–Channel Islands routes while those on the longer Irish Sea overnight services tended to built with three-island type hulls and more extensive accommodation blocks. Ships on the North Sea routes also had raised forecastles and gradually these were extended aft, combining with a bridge deck that in time almost reached the stern.

While Great Britain dominated the cross-channel scene, France, Belgium and Holland also developed their own distinctive fleets. The Belgian diesel-driven ships of the 1930s adopted an entirely new upright design with no rake to the masts and low squat funnel while the Dutch *Koningin Emma* pair of 1939 had 'upturned flower pot' funnels and carried their boats in a lower position on the superstructure than normal. French channel steamers always had a certain *je ne sais quois* about them and the final ships built in the 1950s, *Cote d'Azur* and *Lisieux*, were no exceptions with their streamlined bridge fronts, aerofoil-shaped funnels and sharply knuckled bows.

Multiple funnels were commonplace on cross-channel routes, less so on the short-sea services. The use of four funnels was confined to the City of Dublin Steam Packet Co's *Leinster* quartet of 1860, the Isle of Man Steam Packet Co's rebuilt *Ben-my-Chree* of 1875 and the experimental Dover Strait ships *Castalia* and *Calais Douvres*, which had two pairs of funnels mounted abreast. Three funnels were also comparatively rare, and the most obvious examples Canadian Pacific Railway Co's famous 'Princess' ships on the North West Pacific and the rival Canadian National Railway Co's three 'Prince' steamers of 1930. The only other examples were the Italian turbine steamer *Città di Catania*, first of a quartet of ferries built in 1910 for Naples–Sicily service, and two River Plate vessels built early in the First World War.

The increasing efficiency of boilers allowed the number of funnels to be reduced from two to one and after the Second World War they tended to become shorter and wider. In the 1950s new designs were tested in an effort to push exhaust fumes clear of the after passenger decks. The narrow aerofoil shape of the Strombos-Valensi funnel was used in a number of French Channel and Mediterranean steamers while the Lascroux type funnel adopted by the Belgians had large air intakes at the forward end designed to lift fumes upwards. Fred. Olsen developed its own particular type of combined mast and funnel which was used in a number of ship types including its North Sea passenger ships *Blenheim* and *Braemar*. A later concept that was widely adopted in shipping circles, that of twin funnels placed side by side, was only used by the Spanish ferry company Compania Trasmediterránea for its final conventional-looking ships.

I

Early Paddle Steamers and Experimental Vessels

The development of United Kingdom cross-channel services up to the middle of the nineteenth century had involved a logical development from sailing vessels to private or Admiralty paddle-driven packets. These were often dependant on mail contracts, and one such contract was obtained in 1850 by the British & Irish Steam Packet Co for a Kingstown (Dublin)–Holyhead service. A decade later, it took delivery of a quartet of four-funnelled vessels named after Irish provinces, which were among the fastest ships afloat and in many ways set a benchmark for others to follow.

Other routes came to be closely associated with the still expanding United Kingdom rail network and the owners of the railway companies naturally became more interested in connecting steamer services once their tracks had reached the ports. The parliamentary acts that had established the railway companies did not, however, include powers to operate steamships and as an interim measure they were forced to seek deals with existing operators or help to set up subsidiary companies to run steamer services that connected with train services. This situation changed when the railway companies obtained the necessary powers to run their own steamers and from then on the railways became closely involved in the development of that peculiarly British type of vessel, the cross-channel steamer.

The Victorian era in Great Britain was characterised by inventiveness and innovation and the cross-channel business was no exception. In the mid-1870s three experimental ships were built for the short Dover Strait crossing with the aim of reducing motion in a seaway and thereby enhancing passenger comfort. Two had twin hulls and the third was fitted with a gimballed saloon; but all failed to live up to expectations and were no match for the existing paddle steamers in terms of speed.

Note: An asterisk in a caption indicates the vessel shown in the photograph.

Irish quartet sets the pace

On 1 May 1850, the British government assigned the contract for its Holyhead–Kingstown (Dun Laoghaire) mail service to the City of Dublin Steam Packet Co, which at the time was operating a service between Dublin and Liverpool with two former government packets and two other ships. A decade later the company revolutionised cross-channel travel when it took delivery of four fast, clipper-stemmed paddle steamers named after the four Irish provinces: *Ulster* (1,477 grt), *Munster** (1,492 grt), *Connaught* (1,488 grt) and *Leinster* (1,467 grt). *Leinster* was built on the Thames by Samuda Bros and the others were ordered from Laird Bros, Birkenhead. Some, perhaps all, originally had four bell-mouthed funnels mounted in pairs either side of the paddle boxes. James Watt of Birmingham constructed *Ulster* and *Munster*'s two-cylinder oscillating machinery and that of the other two was supplied by Ravenhill, Salkeld & Co. Piston strokes varied from 6.5 to 7.5 ft and steam was supplied by eight boilers. The open foredecks of the first three to be delivered proved very wet in head seas and they were covered over with long turtle-back forecastles; *Connaught* was altered before delivery but her forecastle was stove in during a severe storm on 9 February 1861. They measured 337 (*Connaught* 343) × 35 ft and were superior to all other channel steamers, particularly in relation to sea-keeping. They offered two daytime departures in each direction and mail was sorted in special rooms on board during the crossing. *Leinster* recorded 17.5 knots on trials and *Connaught* was possibly the first ship anywhere to reach 18 knots. In service they averaged 14.5 knots and in general managed to maintain the contract requirement of a three hours and forty-five minutes passage. In advance of the new mail contract, which came into operation in 1885, all four were refitted by Laird to bring them into line with the new *Ireland* and those with four funnels were reduced to two. In 1896 *Munster* and *Leinster* were sold to S W Higginbottom's Liverpool & Douglas Steam Packet Co, but its planned Liverpool–Douglas service never materialised because they were bought by the Isle of Man Steam Packet Co along with *Ulster*, to remove competition. They were sold for scrap in 1897. *Connaught* was demolished the following year by H E Moss & Co.

The Drogheda Steam Packet Co was formed in 1826 to run a service to Liverpool and in 1862 it received the 697-grt paddle steamer *Colleen Bawn* from Randolph Elder & Co, Govan, Glasgow. She measured 221.5 × 28 ft and was propelled by a simple diagonal engine, but in 1868 this was compounded by her builders with a 5-ft piston stroke, with power output raised to 1,350 ihp. In 1884 her gross measurement was raised to 751 tons after she was given new engines and new boilers by J Jack & Co, Liverpool. The compound oscillating machinery had a 6-ft stroke and developed 1,500 ihp. *Colleen Bawn* was displaced in 1889 and was broken up in Preston in 1901, a year before the Drogheda Steam Packet Co was bought by the Lancashire & Yorkshire Railway Co.

English Channel

The South Eastern Railway Co obtained parliamentary powers to operate its own steamships in 1853 but did not take delivery of its first specially commissioned ship, the clipper-stemmed *Victoria**, from Samuda Bros, Poplar until 1861. An iron vessel of 358 grt, she was followed a year later by a sister, *Albert Edward*. They measured 208.5 x 24 ft and their propelling machinery by John Penn & Sons, Greenwich comprised a simple compound oscillating engine with a 4.5-ft stroke, with steam supplied by a boiler working at 30 psi. They were faster than earlier ships on the Folkestone–Boulogne route and in favourable conditions with the tide underneath them could make the crossing in around one hour and thirty minutes. *Albert Edward* later had her foredeck covered over to provide passengers with protection from the weather but she was wrecked in fog near Cap Gris Nez on 7 April 1893 while proceeding light to Boulogne to deputise for the newer SER paddle steamer *Louise Dagmar*, which had been damaged in a collision. Her sister, *Victoria*, was broken up in 1895 after a creditable thirty-four years' service.

One year after reaching Dover in 1861, the London, Chatham & Dover Railway secured the contract to carry the mails between Dover and Calais and immediately made temporary arrangements to operate the sixteen steamers owned by the previous contract holders, Jenkins & Churchward, on the mail service and other railway connected sailings. During 1861–4, nine new vessels were built, shared between three London shipyards. Samuda Brothers was responsible for *Maid of Kent* (1861; 364 grt), *Foam** and *Scud* (both 1862; 495 grt); Money, Wigram & Sons for *Samphire* (1861; 336 grt), *Etoile du Nord* (1862; 503 grt), later renamed *Petrel*, *Breeze* and *Wave* (both 1863; 385 grt) and finally James Ash & Co for

Prince Imperial (later *Prince*) and *France* (338 grt/365 grt) in 1864, the latter two differing from the remainder in having clipper bows. All were officially acquired by the railway company after it obtained parliamentary powers to operate its own ships in 1864. Early on *Foam*, *Scud* and *Petrel* ran to Boulogne in competition with the South Eastern Railway's service from Folkestone but the Nord railway company remained loyal to the latter. *Samphire* and *Breeze* were slated for night service and were the first to have private cabins, the former having made a trial return crossing to Calais on 12 May 1962, with record passages of eighty-three and seventy-eight minutes respectively. However, on the misty night of 13 December

1865, while on passage to Calais, she was run down by the unlit American barque *Fanny Buck*. Both were damaged and towed back to Dover, but some lives were lost. *Scud* was loaned to the Belgian government in 1863 and withdrawn from service three years later, but the remaining ships performed with great regularity for some thirty years – a tribute to their strong construction and first-class maintenance by the LC&DR's marine department. Latterly, they were used as reserve ships and *Maid of Kent* was broken up in Holland in 1898. The rest became surplus and were demolished following the 1899 merger of the LC&DR and SER, only *Foam* lasting until 1901, when she was broken up.

The iron paddle steamers *Marseilles* and *Bordeaux**
(425/419 grt; 214 × 23.5 ft) were built for the London,
Brighton & South Coast Railway Co by Charles Lungley
at Deptford, London, in 1864–5. Driven by two-cylinder
simple oscillating engines with an output of 820 ihp for a
service speed of 13 knots, piston stroke was 4.75 ft and
steam was supplied at 18 psi by two tubular boilers. They
were virtually identical, but *Bordeaux* was given slightly
finer lines. *Marseilles* took four hours and thirty-five
minutes on her first crossing to Dieppe in roughish
conditions on 17 December, beating her running mate
Alexandra by twenty minutes. *Bordeaux* made three
twenty-four-mile trial runs between Tilbury and the
Mouse Light on 5 September 1865, recording average
speeds of 12.75 knots, 15.75 knots and 12 knots.
Marseilles was reboilered in 1874 and in May 1885 was
sold for excursion work to Liverpool owners, which sent
her for scrapping in 1891. Her sister underwent an
extensive refit by Maudslay in May 1877, during which she
was fitted with new boilers, cylinders and paddle wheels
and a hurricane deck over her forecastle. In 1890 she was
sold to J N C Bull of Newhaven but was little used and
broken up in 1894. *(Newhaven Historical Society)*

The Dover–Ostend service had been maintained jointly by
the South Eastern Railway and the Belgian government,
each responsible for carrying their own mails, since 1846
but the latter took over the running of the whole service
in 1862. In order to offer two daily departures in each
direction, one of these by night, seven steamers were
required and initially other ships were chartered in or
purchased. These included the survey/hydrographic ship

Belgique (1863), the London, Chatham & Dover Railway
Co's *John Penn* (renamed *Perle*) and *Scud*, and SER's *Princess
Clementine* and *Queen of the French* (renamed *Saphir*).
These were beginning to show their age, and as a result the
Belgian government built seven new paddle steamers
during 1867–73: *Louise-Marie* (1867), *Leopold I* (1868),
Marie-Henriette (1869), *Comte de Flandre* (1870), *Comtesse
de Flandre* and *Prince Baudouin* (1872) and *Parlement*

Belge* (1873). Built by Société Cockerill at Hoboken, they
all shared the same dimensions of 200 × 24 ft on 7 ft
draught and were driven at 16 knots by John Penn-type
two-cylinder oscillating engines with an output of 1,500 ihp.
They had clipper bows and bell-topped funnels and their
speed enabled them to reduce the passage time to four
hours and twenty minutes. Most were broken up in the
1890s, but *Leopold I* lasted until 1919.

Completed in 1863–4, *Normandy* and *Brittany** were the first steamers commissioned by the London & South Western Railway Co after it had absorbed the New South Western Steam Packet Co. Intended for the Channel Islands service, they were products of James Ash & Co, Cubitt Town and measured 425/529 grt on dimensions of 215.6/209.75 × 25.5/24 ft. Although not sisters, they had similar looks, having a straight stem and two tall raked masts and funnels. Their two-cylinder simple oscillating engines, built by John Stewart & Co, Poplar, allowed them to reach a maximum speed of 15.5 knots, but 14 knots was service speed. *Normandy* was damaged in collision with the Hamburg America liner *Bavaria* in Southampton Water on 21 April 1864 and six years later, on 17 March 1870, was run down and sunk by the steamer *Mary* in dense fog twenty-five miles south of the Needles. Thirty lives were lost and in the subsequent inquiry she was blamed for steaming too fast under the prevailing conditions. Her sister was reboilered and fitted with a forecastle in 1871 and in 1883 was lengthened by around 20 ft and re-engined with compound oscillating machinery. She switched to the Le Havre route in 1889 and became a relief ship following the introduction of *Alma* and *Columbia* in 1894. She was present at the Jubilee Naval Review at Spithead in August 1897 and was sold in October 1900 to T W Ward for demolition at Preston.

North Sea

The Great Eastern Railway received the twin-funnelled iron paddle steamer *Avalon* from John & William Dudgeon, London in 1865. She was one of three new passenger vessels for service between Harwich and Rotterdam. Measuring 670 grt on dimensions of 239.8 × 27.2 ft, she was driven at 14 knots by a 220-nhp two-cylinder simple oscillating engine. In 1876 she was given new engines and boilers by Victoria Graving Dock Co and twelve years later was sold to Earle's Shipbuilding & Engineering Co, Hull, which lengthened her and converted her to screw propulsion with a triple-expansion engine in 1890. Following further changes of owner, *Avalon* was given a third set of boilers and was eventually wrecked off Jamaica in 1909.

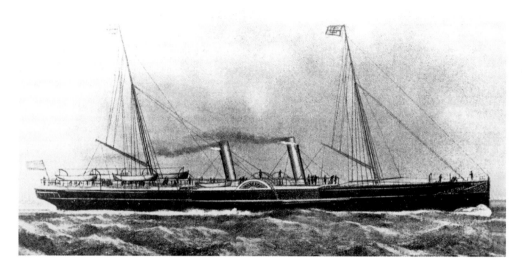

Southern Irish Sea

The iron paddle steamer *Great Western* was built for Ford & Jackson, which operated steamers for the Great Western Railway. Completed by W Simons & Co, Renfrew in 1867, *Great Western* was put into service between Milford and Cork. She had a straight stem and two thin funnels mounted aft of the paddle boxes. She measured 447 grt on hull dimensions of 220.4 × 25.2 ft and her propelling machinery comprised a 190-nhp two-cylinder oscillating engine with 3.75-ft piston stroke, with boiler pressure of 20 psi. In 1872, the GWR obtained powers to run its own ships and in August 1878, *Great Western* was transferred to its Weymouth–Cherbourg route. When the service was closed at the end of June 1885, she returned to Milford but was soon after chartered, in 1887, by the Weymouth & Channel Islands Steam Packet Co to fill the gap caused by the loss of its steamer *Brighton* on the summer Channel Islands service. *Great Western* repeated the exercise over the course of the next two years and in 1890 was running between Preston and Douglas, Isle of Man for Nathaniel Miller's Preston & West Coast Steamship Co. The following year she was sold to David MacBrayne & Co and renamed *Lovedale*. Following service on several of MacBrayne's routes, she was broken up in 1904.

The 1,017-grt paddler steamer *Juno* was delivered in 1868 by the London & Glasgow Engineering & Iron Shipbuilding Co, Govan, Glasgow to the Bristol General Steam Navigation Co for its Bristol–Cork service. She was a twin-funnelled iron vessel measuring 261.5 × 26.5 ft and was propelled by a two-cylinder oscillating engine. Berths were provided for 130 first-class passengers, while 520 could be carried on deck in summer and 390 in winter. *Juno* was the first vessel to use the Cumberland Basin locks in Bristol and also opened the first Avonmouth Dock in 1877. In the same year the name of her owner was changed slightly to the Bristol Steam Navigation Co, when the company was sold to Cork interests. In 1885 her engine was compounded and two years later she rescued thirteen crew members from the wrecked collier *George Moore*. Sold to the City of Cork Steam Packet Co in 1900, *Juno* was reduced to a hulk and towed to Dartmouth two years later and this is where she remained until broken up in 1922.

The Great Western Railway took over the Irish Sea channel service from Waterford to Milford from Ford & Jackson in 1872 and for this service promptly ordered two new steamers. The 914-grt *Limerick* and *Milford* were completed by Renfrew builders E B Mitchell and W Simons & Sons, respectively, in 1873 and were iron paddle steamers measuring 251.8 (*Milford* 250.6) × 29.2 ft. A two-cylinder compound engine of 400 nhp was fed with steam at 65 psi. *Limerick* was wrecked on the Irish coast in 1874 and quickly replaced by a similarly named ship in 1874 along with a sister named *Waterford**, both constructed by Simons. *Milford* was reboilered in 1883 and *Limerick* a year later. The former was broken up in 1901 after suffering serious damage in a storm. *Limerick* went to breakers at Dordrecht, Holland, a year later and *Waterford* was scrapped at Garston in 1905, having spent her later years as a cargo and cattle carrier.

Northern Irish Sea

Launched by J & G Thomson, Govan on 5 August 1868, the 831-grt iron steamer *Racoon* followed a long line of paddle steamers built for G & J Burns and was designed for the Glasgow–Belfast overnight service. She measured 252.3 × 27.8 ft and her two-cylinder oscillating engine with a piston stroke of 6 ft was of 300 nhp, with steam supplied by boilers with a working pressure of 30 psi. On trials between the Cloch and Cumbrae lights, she averaged over 15 knots. In 1880 she was sold to shipbuilders Barclay, Curle & Co in part exchange for new screw-driven steamers but was chartered back to Burns for a short while. The following year she was purchased by the Corporation of the City of London and and was used to transport foreign-sourced cattle upriver to Deptford Market. These had arrived from North America in ocean-going vessels that were too large to proceed above Gravesend because of draught restrictions. *Racoon* was eventually broken up in 1907 after a useful life of almost forty years. The service was discontinued and the vessel was broken up at Belfast during 1895–6.

The 949-grt paddle steamer *Princess of Wales** was the first ship acquired after the takeover of North Lancashire Steam Navigation Co by the railways in 1870, with the Lancashire & Yorkshire Railway Co holding two thirds and the London & North Western Railway Co, one third. *Princess of Wales* was built by Andrew Leslie & Co at Hebburn-on-Tyne in 1878 and measured 260 × 30.25 ft. Her two side lever oscillating engines made by Robert Stephenson & Co were of 300 nhp. Her paddle wheel diameters were 24.25 and 23 ft respectively. In 1883 she was re-engined with Rankin & Blackmore cross-compound four-cylinder diagonal engines fed with steam from four single-ended cylindrical boilers working at 70 psi, and identical to those installed a year earlier in near-sister *Thomas Dugdale*, which had been completed by Leslie in 1873. The latter was sold to the Irish Traders' Cooperative Steamship Co in 1888 and registered in the name of the Irish National Steamship Co. For two years it offered cheap voyages from Londonderry to Glasgow and Fleetwood. Sold again, to Alexander Laird, she was renamed *Laurel* and was scrapped in 1893. *Princess of Wales* also lasted until the 1890s, and was sold to the Naval Construction & Armament Co, Barrow, and delivered in May 1896 for breaking up. Meanwhile two slightly larger paddle steamers, both products of Barrow Shipbuilding Co, were added to the fleet; the 1,082-grt *Duke of Connaught* in 1875 and the 1,107-grt *Earl of Ulster* three years later. Respective lengths were 267.5 and 275 ft on 30 ft beams. *Duke of Connaught* was broken up at Dumbarton in 1893. *Earl of Ulster* was sold to A M Carlisle in 1894, later passing into the ownership of J McCausland of Portaferry for excursion services in Strangford Lough. But after one season the service was discontinued and the vessel was broken up at Belfast during 1895–6. The Barrow yard completed a fifth paddler, the 1,429-grt *Prince of Wales*, in 1886 but she was sold to Spain after only a decade of service and became the Spanish navy's *General Valdes*. She foundered at Cadiz arsenal in 1901, was raised and became a hulk only to sink again in 1907.

The 497-grt *Princess Louise* was the first ship built for the Larne & Stranraer Steamboat Co. Completed by Tod & MacGregor at Meadowside, Glasgow, in June 1872, she was an iron paddle steamer measuring 211.4 × 24.1 ft, and was driven by two-cylinder steeple machinery of 200 nhp fed with steam by two boilers with a working pressure of 35 psi. Her top speed on trials was 14 knots. Her two funnels were painted red with a black top. Her engines gave constant trouble and she was reboilered with higher-pressure units in 1878. In January 1890,

yellow funnels were adopted following takeover by the Portpatrick & Wigtownshire Railways Joint Committee and in June of the same year, *Princess Louise* was sold to a Mr Lowther of Belfast but quickly passed to David MacBrayne, who renamed her *Islay* in the following January. Placed in service between Glasgow and Islay, she was wrecked in fog on Sheep Island near Port Ellen on 15 July 1902. A slightly larger version, the 556-grt *Princess Beatrice**, was completed by Harland & Wolff, Belfast in 1875, entering service on 4 February the following year.

She measured 234.6 × 24 ft and enjoyed a better arrangement of accommodation below deck. Externally, she differed in having a single funnel abaft the paddle boxes and her propelling machinery comprised a simple double diagonal engine but this was replaced by a compound diagonal unit by David Rowan, Glasgow in 1893. In her later years she was in a poor state of repair and her boiler pressure had sunk to 90 psi, reducing service speed to less than 14 knots. She was finally broken up at Dumbarton in 1904.

The paddle steamer *Tredagh* was built by A & J Inglis, Pointhouse, Glasgow, for the Drogheda Steam Packet Co and entered service to Liverpool and Fleetwood in June 1876. A ship of 878 grt on hull dimensions of 241.2 × 29.3 ft, she was propelled by compound diagonal machinery with a 6-ft piston stroke and developing 1,400

ihp. Her arrival in Drogheda aroused much interest because she was the first cross-channel steamer working to Ireland to have steam steering gear, steam winches for cargo handling and a steam capstan for her anchor. There was good quality berth accommodation for fifty saloon passengers and steerage passengers also had sleeping

accommodation. *Tredagh* was reboilered in 1887 and broken up at Preston in 1904, two years after she had passed into the hands of the Lancashire & Yorkshire Railway Co, following its acquisition of the Drogheda company.

Isle of Man

The handsome 806-grt paddle steamer *King Orry* was delivered to the Isle of Man Steam Packet Co by the Port Glasgow yard of Robert Duncan & Co in 1871. She measured 271 oa × 29.4 ft (54 ft over the paddles) and her simple oscillating engine by Rankin & Blackmore had a 7-ft piston stroke and was supplied with steam by two boilers working at 30 psi and placed either side of her engine-room. Total output was 1,700 ihp and on trials between the Cloch and Cumbrae lights she reached 15.75 knots at 32 rpm, but her normal service speed was 14 knots. Her main saloon was 70 ft long and 8 ft high and in addition she had a full-width dining saloon. In 1888, coupled with a major refit by Fairfield Shipbuilding & Engineering Co, she was lengthened by 30 ft, her funnels were increased in height and a new deck saloon added aft; gross tonnage was increased to 1,104. At the same time she was fitted with a new and more powerful compound diagonal engine with a 7.5-ft piston stroke manufactured by Westray, Copeland & Co; together with new boilers, this increased speed to 17.75 knots. She was also reboilered. After a respectable career of forty-one years, she was disposed of in 1912 and broken up at Llanerch-y-Mor near Mostyn.

The Isle of Man Steam Packet Co's 1,030-grt *Ben-my-Chree* was a product of Barrow Shipbuilding Co in 1875. The first in the company fleet to exceed 1,000 tons, she measured 318 oa × 31 ft and her iron hull incorporated a raised forecastle. She was driven at 14 knots by a simple oscillating engine with the company's longest piston stroke to date at 7.5 ft. Initially, she had two funnels but during a major overhaul in 1884 she was reboilered, emerging as shown with a new promenade deck aft and four funnels mounted in pairs fore and aft of the paddle boxes, similar to the City of Dublin Steam Packet Co's earlier ships. These alterations raised her gross measurement to 1,192 tons. She remained in service for thirty-one years until withdrawn in 1906 and broken up by T W Ward at Morecambe.

Holyhead steamers

The London & North Western Railway opened a new service between Holyhead and Greenore, County Louth, on 2 May 1873, using the paddle steamers *Countess of Erne*, which had been transferred from the Dublin North Wall service, and the brand-new *Eleanor*. The latter was a 917-grt iron steamer built by R Stephenson & Co, Newcastle and her hull measured 252.9 x 30 ft. She was propelled by two oscillating engines with a 6.5-ft piston stroke, which had 350 nhp and were supplied with steam by boilers working at 20 psi. A near-sister, *Earl Spencer**, was launched by Laird Bros, Birkenhead on 4 July 1874. Measuring 859 grt on dimensions of 253.7 x 29.4 ft, she was propelled by similar machinery with a 6-ft piston stroke and had a service speed of 13.5 knots. *Eleanor's* career was cut short on 27 January 1881, when she drove ashore on Leestone Point near Kilkeel, Co Down, while *en route* to Greenore and became a total loss. *Earl Spencer* was withdrawn in February 1896 and broken up in Preston.

The London & North Western Railway Co built two paddle steamers for a new express daytime service between Holyhead and Dublin North Wall, which was inaugurated in July 1876. *Rose** and *Shamrock* were constructed by Laird Bros, Birkenhead and were designed to compete more effectively, especially in terms of speed, with the ships of the City of Dublin Steam Packet Co. At 1,178 grt, they were larger than anything hitherto and their hulls measured 291.8 x 32.2 ft. Their two-cylinder simple oscillating engines of 650 nhp had a 7-ft stroke and maximum speed was 20 knots. The sisters were fitted with new boilers in 1887 and 1886, respectively. *Rose* was sold in 1894 to R Smith of Birkenhead for demolition and scrapped two years later at Tranmere, while *Shamrock* was demolished at Dumbarton in 1898. In 1877 and 1881 Laird completed two smaller versions, *Isabella* and *Eleanor*, for the railway company's Greenore service. The latter, a replacement for an 1873-built namesake lost on 27 January 1881, was constructed of steel and they measured 842/903 grt on dimensions of 254 x 30 ft. Their propelling machinery differed; *Isabella* had a 350-nhp simple oscillating engine with a 6-ft piston stroke and *Eleanor* was fitted with two sets of compound oscillating engines with a 6.5-ft stroke producing 530 nhp; service speed for both was around

14.5 knots. *Isabella* ceased sailing and was broken up early in 1898 and at around the same time *Eleanor* was downgraded to a cargo carrier for the Holyhead–Dublin North Wall service. She was finally withdrawn in March 1902 and broken up.

North Sea

In 1875, Société Anversoise de Bateau á Vapeur (Antwerp Steamship Co) took delivery of the 961-grt paddle steamer *Baron Osy* from the yard of Charles Mitchell & Co, Low Walker. She was the third vessel with this name to operate on the Antwerp–London route and replaced the second of these, a clipper-bowed, twin-funnelled paddle steamer built by John Scott Russell & Co, Millwall, which had been sunk in collision in the Thames in 1863 but later raised and repaired. The new ship, which had two black funnels, measured 237.75 × 30.3 ft and her hull was subdivided by four watertight bulkheads and featured a raised forecastle and long raised poop. Her machinery comprised a pair of compound diagonal engines made by Thompson & Co, Newcastle, with a 6-ft piston stroke. Fed with steam at 65 psi, they were of 250 nhp for a service speed of 12.5 knots. The service ran twice weekly to St Katherine's Wharf near Tower Bridge. Some forty first-class passengers were carried in the poop with third class housed forward and space was provided under the bridge for the carriage of horses and cattle. In 1891 she was sold to Hill, Gomes of Manchester, renamed *Nebula* and converted to twin-screw propulsion by Blackwood & Gordon, Port Glasgow. Her forecastle was raised one deck and a new deck was fitted between its original level and the poop. Her new triple-expansion engines with Morton valve gear were constructed by Kincaid & Co, Greenock, and steam was supplied by a single boiler with three furnaces. She was despatched to Brazil and sailed for the Carioco Navigation Co until lost by fire off Caravellas in 1892.

The popular 962-grt paddle steamer *Claud Hamilton* was completed by John Elder & Co, Glasgow, in 1875 for the Great Eastern Railway Co, following *Richard Young* of 1871, which was the first ship to arrive in Rotterdam via the New Waterway instead of the previous sandbank-strewn Maas estuary. Named after the company's chairman, *Claud Hamilton* measured 251.6 × 30.2 ft and was the first in the fleet to be propelled by a two-cylinder compound oscillating engine, which was of 350 nhp and had a piston stroke of 5.25 ft. She was reboilered in 1888 and nine years later was sold to the Corporation of the City of London and used to convey cattle between Gravesend and the foreign cattle market at Deptford. These had arrived from the Americas in large ships that could not proceed above Gravesend because of draught restrictions. She was sold to breakers at Hendrik-Ido-Ambacht, Netherlands, in August 1914, by which time she was the sole survivor of the former GER paddle steamers.

Experiments on the Dover Strait

Victorian ingenuity knew no bounds and this led to some interesting experiments on the Dover–Calais crossing encouraged by the London, Chatham & Dover Railway Co. In 1874, English Channel Steamship Co took delivery of the unusual-looking 1,533-grt *Castalia* from the Blackwall shipyard of Thames Ironworks & Shipbuilding Co. She was built on the catamaran principle with a broad deck supported by two half hulls with the straight edges pointing inwards and measured 290.4 × 60 ft on a shallow draught of 6 ft. She had four funnels, two on

each hull, and was propelled by two paddle wheels that operated in the 26-ft space between the hulls and were driven by two separate diagonal compound engines with a piston stroke of 5 ft and constructed in London by J & A Blyth. With power of 250 nhp, her speed in service was a disappointing 11 knots. She was also a poor sea-keeper, which did not endear her to the travelling public and after only a few years in service was laid up in Gallions Reach on the Thames. In 1883, she was bought by the Metropolitan Asylums Board, which had used the

old battleship *Atlas* and the frigate *Endymion* for isolation at Dartford of smallpox victims. *Castalia* was converted by R & H Green and emerged looking more like a row of houses than a ship, with five separate ward blocks placed athwartships. She was moored in Long Reach in company with the two older ships and was officially opened in June 1884. The MAB ceased operations in 1902 and *Castalia* was eventually broken up at Garston.

The slightly more conventional twin-hulled, four-funnelled *Express*, built for English Channel Steamship Co by A Leslie & Co, Newcastle in 1877 virtually bankrupted her owner. She was bought at a bargain price by the London, Chatham & Dover Railway Co and after undergoing trials, was more appropriately

renamed *Calais-Douvres* before entering that service in May 1878. Her two normal hulls were connected by strong wrought-iron girders and a single large paddle wheel placed between these. Measuring 1,924 grt and 302 × 61 ft, she was by a long way the largest cross-channel steamer at the time and was initially popular,

but her slow speed of around 13 knots was not sufficient for daytime service and she was too large for the less well patronised night service. As a result, *Calais-Douvres* was withdrawn in 1887 and laid up in Tilbury. Eventually she was sold to coal erchants for use as a hulk on the Thames.

Intended for operation by the London, Chatham & Dover Railway Co, the Bessemer Saloon Ship Co's equally strange 1,886-grt *Bessemer* made her appearance from Earle's Shipbuilding & Engineering Co, Hull, in January 1875. Designed by Sir Henry Bessemer of blast furnace fame, she measured 349.6 x 40.2 ft and featured a double-ended hull with an exceptionally long bridge deck, which dropped down vertically to short, low-freeboard bow and stern sections that Bessemer hoped would reduce pitching by allowing heavy seas to roll over them. Amidships was a large well which contained an 86-ft long swinging saloon that was designed to remain level while the ship moved around it. In the event it was only

possible to counter the transverse motion and even then the hydraulic controls required assistance of skilled manual engineers. Later plans to use gyroscopes for automatic operation never materialised. Her main machinery comprised four sets of simple oscillating engines manufactured by Earle's and which drove two pairs of 30-ft diameter paddle wheels placed 106 ft apart and fitted with feathering floats. Boiler pressure was 30 psi and power amounted to 8,000 ihp, which gave her a speed of about 17 knots on trials. She proved unwieldy to steer in confined areas and collided with Calais Pier on her private trial in April 1875. On the first public voyage, which took place on 8 May 1875, she crashed into Calais

pier again, but this time partly demolishing it. The ship's poor performance lost the confidence of investors and this led to the winding up of the Saloon Ship Co in 1876. The ship, which was returned to Bessemer, remained in dock at Dover until she was sold in 1879 to W Sugden of Hull. She was broken up about a year later. Her swinging saloon ended up in a private house at Swanley, Kent, where it became a billiard room. When the house later became Swanley Agricultural College, the old saloon became a lecture hall, but it was destroyed by a direct hit when the college was bombed during the Second World War.

Newhaven paddlers

The London, Brighton & South Coast Railway Co along with France's Ouest railway company obtained powers to run their own ships on the Newhaven–Dieppe service in 1862 and five years later took the operation from Maples & Morris. In 1875 it took delivery of a more advanced iron paddler steamer, the 483-grt *Paris*, from John Elder & Co, Govan. She measured 220 x 25.2 ft and her two-cylinder compound oscillating engine developed 775 ihp for a service speed of 13 knots. Steam was supplied by two circular boilers working at 60 psi and the piston stroke was 5 ft. Once in service, her speed proved to be disappointing even after curved floats had been substituted for the original flat floats on her paddle wheels. *Paris* only once accomplished the crossing in under five hours, taking ten minutes less on 3 March 1888 a few months before she was sold to Fairfield Shipbuilding & Engineering Co. The yard fitted new boilers with a working pressure of 80 psi and in 1890 *Paris* was sold to Richard Barnwell, managing director of Fairfield. She was operated by New North Wales Steamship Co on excursion services in North Wales for a couple of seasons under the name *Flamingo*. She then passed on charter to Albert Ballin for Elbe–Heligoland service and returned to Barnwell in 1895. Two years later she was sold to W M Rhodes, who

renamed her *La Belgique* and ran her for a season between Tilbury and Ostend. In 1902, she changed hands for the fifth time and became David MacBrayne's *Glendale*. She was wrecked in July 1905. *(Newhaven Historical Society)*

The London, Brighton & South Coast Railway Co ordered two paddle steamers from John Elder & Co, Govan, in anticipation of extra traffic arising from the Paris International Exhibition of 1878. *Brighton* and *Victoria** were of 531 grt and the first on the Newhaven service to be built of steel. They measured 221.3 x 27.7 ft but drew only 7 ft due to a lack of water at low tide in both Newhaven and Dieppe. They had two funnels, which were distinctive because they were not fully cased, and were driven by two-cylinder compound diagonal engines with a 5-ft stroke, with steam supplied by four Stroudley cylindrical boilers working at 80 psi. Power output was 2,000 ihp and the contract speed of 15 knots was comfortably exceeded when *Brighton* recorded 17.5 knots on trials in March 1878. Two years after entering service, their paddle wheels were replaced by a new feathering type designed by William Stroudley, the railway company's renowned locomotive engineer. *Victoria* was the more accident-prone of the pair, hitting the pier at Newhaven on her first arrival and grounding near Rottingdean on her first crossing. Her next grounding in fog on the French coast on 13 April 1887 proved to be her last. Due to a fog signal not operating, she struck rocks near Point d'Ailly and in the ensuing panic one of her lifeboats upended in the falls and nineteen of its twenty-one occupants drowned – the only deaths ever recorded on the Newhaven–Dieppe route. She quickly broke up and was a total loss. Just two years later, *Brighton* struck the pier while entering Dieppe in fog and sank in the inner harbour. She was purchased 'as lies' by a French broker who raised and repaired her and sold her to Pockett's Bristol Channel Steam Packet Co for excursion work between Swansea, Ilfracombe and Lundy. Later her mainmast was removed and her saloon was widened and extended aft. During the First World War, she was requisitioned by the Admiralty for use as a minelayer in the Dardanelles campaign and after the war was sold to a Turkish company, which ran her in local waters until 1927 when she was broken up, in her fiftieth year. *(Newhaven Historical Society)*

Dutch North Sea paddle steamers

The 1,652-grt iron paddle steamers *Prinses Marie** and *Prinses Elisabeth* were the first new ships ordered by Stoomvaart Maatschappij Zeeland (Zeeland Line). Designed for the overnight Vlissingen (Flushing)–Queenborough (Medway) service, they were constructed in Glasgow by John Elder & Co and entered service in March and April 1878. Hull measurements were 278.2 x 35.1 ft and they were propelled by two-cylinder compound oscillating machinery developing 3,000 ihp for a speed of 16 knots in service. Sleeping berths were supplied for 240 passengers, of which around 150 were in first class. In 1889 the vessels were reboilered by Elder, after which *Prinses Marie* attained

just over 17 knots on trials. In 1896 *Prinses Marie* was chartered to Albert Ballin for one season on the Elbe–Heligoland service as *Prinzess Marie* with a white hull. Both were sold in 1898, *Prinses Marie* to Stettiner DG with the new name *Germania* and her sister to G O Wallenberg of Stockholm (Svea Line), which rechristened her *Svea* in 1901. Both were employed in a joint service between Stettin and Stockholm until *Germania* was broken up at Zwijndrecht in 1902. *Svea* continued until 1909 and was broken up at Stettin the following year. Zeeland Line had returned to John Elder for a similarly-dimensioned steamer to cope with the anticipated extra traffic arising from the opening in 1880 of a through-rail

service from London to Berlin. The 1,573-grt *Prins Hendrik* was delivered on 11 May and was driven by similarly powered compound oscillating engines. A fourth ship, *Willem Prins van Oranje*, entered service on 12 July 1883 after attaining over 18 knots at 4,628 ihp during trials. Both ships were given new boilers by their builder in 1889 and 1896 respectively and their funnels were possibly heightened at this time. *Prins Hendrik* was laid up at Flushing in 1895 and broken up by Gebrüder Specht in Bremen in 1902. Her sister became a reserve ship and was demolished in 1908 at Hendrik-Ido-Ambacht.

2

Screw Begins to Challenge Paddle

While paddle steamers continued to dominate on most cross-channel routes, several operating companies began to adopt screw propulsion, initially for small, mainly cargo-carrying steamers. Among these were Glasgow-based J & G Burns and the London & South Western Railway and the latter together with another Clyde company, Laird Line, and the Great Eastern Railway were among the first to make a complete switch from paddle to screw. The early passenger ships were single-screw vessels driven by compound machinery, but the Great Eastern Railway introduced twin screw installations with its first such vessels in 1883.

A notable feature of this period was the delivery in 1888 of two paddle steamers to the Belgian government by the small Clyde shipyard of William Denny & Brothers, which had won the contract on the strength of calculations derived from its novel ship testing tank. The success of these vessels marked the beginning of the yard's long association with building cross-channel steamers that was to last for some eighty years.

Note: An asterisk in a caption indicates the vessel shown in the photograph.

Screw steamers for Clyde and Channel Islands services

The twin-screw sisters *Azalea** and *Cedar* were delivered to the Glasgow & Londonderry Steam Packet Co (managed by A A Laird & Co, and also known as Laird Line) in 1878 by A & J Inglis and D & W Henderson, Glasgow. They measured 706 grt on dimensions of 217.7 x 30.4 ft and were propelled by two-cylinder compound engines of 242/260 nhp respectively. *Azalea* made 13.5 knots on trials on 2 October. Intended for the Glasgow–Londonderry service, they carried seventy saloon-class passengers but *Azalea* spent her initial year on the Dublin station. During the next few years, both vessels had changes of registered owner, and in the 1890s both underwent major refits – *Cedar* in 1892 and *Azalea* the following year – receiving improved accommodation and new high-pressure boilers, which raised trial speed to 14 knots. After this, *Azalea* mainly operated on the Gourock–Portrush or Ardrossan–Portrush daytime services, inaugurating the latter on which she alternated every other day with the Laird steamer *Lily*. *Cedar* was sold to the Ayr Steam Shipping Co in July 1906 and renamed *Dunure* and following the acquisition of the Ayr company in May 1908, *Azalea* was transferred to the Ayr–Belfast route until sold in June 1914 to G Yannoulatos Frères, Navigation à Vapeur 'Ionienne', of Piraeus, initially as *Chalkis* and later as *Nafktratoussa*. From 1933 she sailed as *Psara* for the newly-formed Hellenic Coast Lines and was broken up on the eve of the Second World War in May 1939. In the meantime, her sister *Dunure* had returned to Laird Line in 1921 and passed to the newly-merged Burns & Laird Lines the following year. In February 1924, she followed *Azalea* to Greek waters, sailing under the Kavounides banner in turn as *Nicholaos Kavounides*, *Bosphoros*, *Express* and *Zephiros*. Her final name was *Spetsai* and she was sold for scrap in January 1938.

The involvement of Glasgow shipowner J & G Burns with the mail service to Belfast began in 1849 and it was one of the first companies engaged in the Irish Sea cross-channel trade to adopt screw propulsion. Improved ships were introduced at regular intervals and the first screw-driven passenger ship on the Belfast run was *Walrus* in 1878. Three years later, the company took delivery of the larger sister ships *Alligator*, *Dromedary** and *Gorilla* from Barclay Curle, Whiteinch. Measuring around 930 grt on dimensions of 250.25 x 30 ft, they were driven by two-cylinder compound engines of 280 nhp that gave a maximum speed of around 14 knots. They received new boilers in 1891–2, after which speed was increased by around one knot. *Gorilla* was transferred to the Glasgow–Liverpool coastal service in 1906 and the following June *Alligator* was sold to Hellenic Steam Navigation Co (the manager of which was J McDowall & Barbour) and was renamed *Ismene*. *Dromedary* was disposed of in August 1909 to Reid Newfoundland Co, St John's, and became *Invermore* but was wrecked at Brigpoint, Labrador, on 10 July 1914 on voyage from St John's with provisions and fishery supplies. *Gorilla* followed *Alligator* to Greek waters in 1913, becoming G Yannoulatos Frères' *Nafkratoussa*, but had to be sunk by Royal Navy gunfire off the Gallipoli peninsula on 30 January 1918 after she had caught fire while loading cased petrol. *Ismene* was sold to A G Yannoulatos in 1927 and sailed as *Afovos* until 1933 when her name was changed to *Rodos* following the setting up of Hellenic Coast Lines. She was broken up in 1934.

The London & South Western Railway Co abandoned its usual London shipyards and in 1876 turned to Aitken & Mansel, Whiteinch, for the new steamer *Diana*. Notable as the first passenger ferry on the English Channel to be driven by screw propulsion, she had a raised forecastle and single funnel, and her main particulars were 738 grt on dimensions of 232.6 x 28.2 ft. Her two-cylinder compound engine made by J & J Thompson developed 1,650 ihp and gave her a speed of 14 knots on trials in Stokes Bay. A boat deck was added in October 1881 and she was transferred to the St Malo service in 1890. Her engine was tripled in 1892 but when northbound on 21 June 1895, *Diana* struck rocks in fog near Cap de la Hague and sank two days later. Two improved and slightly larger versions, *Ella** and *Hilda*, were delivered by the same yard in 1881 and these measured 820 grt on dimensions of 235.5 x 29.1 ft. Their twin-cylinder compound engines constructed by J & J Thomson fed by a single boiler developed 1,530 ihp for a maximum of 14 knots, with 1,330 ihp sufficient for 13.5 knots in service. The iron hulls featured a single deck with a long raised forecastle and a tall funnel was set between two tall closely-spaced masts that gave them an elegant yacht-like appearance. They carried 450 passengers and *Ella* was generally employed on the Le Havre service, while her sister ran to the Channel Islands and St Malo. In 1896 the former was reboiled and had electric lighting installed by Day, Summers in Southampton; *Hilda* was

treated likewise during a winter 1896–7 refit. Tragedy struck on the night of 18 November 1905, when *Hilda* was entering St Malo in blizzard conditions. She struck the Rocher du Jardin (Garden Rock) and broke her back, foundering with the loss of 128 lives. *Ella* continued to serve the railway company until the end of July 1913, when she was sold to the Shipping Federation and left for Liverpool. She was used to house workless persons and was eventually sold to T W Ward in February 1929 and broken up at Grays, Essex.

Paddle developments

Irish Sea

The Great Western Railway's last and largest paddle steamer, the 977-grt *Pembroke*, was completed by Laird Bros at Birkenhead in 1880. A steel vessel measuring 235.5 x 27.6 ft and 15 ft draught, she was based at Milford and made some fast passages to Waterford. She was propelled at 14 knots by twin two-cylinder compound oscillating engines of 400 nhp with a 7-ft piston stroke and steam was supplied by two double-ended return tube boilers. On 16 March 1895 she was disabled when approaching Waterford due to a fractured low-pressure cylinder piston rod and in June was sent back to Lairds which converted her (as depicted) to twin-screw propulsion with two triple-expansion engines and new boilers. The combined output of 3,500 ihp gave her a trials speed of 17.5 knots and her normal speed was 16 knots. Gross tonnage was now 976 grt and hull dimensions 254 x 30.9 ft. She returned to service on 17 May 1896 and in thick fog on 13 February 1899 stranded on rocks off Saltee Island, but was refloated after five days and towed to Waterford, later steaming to Birkenhead for repairs. In 1906 she was transferred to Fishguard on the closure of the Milford service and officially opened the new Fishguard–Waterford service on 21 July. She occasionally acted as a tender during the brief period when ocean liners called at the Welsh port

to land passengers and mail for onward carriage to London by rail. Displaced by *Waterford* in May 1912, she was converted to a 665-passenger tender but was either used for cattle carriage or laid up. *Pembroke* was transferred to the Weymouth–Channel Islands station in March 1916, acting mainly as a cargo carrier but

occasionally taking up to forty passengers, and after the First World War sailed in summer only with agricultural produce. Replaced by the new cargo ship *Roebuck* in 1925, she made her last crossing on 25 July and the following month was towed to the Firth of Forth for demolition by Alloa Shipbreaking at Charlestown.

The London & North Western Railway Co paddle steamers *Lily* and *Violet** were built by Laird Bros, Birkenhead in 1880 to inaugurate a new overnight service between Holyhead and Dublin North Wall. Their entry into service coincided with the completion of a new inner harbour at the Anglesey port, which allowed steamers to berth next to the boat trains. Gross measurement was 1,035 tons and hull dimensions 300 × 33.1 ft. As built, they had simple oscillating engines, which developed 3,200 ihp and allowed them to reach a speed of 17.75 knots, but in 1891/1890 respectively they were re-engined and reboilered to increase speed to 19.5 knots. The railway company stipulated that the changes were in no way to impinge on the existing passenger spaces, so the new engines were triple-expansion steeple units with Joy's valve gear. Steam was supplied by six locomotive-type boilers and the improved power output amounted to 4,087 ihp at 35 rpm. The alterations resulted in marginal increase in gross tonnage to 1,175 and 1,114. The two sisters spent their entire career with the railway company on the Dublin service and *Lily* was eventually withdrawn in April 1900 and her sister two years later. Both were sold to the Liverpool & Douglas Steamers Co, which ran a short-lived service from the Mersey to the Isle of Man, *Violet* being scrapped in 1903 and *Lily* in 1905 by T W Ward at Preston.

The 1,564-grt paddle steamer *Mona's Isle** was delivered to the Isle of Man Steam Packet Co by Caird & Co of Greenock in May 1882. She was the first of the company's ships to be built of steel and was considerably larger than her predecessors at just over 338 oa × 38.1 ft. She was propelled by surface condensing, compound oscillating machinery with a 7.5-ft piston stroke and the diameter of her low pressure cylinder was over 9.25 ft. The combined output of 4,500 ihp provided a service speed of 17.5 knots, which enabled her to reduce the Liverpool–Douglas passage time by forty-five minutes to three hours and thirty-five minutes. In 1886 her paddle wheels were strengthened and given new floats after she had suffered damage in heavy seas the previous May. Inbound from Dublin on 6 September 1892, she grounded on Scarlett Point near Castletown with 500 passengers on board but all were safely disembarked and she was refloated two days later. After thirty-three years serving the Isle of Man, *Mona's Isle* was bought by the Admiralty in 1915 and engaged in laying anti-submarine net defences around the UK in addition to patrolling off the west coast of Ireland to counter the threat of gun running. She helped salve guns from the torpedoed HMS *Arethusa* and acted as a base ship for a further salvage operation on a Dutch steamer that had been torpedoed off the Cork light vessel. After the war she was broken up by T W Ward at Morecambe in 1919. In 1885, Barrow Shipbuilding Co delivered the similar *Mona's Queen*, which arrived in Douglas in July and was placed on the Fleetwood service. Priming trouble with her boilers necessitated a return to her builders after her first season

but she proved a popular vessel and often completed the voyage between Douglas and the Wyre Light off Fleetwood in less than three hours. Taken up in the First World War, *Mona's Queen* rammed and sank a U-boat in

the English Channel on 6 February 1917. When broken up at Port Glasgow towards the end of 1929, she was the last paddle steamer in Europe.

North Sea

The 995-grt *Lady Tyler* was completed by T & W Smith at North Shields in May 1880 for the Great Eastern Railway's Harwich–Rotterdam service. Her iron hull measured 261 x 30.2 ft and her main machinery constructed by R & W Hawthorn comprised a compound engine with two high pressure and four low pressure cylinders and a 5-ft piston stroke. Power output was 1,400 ihp for a service speed of 13 knots. Her single raked funnel placed abaft the paddle boxes gave her a somewhat unbalanced look and she could carry around 700 passengers in two classes, her main saloon being 40 ft in length. She was soon displaced by more efficient screw-driven ships and after only thirteen years was sold in 1893 to Earle's Shipbuilding & Engineering Co, Hull, in part payment for a new vessel. Two years later she was chartered to Mutual Line of Manx Steamers, which was attempting to run a service from Liverpool to the Isle of Man in opposition to the old-established Isle of Man Steam Packet Co. Her lack of speed counted against her, earning her the soubriquet 'the lazy toiler', and she was laid up when her owners went bankrupt after less than three months. In 1897 she was bought by Earle's and renamed *Artemis* and in March 1900 was reduced to a coal hulk for George Sandford, serving for the next half century at Gravesend until broken up in 1955.

The last paddle steamer built by the Great Eastern Railway was the 969-grt *Adelaide*, which was launched by Barrow Shipbuilding Co on 8 May 1880. On completion, she underwent a 100-mile trial during which she averaged 14.5 knots. Marginally larger than the preceding *Lady Tyler*, she measured 260 oa x 32.3 ft and was driven by two-cylinder compound oscillating machinery with a 6-ft piston stroke and which developed 1,600 ihp for a service speed of 14.5 knots. She was a handsome two-deck steamer with two well-raked masts and funnels and her accommodation was described as being the equal of the Barrow-built Atlantic liners. She could carry 682 passengers and overnight berths were provided for 113 in first class and fifty-eight in second class. *Lady Tyler* had a comparatively short career and was sold to T W Ward for scrap in 1896, but was handed on to J Bannatyne & Sons and was hulked at Preston in June 1897.

English Channel

The South Eastern Railway built two more iron steamers at Samuda Bros, the 276-grt *Alexandra* and the 388-grt *Napoleon III*, in 1864–5 before it embarked on a programme to build larger packets to increase the popularity of the Boulogne route. Sisters *Albert Victor* and *Louise Dagmar** were also Samuda products, completed in 1880, and were the first of the company's ships to be built of steel and the first to have bow rudders. They measured 782 grt on dimensions of 250 x 29.2 ft and oscillating engines by John Penn produced 2,800 ihp, which was sufficient to maintain a service speed of 16 knots (*Albert Victor* averaged 18.5 knots during six trial runs off Maplin). Passenger capacity was around 600 and from April 1885 fixed schedule running became possible following the deepening of Folkestone harbour. On 7 April 1893, *Louise Dagmar* damaged her bow following collision with the French steamer *Alberte*, while on passage to Folkestone and required ten days for repairs by R & H Green. The merger of the SER with the London, Chatham & Dover Railway in 1899 produced a surplus of steamers and both ships were broken up after just twenty years of service. A near-sister, *Duchess of Edinburgh*, was completed at Clydebank in spring 1881 by J & G Thomson (later John Brown & Co) but averaged just over 17.5 knots on trials and proved disappointing in service. She was withdrawn after a few trips in August 1882 and was soon sold to J Little and Co, Barrow-in-Furness, for service to the Isle of Man. Lengthened in 1883 by almost 30 ft, the renamed 989-grt *Manx Queen* in 1883, she was chartered to Belgium in 1888–9 to stand in for the new *Prince Albert* on the Ostend service and was reboilered in 1895. A

decade later she passed into the hands of the Midland Railway and was broken up by J J King at Garston in 1908. To replace her in the SER fleet, Samuda built *Mary Beatrice* in 1882, which echoed the original pair in all particulars except she was 5 ft longer, raising gross registered measurement to 803 tons. The bell tops to her funnels were removed during a major refit in 1898 and after lying alongside Dover's Admiralty Pier for a while, she was sold for scrap in January 1900.

The London, Chatham & Dover Railway Co's *Invicta* was the first 'modern' paddle steamer built for the Dover–Calais service and the last of her type to come from the Thames, namely the Blackwall yard of Thames Ironworks. Measuring 1,197 grt on dimensions of 312.3 x 33.6 ft, she was the largest conventional channel paddle steamer of her day when delivered in 1882, but she retained the double-ended hull design employed in the three experimental vessels that preceded her, which facilitated manoeuvring astern into both Dover and Calais. Her simple oscillating machinery by Maudslay, Sons & Field had a piston stroke of 6.75 ft and steam was supplied by box return tube boilers, the whole generating some 4,000 ihp for a speed of 18.5 knots on trials. She was a fine-looking vessel with two raked funnels and masts, the former with horizontal tops. In April 1888, she was stranded off Calais for several days after stormy weather had shifted the sandbanks but although continuously swept by the seas, she was eventually refloated by five tugs without serious damage. Some six years later, she repeated the mishap and in 1896 was chartered to Compagnie du Chemin de Fer du Nord following an Anglo–French mail sharing agreement. She ran under French colours and with a French crew for two years until the French railway company's two new paddle steamers were ready, after which she was returned to the LC&DR and laid up. She was broken up at Hendrik-Ido-Ambacht, Netherlands, in 1899.

In July and August 1882, the London, Brighton & South Coast Railway took delivery of the 605-grt paddle steamers *Brittany* and *Normandy** from John Elder & Co. Larger than the preceding *Brighton* and *Victoria*, they measured 231 x 27.7 ft and the design incorporated fully-cased funnels and Stroudley's feathering paddle floats. The latter were complex and prone to breakdown but these drawbacks were more than compensated for by an increase in both efficiency and speed. Both ships recorded their fastest crossing times within a month of each other in summer 1885, *Brittany* taking three hours and thirty-seven minutes and *Normandy* five minutes less. The latter grounded on rocks near Beachy Head in thick fog in June 1891 but was refloated at high water and taken to London for repairs. The following year *Brittany* was reboilered in Glasgow and at the same time taller funnels were fitted and her after deckhouse extended forward to the second funnel. Both ships were sold in 1902 to Liverpool & Douglas Steamers, which had begun a service in opposition to the established Isle of Man Steam Packet Co, but the company folded before they could be used. *Brittany* was broken up at Preston in 1904, but her sister was bought in 1903 by James R Richards of Swansea for his newly-formed Normandy Steamship Co, for excursion work in the Bristol Channel. With red funnels under black tops, she frequently raced her former Newhaven running

mate *Brighton* – both vessels were evenly matched. Normandy Steamship Co was wound up in 1907 and *Normandy* was broken up at Voryd Harbour, Rhyl in 1909.

River Plate paddle steamers

William Denny & Bros had built a number of paddle steamers for River Plate service, including the 1,255-grt *Apolo* and *Minerva* in 1883 for the Paris-registered Compagnie La Platense's mail and passenger service linking Buenos Aires with Montevideo. In 1886 Wm Denny and Paddy Henderson formed a joint venture in Argentina and styled La Platense Flotilla, for which Denny built two larger paddle steamers for the Montevideo service, the 1,749-grt *Venus** and *Eolo*, which measured 299 × 35.1 ft on draught of 8.5 ft. They were driven at 14.5 knots in service by 524-nhp compound oscillating engines fed by one single- and one double-ended boiler. Their paddles were fitted with ten feathering floats and electrically lit accommodation was provided for 244 first- and seventy-two second-class passengers. Their hulls were painted black and the funnels red with a black top. Boarded up for the delivery journey, they steamed out to Argentina about a month apart in August and September. In 1896 *Eolo* was sold to Saturnino Ribes of Montevideo and was operated under the Uruguayan flag by Mensajeries Fluviales de Plata, but when Ribes died four years later, *Eolo* was acquired by Nicolas Mihanovich's Argentine Navigation Co. Both ships were rebuilt in 1904, with accommodation altered to cater for ninety first-class and fifty-two second-class passengers, and in 1919 they were transferred to Uruguayan flag. On 19 September 1928, the Rosario-bound *Eolo* sank at Km

227 in the Parana River following collision with the steamer *Olympier* and *Venus* was sold in 1930 for use as a hotel at Puerto Aguirre, about twenty kilometres from the Iguaçu Falls.

New screw steamers for North and Irish seas

Anticipating completion of its new Parkeston Quay, which was being constructed on marshland on the south bank of the River Stour two miles upstream from Harwich, the Great Eastern Railway ordered its first screw-driven steamers from Earle's Shipbuilding & Engineering, Hull, a company that had previously carried out repair work on its paddle steamers. The 1,065-grt *Norwich** and *Ipswich* were completed in July and October 1883 to coincide with the opening of the new quay, which replaced the old Continental Pier at Harwich. Built of iron, their hulls measured 260.2 × 31.3 ft and were of the three-island type with the well decks hidden by high-sided hinged doors. Propulsion was by a pair of two-cylinder inverted surface-condensing diagonal compound engines fed with steam by two double-ended boilers. Power output was around 2,000 ihp for a service speed of 14 knots and *Norwich* made 16 knots on trials. First-class accommodation was provided for eighty-four passengers forward of the machinery space with forty-two second class housed beneath the poop. The two ships were generally employed on the Antwerp service and were reboilered in 1895 and 1897 respectively. Disposal came in 1905: *Ipswich* was sold in 1906 to the Shah Steam Navigation Co of Bombay, passing two years later to the Bombay & Hujaz Steam Navigation of India Co and broken up locally in 1909. *Norwich*, meanwhile, had been bought by Channel Dry Docks & Engineering Co but ownership passed to Queenstown

Dry Docks Shipbuilding & Engineering Co in 1906. Between 1908 and 1911, she was registered to The Shipping Syndicate, before passing to Portugal's Empreza de Navegaçao as *Fortuna* and was based at Fogo in the Cape Verde Islands. In 1913 she crossed the South Atlantic to Montevideo and ran as F Alessi's *Evelyn* but two years later was registered in New York as Continental Trading Co's *Neptune*. She sailed under this name for three more New York owners, Cuneo Importing, Federal Operating and Mexican Fruit & Steamship Co before she was finally wrecked on Palas Rock near Cardenas on 18 March 1921 after an interesting and varied thirty-eight-year career.

In 1882, the Belfast Steamship Co turned for the first time to local yard Harland & Wolff for a new steamer for its Belfast–Liverpool express service. *Dynamic* was built of iron and was both larger and faster than the company's previous tonnage, measuring 937 grt on dimensions of 243.3 x 31.9 ft and her two-cylinder compound engine drove her at 14.5 knots. She entered service on 18 December 1883, but her popularity and more importantly her speed soon attracted the attention of the Admiralty, which chartered her in May 1885 for a voyage to the Mediterranean and again the following year for a round trip to Malta. After this her passenger accommodation was improved and electric lighting fitted to bring her into line with the newer *Caloric* and *Optic* but later in her career she ran a twice-weekly cargo service to Liverpool together with Saturday excursions down Belfast Lough and to Larne. In 1894–5 she sailed for a while to Londonderry and in 1899 she was sold to Union Comercial de Vapores, Mallorca, which renamed her *Mallorca* the following year and placed her in service to Barcelona. She later sailed on a more coastal route and in 1904 was on a Palma–Tangier–Gibraltar run. In 1905 she was sold to Greek owner A Diakaki and as *Principessa Sophia* ran mainly to the Cyclades and also occasionally to Alexandria. In 1912 *Mallorca* was renamed *Ittihad* by Ibrahim Scounaki's Ittihad Steamship Co but was seized by Greece during the First Balkan War. She reverted to her Greek name but was captured by the Russian navy in 1916 and used as the submarine depot ship *Dobycha*. At the conclusion of the Bolshevik revolution, she was one of the White Russian ships that escaped from the Black Sea and ended up in Bizerta. In December 1922, she became *Ambro* of Transitaria Italiana Marittima, Genoa, and was finally broken up in 1925.

Pleased with *Dynamic*, Belfast Steamship Co returned to Harland & Wolff for a pair of more advanced steel steamers for its express Liverpool service. *Caloric* and *Optic* were completed on 12 December 1885 and 29 January 1886 respectively and were elegant ships with a single funnel and considerably more superstructure than *Dynamic*. They measured 982/980 grt on dimensions of 243.9 x 31.9 ft and their hulls were fitted with bilge keels. Two compound engines gave a service speed of 15 knots, which allowed the 137-mile passage to be completed in eleven hours. Lit by electricity, they were fitted with overnight berths for about 125 passengers. *Optic* briefly relieved *Dynamic* on the Liverpool cargo

service and on 25 February 1892 collided with the Antrim Iron Ore Co's steamer *Rathkenny* off Belfast Lough. In June 1895, *Caloric* made a round-Ireland cruise with seventy-five passengers and the following month cruised from Belfast to Galway. Replaced by new tonnage, *Optic* was sold in May 1907 to Sociedad Navegacion y Industria, Barcelona, and renamed *Delfin**. Initially she ran from Cadiz to the Canary Islands, but after the formation of Compania Trasmediterranea in 1917 she served on most routes, including to the Balearics. During the Spanish Civil War, she was briefly used as a prison ship in Malaga in summer 1936, after which she put in a coastal service to Alicante via Almeria

and Cartagena. While returning to Malaga from Almeria on 30 January 1937, she was attacked by torpedo-carrying aircraft and beached herself at La Herredura, off Torrox. The following day she was torpedoed by the Italian submarine *Ciro Menotti* and on 2 February her wreck was bombed. *Caloric* was given improved accommodation and acted as reserve ship until replaced by *Patriotic* in 1912. She was sold to Greece in November 1914 and sailed initially as *Adriaticos* but was renamed *Syros* by Hellenic Coast Lines in 1933. After further changes of name and owner, she was scrapped at La Spezia in 1952 as *Costas* after a career of over sixty-five years.

Further Irish Sea and English Channel paddle steamers

The London & North Western Railway's final cross-channel paddle steamer, *Banshee*, was launched at Birkenhead by Laird Bros on 30 January 1884. A steel two-funnelled ship, she measured 310 x 34.1 ft and had a gross tonnage of 1,250, while simple oscillating machinery with a 7-ft piston stroke provided a speed of 19 knots. Steam was provided by eight boilers and she was fitted with electric light. After a decade working the Holyhead–Dublin service, *Banshee* was re-engined with triple-expansion machinery with a 6.5-ft stroke, which provided an output of 1,030 nhp and increased her speed to 21 knots. She was reboilered at the same time. In February 1906, she was sold for scrap to J J King of Garston but was resold to breakers at Genoa.

The City of Dublin Steam Packet Co's final paddle steamer, the 2,049-grt *Ireland*, was launched by Laird Bros at Birkenhead on 30 April 1885. The longest and largest cross-channel ship of her day, she had two funnels and was the last to have a clipper bow. She measured 380 oa x 38 ft and was propelled by a two-cylinder simple oscillating engine fitted with jet condensers and having an 8.5-ft piston stroke. The total power output of 5,000 ihp using natural draught and 6,000 ihp with forced draught gave her a speed of 20.25 knots on trials. Her paddle wheels measured 33.3 ft over the floats, which were 13 ft long and 5.75 ft wide. On 27 June 1887, she made the passage from Holyhead to Kingstown in just two hours and forty-four minutes when transporting the Dukes of York and Clarence to Ireland for the Golden Jubilee celebrations. In service, she generally proved to be less successful than her predecessors because her huge cylinders suffered from constant trunnion problems and she was sold in 1899 to S W Higginbottom's Liverpool & Douglas Steamers Co. She was slow by this time and being completely outclassed by the rival Isle of Man Steam Packet Co's newer ships, was sold for demolition in France, arriving in Brest on 16 October 1900. The company folded after Higginbottom's death in December 1902.

In 1886 a new company, the Isle of Man, Liverpool & Manchester Steamship Co (or Manx Line), was formed to run in opposition to the long-established Isle of Man Steam Packet Co, and it ordered two large paddle steamers from Fairfield Shipbuilding & Engineering Co, Glasgow. Completed in April and May the following year, *Queen Victoria** and *Prince of Wales* measured 1,657 grt on dimensions of 341.5 oa × 39.1 ft and their design featured two funnels and a flush hull offering passengers almost unobstructed use of the weather deck, save for mooring areas at the bow and stern. In the engine-room, four double-ended boilers supplied steam to two-cylinder compound diagonal engines with a piston stroke of 6.5 ft and output of 6,500 ihp for a speed of 20 knots. Passenger complement was 1,600 persons, served by sixty crew members. In service, they proved to be thirty minutes faster than the Packet Company's ships and *Prince of Wales* made a passage from the Rock Lighthouse to Douglas in one minute under three hours. The Steam Packet Co cut its fares in retaliation and Manx Line followed suit, with the result that both lost money and after only two seasons the IOMSP Co bought out its rival. In 1915 both ships were bought by

the Admiralty and employed as anti-submarine net layers in the Mediterranean, for which *Prince of Wales* was renamed HMS *Prince Edward*. After the war they were of

no further use and were scrapped in 1920 by T C Pas in Scheveningen.

In 1885 the Seacombe yard of A Jack & Co delivered the 988-grt steel paddle steamer *Kathleen Mavourneen* to the Drogheda Steam Packet Co. A steel paddle steamer with single funnel abaft the paddle boxes, she measured 260.5 × 31 ft and was fitted with a two-cylinder compound oscillating engine with a 6-ft piston stroke and developing 2,000 ihp. The 995-grt *Iverna**, completed by A & J Inglis in November 1895, was similar in appearance but her hull dimensions were slightly

smaller at 255 × 30.2 ft. *Iverna's* triple-expansion engine developed 1,800 ihp but had a piston stroke 6 in longer than the earlier ship. Both vessels were transferred to the Lancashire & Yorkshire Railway Co in 1902, when that company acquired Drogheda SP Co. *Kathleen Mavourneen* was broken up in in Holland in 1903 after a fairly short eighteen-year career and *Iverna* lasted one year less when she was sold in July 1912 to T W Ward for demolition at Preston.

The London, Chatham & Dover Railway Co's *Victoria* and *Empress* followed the pattern set by *Invicta*, but both were products of Fairfield Shipbuilding & Engineering Co, Glasgow, in 1886 and 1887. *Victoria* was shorter at 309.4 × 34.1 ft with a corresponding gross measurement of 1,042 tons but *Empress* was larger at 1,282 grt on dimensions of 324.6 × 35.9 ft. They were, however, somewhat more powerful with compound diagonal engines delivering 5,000 ihp, and the former 18 knots and the latter, due to her greater length, over 19 knots in service. The piston stroke was 6 ft and steam was supplied by two double-ended and two single-ended cylindrical boilers. Boilers had comparatively short lives in those days and the latter had new boilers fitted in 1895. On 4 March 1895, *Empress* damaged a paddle wheel after hitting Calais Pier and drifted until grounding the next morning, spending several weeks on the sand. The following year *Victoria*, along with *Invicta*, was loaned to France's Nord railway company for two years in 1896 but on return to UK flag, continued to operate until 1904, when she was scrapped by the Shipbreaking Co, London. *Empress* was broken up two years later.

Resuscitating the name of the ill-fated catamaran of 1877, *Calais-Douvres** was another Fairfield product, launched in April 1889 and completed in time for the additional traffic expected to be generated by the Paris Exhibition of that year. Broadly similar to the preceding *Empress*, she differed in having 4.5 ft greater beam and slightly more powerful machinery developing 6,450 ihp, with her four double-ended boilers working under forced draught. On trials on the Skelmorlie mile, she

recorded maximum of 21.25 knots and averaged 20.75 knots. The formation of the new SE&CR in 1899 rendered her surplus and she was sold after only eleven years in service to S W Higginbottom's Liverpool & Douglas Steamers, which failed in its attempt to rival the Isle of Man Steam Packet Co. The latter acquired her in 1903 and she was renamed *Mona*, after which she operated the island service from Liverpool until 1909 when she was broken up at Briton Ferry.

In 1886 the Belgian government ordered two new large paddle steamers from John Cockerill's yard at Hoboken to meet increasing demand on the Ostend–Dover run by offering a thrice-daily service. *Prince Albert* and *Ville de Douvres** measured 797 grt on dimensions of 256 × 29 ft and were propelled by two-cylinder simple oscillating engines. They made their maiden crossings in April and May 1887 respectively, but failed to live up to expectations in service. *Prince Albert* was returned to her builders for replacement of engines and boilers, while at the same time she lengthened by 16 ft and increased in gross registered tonnage to 861. She returned to service in September 1889, having in the meantime been replaced by the chartered *Manx Queen* (formerly the South Eastern Railway's *Duchess of Edinburgh*) and was now capable of a respectable 19 knots from her new compound diagonal machinery, which had a 6-ft piston stroke. Her sister was treated likewise and emerged from Cockerill the following February. In the meantime, a third sister, *La Flandre*, which incorporated the improvements from the outset, had made her debut in December 1889. All three ships performed satisfactorily until 1908, when *Prince Albert* was sold to Turkish owners in Constantinople and *Ville de Douvres* was scrapped in the north of England. *La Flandre* lasted until October 1918, when the retreating German army sank her as a blockship at Ostend.

The Belgian government ordered a fast new mail steamer from the Dumbarton firm of Wm Denny & Bros towards the end of 1887. She was to achieve 20.5 knots on a length of no more than 300 ft, but thanks to its new testing tank and a new type of lighter, more powerful compound diagonal machinery, the yard met the specifications within the stipulated seven months and thus began its long history as a noted builder of high-class cross-channel vessels. *Princesse Henriette** and sister *Princesse Josephine*, ordered while the former was under construction, were delivered in June and November 1888 and were unique in the Belgian channel fleet in that they were double-ended due to length restrictions in Ostend. They were fitted with bow rudders to facilitate entering or leaving harbour astern. The gross tons measurement was around 1,100 on dimensions of 300 × 38 ft and steam was supplied by six Admiralty-type boilers. Their two-cylinder compound diagonal machinery had a maximum output of 7,000 ihp and *Princesse Henriette* made over 21 knots on the Skelmorlie measured mile and on her first crossing ran from Ostend to Dover in two hours and fifty-five minutes. The sisters reduced the scheduled crossing to three hours and twenty minutes and both had long careers marred only by an unfortunate collision between *Princesse Henriette* and the older *Comtesse de Flandre* in fog off Ruytingen on 29 March 1889, which led to the sinking of the latter with some loss of life. *Princesse Josephine* was out of commission when the Germans invaded in 1914 and was seized, but her sister escaped to England with most of the National Bank's gold reserves and was thereafter employed on trooping duties. The Germans sank *Princesse Josephine* as a blockship at Bruges in October 1918 but *Princesse Henriette* made a brief return to service after the Armistice. She was withdrawn in 1920 and scrapped in Holland the following year.

North Sea contrasts

Pressed by the Dutch and German governments to introduce a daytime service, Stoomvaart Maatschappij Zeeland (Zeeland Line) ordered three new steel paddle steamers from John Elder & Co. The 1,653-grt *Duitschland* and sisters *Engeland* and *Nederland**, named after the three principal countries they served, were completed in the first few months of 1887 and inaugurated the new day service on 1 June 1887. Measuring 286.5 × 35.3 ft, they were marginally larger than the earlier Elder-built night vessels and were propelled by the same two-cylinder compound oscillating machinery with steam supplied by four single-ended boilers. Total power output was 4,600 ihp, which produced a trials speed of 19.25 knots; the normal service speed was 17 knots. Externally, they differed from the earlier ships in having solid bulwarks forward and a more substantial superstructure, but their original short funnels with narrow black tops were later heightened and give deeper black tops. In 1910, *Engeland* and *Nederland* were replaced by new twin-screw steamers and were sold to be broken up at Hendrik-Ido-Ambacht. The remaining sister, *Duitschland*, was renamed *Zeeland* in 1916 to emphasise her Dutch neutrality and in 1918 was used as a hospital ship for repatriating wounded prisoners-of-war from Rotterdam to the Lincolnshire port of Boston. She was broken up at Bremen in 1922.

The twin-screw *Cambridge** and *Colchester* were delivered to the Great Eastern Railway by Earle's of Hull in 1886 and 1889. Improved versions of the *Norwich* pair, they retained their strong scantlings but were built of steel and were 20 ft longer at 280.8 × 31 ft, giving gross measurements of 1,196/1,160 tons respectively. Externally, they differed in having a more extensive deckhouse and an extra pair of boats. Electrically-lit and steam-heated accommodation berthed 134 in first class under the bridge and a further fifty-six in second class under the poop, with a maximum capacity of 730. The two-cylinder compound machinery echoed that of *Norwich*, but their greater length made them a fraction faster at 14 knots. They appear to have started on the Antwerp run but later sailed to Rotterdam and the

Hook of Holland – all night crossings. In 1900, *Colchester* was fitted with a pair of more economical four-cylinder triple-expansion engines and new boilers. Her sister collided with the destroyer HMS *Salmon* on 12 December 1911, killing two of her crew, and the following November was sold to the Anglo Ottoman Steamship Co (the manager of which was Demetrius Lambiri) and renamed *Kembric*. Management passed to S Kavounidis in 1913 and in 1914 she became part of Turkey's state fleet Administration de Navigation à Vapeur Ottomane and was renamed *Gulnihal* – later used as a hospital ship by the Red Crescent during the Gallipoli campaign. *Colchester* continued normal service during the First World War, using her speed to escape from enemy submarines on four occasions between December 1914

and May 1915; but she was captured by torpedo boats off the Dutch coast on 22 September 1916 and taken to Zeebrugge, where her crew was interned. Declared a war prize, she was converted to a naval minelayer in Bruges and later served in the Baltic, including the Oesel operation, but stranded and sank off Laboe in Kiel Bay on 2 March 1918. Raised after the war and returned to the UK, she was scrapped in 1919. After the war, her sister sailed in the Turkish state fleet, which underwent several name changes and later became Turkiye Seyrisefain Idaresi and then Denizyollari Idaresi, all antecedents of Turkish Maritime Lines. She was broken up in Istanbul in 1938 after a fifty-year career.

3

From Paddle to Triple-Expansion Engines

The advent of the triple-expansion marine steam engine in 1881 had a marked effect on marine propulsion, because it was more efficient and better able to cope with the higher boiler pressures than those achieved by compound engines. Single engines were first used on Irish services from Glasgow in G & J Burns' *Hare* of 1887 and Laird Line's *Ivy* of 1888.

On the English Channel, the London & South Western Railway followed suit with its *Dora* of 1889 which within a few months was quickly outclassed on the Channel Islands run by the rival Great Western Railway's twin-screw *Lynx* trio. The London & South Western responded a year later with its own *Frederica* trio. In 1891 the French partner in the Newhaven–Dieppe service introduced the twin-screw *Seine*, which was one of the first ships to have a rudimentary cruiser stern as well as watertube boilers, while the Isle of Man Steam Packet Co's handsome *Tynwald* was the company's first true screw-driven passenger ship. In 1893 both the Great Eastern Railway and Belfast Steamship Co also made the switch to triple-expansion machinery.

At around the same time the final paddle steamers were delivered to the London, Brighton & South Coast Railway (*Rouen* and *Paris*), J & G Burns (*Cobra* and *Adder*) and the Portpatrick & Wigtownshire Railways Joint Committee (*Princess Victoria* and *Princess May*).

Note: An asterisk in a caption indicates the vessel shown in the photograph.

Final Newhaven paddle steamers

The London, Brighton & South Coast Railway ordered two new steel paddle steamers for its Newhaven–Dieppe service in anticipation of extra traffic for the Paris Exhibition of 1889. Fairfield of Govan was the chosen builder and the handsome 760-grt *Rouen* and *Paris** were completed in 1888. Designed by Stroudley, the famed locomotive designer, they ranked among the finest of their day and featured a long turtle-back forecastle and two heavily raked masts and funnels. Their hull dimensions were 250.6 x 29.1 ft (55 ft over the paddle boxes) and they carried 706 passengers. Main machinery comprised a two-cyinder compound diagonal engine with a 6-ft piston stroke and steam was supplied by four Stroudley boilers. Power output amounted to 3,500 ihp, and this gave a service speed of around 19 knots. Initial paddle problems were overcome and on 12 September 1888 *Rouen* made a passage of three hours and twenty minutes, equating to around 19.25 knots. Early in 1890, her sister was disabled in a fierce storm when several floats on her starboard paddle wheel came loose and she drifted up-channel for some sixty miles. Off Cap Gris Nez the damaged floats fell off and she restarted her engines and crawled into Dover, having been at sea for about thirty-six hours. A different problem beset *Rouen* on 2 February 1897 when she grounded in fog between Beachy Head and Seaford, but

managed to refloat herself and reach Newhaven despite leaking badly. Following the arrival of the new turbine steamer *Brighton* in 1903, *Rouen* was sold to J W & R P Little (managers of the Barrow Steam Navigation Co) and renamed *Duchess of Buccleugh*. She operated a summer service to Douglas until disposed of for demolition in 1910. *Paris* remained with the railway

company, latterly as a reserve ship, until December 1912 when she was sold to the Shipping Federation, London. Leased to the Admiralty for minesweeping duties in March 1916, she was renamed *Verdun* but had the suffix *II* added a year later when the Admiralty bought her. She was repurchased by the Shipping Federation in April 1922 and scrapped at Upnor on the Medway in 1924.

Paddle bows out on the Irish Sea

The 1,146-grt steel paddle steamer *Cobra* was delivered to J & G Burns by Fairfield Shipbuilding & Engineering Co in 1889 for a new day service to Belfast from the Caledonian Railway's new pier at Gourock. The first pure passenger ship on any Irish Sea service, she was electrically lit and measured 275 oa x 33.2 ft. Her two-cylinder compound diagonal, surface condensing engine with a 5.5-ft piston stroke fed by four single-ended boilers, produced 4,500 ihp for a service speed of 19 knots. She had a full-length promenade deck and spacious main deck saloon but failed to match the popularity of the night ships. After only one season, *Cobra* was returned to her builders in part exchange for a new ship. Registered to Fairfield managing director Richard Barnwell, she was placed on a Liverpool–Llandudno run as *St Tudno* and operated by the New North Wales Steamship Co. Again, after only a single season, she was sold to Albert Ballin's Nordsee Line in 1891 and used under her original name as a summer excursion ship on the Hamburg–Cuxhaven–Heligoland run. In 1905 she was bought by Hamburg America Line and started making occasional winter trips to the Mediterranean running between Genoa and Nice. In 1912, she was used as a tender at Southampton by the Maciver Steamship Co and in 1914 was taken over by the UK government for war trooping duties. She was ceded to France in

1919 and broken up at Wismar in 1922. Her replacement, *Adder** (951 grt), was 5 ft longer with a more powerful engine with 7-ft piston stroke, which developed 5,500 ihp for 20 knots in service, with steam supplied by two double-ended boilers. During trials on 31 May 1890, she averaged 19.5 knots in the course of six runs between Cloch and Cumbrae lights and a mean rate of 20.25 knots on the Skelmorlie Mile. For most of the 1901 season, she was replaced by Burns' *Vulture* and the following year switched her Scottish terminal to

Ardrossan, her speed allowing passengers nearly three hours ashore in Belfast. Her all-black livery was greatly improved by yellow painted funnels with a black top. In 1906 she was replaced by the new turbine steamer *Viper* and was sold to Argentine owner Santiago Lambruschini for service between Buenos Aires and Montevideo as *Rio de la Plata*. She was wrecked near Maldonado on Christmas Eve 1918 on voyage from Buenos Aires to Santos with general cargo.

Due to a full order book at Harland & Wolff, the Portpatrick & Wigtownshire Railways Joint Committee switched to Wm Denny & Bros for its new 1,096-grt paddle steamer *Princess Victoria*, which was completed in April 1890. Her hull, which was extensively tested in Denny's tank, measured 280.5 x 35.6 ft and had a bow rudder, while her two funnels were painted buff instead of the previous red with a black top. She was driven by a compound diagonal engine with a 6.5-ft stroke fed by four single-ended return tube boilers employing forced draught. On a double trial between the Cloch and Cumbrae lights she averaged 19.75 knots at 4,440 ihp. Passengers enjoyed electically-lit saloon accommodation and a new form of ventilation was fitted to prevent inconvenience caused by the 700 head of cattle and fifty horses that could also be

carried. Deck passengers were carried beneath the forecastle. *Princess Victoria*'s increased speed permitted an extra daylight return trip to be made from 14 July, but she was a poor sea boat and suffered endless paddle wheel trouble. She was disabled on 4 June 1891 after her port wheel struck wreckage and Denny replaced the original steel wheels with wrought iron wheels in December 1892. The previous May, Denny had completed a sister vessel, *Princess May**, which measured 1,123 grt due to a continuous promenade deck and a small shelter deck around the funnels. She was given strengthened paddle wheels and averaged 20 knots on a forty-eight-mile trial. Her entry into service permitted two round trips a day and both ships ran weekend excursions to Ailsa Craig and Larne. On 22 December 1894, she was torn from her

moorings in Stranraer and driven ashore, remaining fast for three weeks. Her accommodation was later altered for day crossings and both ships were fitted with sleeping berths in 1898 to allow first-class passengers to sleep on board before the early morning sailing. In addition, the ladies' deck saloon was converted to four two-berth cabins, while a pair of two-berth cabins were added either side of the engine-room skylight. *Princess Victoria* was withdrawn in September 1910 and scrapped at Blackwall by Shipbreaking Co of London and her sister was bought by the Admiralty in December 1914 and altered for use as an accommodation ship at Scapa Flow. Some reports say she later sailed to the Mediterranean from Swansea but after the war she was laid up in Holy Loch and was sold to Garston breakers in January 1920.

Paddle steamers in the Americas

While the majority of fast paddle-driven passenger ferries were for northern European routes, a few notable examples were built for service overseas. Among these was *Prince Rupert*, ordered by the Canadian Pacific Railway from Wm Denny & Bros, Dumbarton, in October 1893. She was intended to run between Vancouver and Victoria, Vancouver Island, but after some delay this was changed to the forty-five-mile route across the Bay of Fundy linking St John NB with Digby NS, with both of roughly the same duration at just over two hours. A steel, single-funnelled vessel measuring 1,158 grt on dimensions of 260 x 32.2 ft, she was propelled by a triple-expansion diagonal surface condensing engine developing over 3,000 ihp for a service speed of 17–18 knots. Steam was supplied by two single-ended boilers and on trials she recorded nearly 18.75 knots at 3,572 ihp. Initially she could accommodate seventy-four first-class passengers in staterooms situated mainly aft but this figure was later increased to 103 while provision was also made for some 900 deck passengers and a limited number in steerage space forward. Public rooms included two dining saloons and a smoking room. Although completed in September 1894, she was towed across the Atlantic from Southampton to Halifax in June 1895 and the following month was transferred to the newly-

incorporated Dominion Atlantic Railway Co, which numbered two Denny family members among its management board. Her original white livery and buff funnel was changed to a black hull with red funnel and black top. In service, *Prince Rupert* suffered frequent paddle damage caused by floating logs and debris from the local sawmills, while strong tides on the beam caused

her to list badly on passage. In 1911, DAR was leased to the CPR for ninety-nine years and in May 1913 she was joined by *St George*, purchased by the CPR from the Great Western Railway. She continued in operation until 1919 when she was sold to US owners and broken up in 1924.

The near-sisters *Triton* and *Paris** were completed respectively by Scotswood Shipbuilding Co, Tyneside, in May 1894 and A & J Inglis, Pointhouse, in January 1897 for Saturnino Ribes' Mensajeries Fluviales del Plata for overnight Montevideo–Buenos Aires service. They had gross measurements of 1,915/2,311 tons on dimensions of 292 x 36 ft and were driven at 15 knots by triple-expansion machinery, built in both cases by Inglis, which was supplied with steam by four boilers and developed

around 1,262 ihp. They could carry 265/291 (187 first/104 second) passengers respectively. Senor Ribes died in 1900 and his fleet was acquired by his great rival Nicolas Mihanovich and transferred to the Argentine Navigation Co, with the two ships switched to the Argentine flag in 1907 and 1911. In 1919 Mihanovich sold out to Owen Phillips' Royal Mail Group, but the company retained its original name until 1942, when both vessels were re-registered to Compania Argentina

de Navegacion Dodero. Two years later, *Triton* was converted to a barge but after the fleet was nationalised into Compania de Navegacion Fluvial Argentina in 1949, *Paris* was assigned to the province of Buenos Aires and renamed *Justicia Social* to house political prisoners. She reverted to *Paris* in 1955 and undertook several river excursions until 1958, when she was withdrawn and laid up in Rio Santiago. She was broken up locally in 1961. *(Histarmar)*

Final European paddle steamers

Dover Strait

The Belgian government received two new paddle steamers for the Ostend–Dover mail service in 1893. The 1,461-grt *Leopold II* was completed by Wm Denny & Bros in March and *Marie Henriette** by Société Cockerill in August. Built to similar dimensions of 340 × 38 ft, they differed slightly in looks, the former having two lofty raked funnels, while those of the Belgian-built ship were shorter with horizontal tops. Both were driven by two-cylinder compound diagonal engines that gave trials speeds of just over 22 knots, and those of *Marie Henriette* were marginally more powerful at 8,300 ihp, with larger cylinders and a 7-ft piston stroke. She was fitted with eight single-ended boiler. Luxurious accommodation was supplied for about 400 passengers. When less than one year old, *Leopold II* had to return to Denny to have her high-pressure cylinder replaced due to scaling and in January 1902 *Marie Henriette* lost her starboard paddle in a severe storm and after drifting for many hours, finally reached Ostend in tow of *La Flandre* after a passage of sixty-four hours. Both were taken up for trooping duties after the outbreak of the First World War but on 24 October 1914 the Cherbourg-bound *Marie Henriette* was wrecked on Les Equets Shoals near Cap Barfleur due to the lighthouse not working. All 650 persons on board were rescued by a destroyer. *Leopold II* was sold to the British shipping administration in 1920 in exchange for two trawlers and was broken up in Germany in spring 1922. All subsequent Belgian channel packets were built by Cockerill.

Two larger paddle packets were delivered to the South Eastern Railway in 1895 and 1898, the 996-grt *Duchess of York** from R & H Green of London and the 1,009-grt *Princess of Wales* from Laird Bros of Birkenhead. Both were 270 ft in length but the latter was some 2 ft broader at just over 32 ft. They were propelled by three-cylinder (one HP, two LP) compound diagonal engines fed by four single-ended boilers, which developed around 4,000 ihp for a service speed of 18–19 knots. The former had to return to her builders for about nine months and did not make her maiden voyage until June 1897, when she inaugurated an afternoon sailing to Boulogne to connect with a new express train to Paris. Despite a rise in passenger numbers, it is possible that her unreliability led to the ordering of the second vessel that arrived in Folkestone just a few months after her and this is backed up by her early demise at the hands of Dutch breakers in November 1904 after only seven years' service, latterly just running cheap coastal cruises. *Princess of Wales* proved a little heavy on coal consumption, burning 18 tons per trip compared with just 15 tons for the London, Chatham & Dover Railway Co's *Dover* trio, and she became a reserve vessel after the appearance of the South Eastern & Chatham Railway's more efficient new turbine steamers. While substituting for the damaged *Empress* in August 1908, her saloon bulkhead was smashed by a rogue wave and a year later she was employed on cheap day excursions to Boulogne on summer Mondays. In 1910 she was sold to Santiago Lambruschini of Buenos Aires and joined the former Burns' paddler *Adder* on the express service between Buenos Aires and Montevideo, for which she was fitted with radio and renamed *Rio Uruguay*. Her ownership passed in 1921 to Carlos Pujol, who converted her to a cargo ship and she was finally scrapped in 1930 after a creditable career of thirty-two years.

The last channel steamers to be ordered by the London, Chatham & Dover Railway Co were *Dover**, *Calais* and *Lord Warden*. William Denny & Bros of Dumbarton won the contract, no doubt emboldened by its success with the *Princesse Henriette* pair of 1888 for the Belgian government and nine subsequent cross-channel type ships including the screw-driven *Duke of York* for the Lancashire & Yorkshire Railway in 1894. *Dover* and *Calais* were contracted for in May 1895 and delivered a month apart in early 1896. Although still double-enders, they were the railway company's first single-funnelled paddle steamers and their smaller size, 979 grt on dimensions of

280 x 35 ft, reflected their intended overnight service, although they later also made some daytime runs. On trials, their three-cylinder diagonal machinery fitted with Brock's valve gear and having a 6-ft stroke, fed with steam from four single-ended return tube boilers, helped them reach 19.3 and 19.6 knots respectively at around 4,100 ihp. They enjoyed excellent performance in service: *Dover* averaged over 18.5 knots during her first month, and their greatly improved coal consumption of 13 tons per return trip, less than half the amount used by their predecessors, led to the ordering of a third sister, *Lord Warden*, which was delivered on 1 December 1896. The introduction of

new turbine-driven steamers from 1902 rendered them obsolete and they were relegated to lesser duties and excursion sailings such as on 12 July 1904 when *Lord Warden* was chartered by the French to bring a party of guests to Folkestone to witness the opening of the pier extension by the French ambassador. All three sisters were sold in 1911 after only fifteen years' service. *Dover* and *Lord Warden* went for scrap in Norway and Holland, but *Calais* was bought by P Hattemer and renamed *Au Revoir* for tendering passengers to and from ocean liners in Boulogne outer harbour. She was torpedoed and sunk by *U 18* on 26 February 1916.

The 1,474-grt *Princesse Clémentine** was the last paddle steamer to be built by Société Cockerill for the Ostend–Dover service. She followed the 1,195-grt *Rapide*, completed in 1895 for the night service and which was the only Belgian-built paddler to have sloping funnel tops, resembling a smaller version of *Leopold II*. *Princesse Clémentine* was generally similar in looks and size to the earlier *Marie Henriette* and was launched at Hoboken by Crown Prince Albert in October 1896, but did not enter service until the following June after trials in the Firth of Clyde where she recorded a speed of over 22 knots at 8,500 ihp in poor weather conditions.

This was later improved to 22.5 knots at around 9,300 ihp. Her mild steel hull measured 341.3 x 37.8 ft and was subdivided by twelve watertight bulkheads, while her main machinery consisted of a compound diagonal engine fed with steam from eight single-ended Serve type boilers. She could accommodate around 700 passengers in luxurious surroundings and had three large royal staterooms, a dozen private cabins and a smoking room. *Princesse Clémentine* was the first steamer to be fitted with radio. After the outbreak of war in 1914, together with the other Belgian mail ships, she briefly used Folkestone instead of Dover and later transported

the Royal Marines to Belgium. She then moved to Cherbourg under the control of the Belgian War Office but was loaned to the British government in May 1915 for transporting troops to France from Folkestone and Southampton. She proved she could still steam at 22 knots following her return to the Ostend–Dover service after the war but was placed in reserve in 1923 following the arrival of the new *Princesse Marie-José*. She remained more or less inactive in Ostend until sold at auction to Dunkirk breakers in June 1928, but this last surviving example of a European cross-channel paddle steamer was resold for demolition in Copenhagen.

North Sea

Stoomvaart Maatschappij Zeeland (Zeeland Line) built its last and finest paddle steamers in 1896 to meet increased competition from the Great Eastern Railway's twin-screw *Amsterdam* trio on the Harwich–Hook of Holland route. Once again, Fairfield Shipbuilding & Engineering Co, Govan, won the contract and *Koningin Wilhelmina*, *Koningin Regentes** and *Prins Hendrik* were launched on 27 May, 9 July and 22 August respectively. At 1,947 grt and measuring 320 × 35.8 ft, they were the equals in size of the large Belgian and Isle of Man paddle steamers and were much more imposing than the earlier Zeeland ships. They were driven by triple-expansion diagonal engines with a 6.5-ft piston stroke and steam was supplied by six single-ended boilers. A power output of 9,000 ihp guaranteed a service speed of 21 knots. Designed for overnight service between Flushing and the Medway, they were fitted with 244 sleeping berths. Reboilered in November 1901, July 1903 and December 1904 respectively, they were displaced in 1910 by Zeeland's new twin-screw steamers and as a result were converted for daytime service. On the outbreak of the First World War, the UK terminal was switched from Queenborough to Tilbury and on 31 July 1916 *Koningin Wilhelmina* was sunk with the loss of three lives in the vicinity of the North Hinder light vessel after striking a mine laid by the German submarine *UC 1*. On 23 September, *Prins Hendrik* was escorted into Zeebrugge by German torpedo boats but later released and on 10 November *Koningin Regentes* was captured by the submarine *UB 19* west of the Nord Hinder and taken to Zeebrugge and later Ostend. After her release on 17

December, the regular mail service was abandoned. In 1918 *Koningin Regentes* joined the older *Zeeland* on ambulance duties ferrying wounded POWs but while *en route* from Boston to Rotterdam on 6 June was torpedoed about twenty-one miles from the East Leman lightship with the loss of seven lives. After the Armistice,

Prins Hendrik inaugurated a day service from Flushing to Gravesend on 31 January 1919 but was soon transferred to Folkestone as reserve ship for the night service. In November 1922 she was sold for scrap to Diedrichsen of Bremen.

Isle of Man

The Isle of Man Steam Packet Co's last paddle steamer was completed by Fairfield Shipbuilding & Engineering Co in 1897. Originally to be called *Douglas*, she was in fact named *Empress Queen* in honour of Queen Victoria's Diamond Jubilee and was the largest and fastest example of her type to be built for cross-channel service in the United Kingdom. Her gross measurement was 2,140 tons on hull dimensions of 372 oa × 42.3 ft and her main machinery comprised a three-cylinder compound diagonal engine with a 7-ft piston stroke. The combined power output was around 10,000 ihp, which provided a speed of over 21.5 knots. She was the first in the Steam Packet fleet to be fitted with a bow rudder and entered Liverpool–Douglas service in July, carrying up to 2,000 passengers. On 13 September 1897 she set a new record, steaming from the Rock Lighthouse to Douglas Head in two hours and fifty-seven minutes, eclipsing the previous best time by the *Prince of Wales* by two minutes, and taking five minutes over three hours for the full voyage. *Empress Queen* became a great favourite but only sailed during the summer months, returning to lay up in Birkenhead every winter. During the First World War, she was converted to a troop transport in Barrow and steamed south to the English Channel in February

1915 on charter to the British government. A year later, on 1 February 1916 with 1,300 soldiers on board, she stranded in fog on Bembridge Ledge at the eastern end

of the Isle of Wight. Salvage efforts proved abortive and this fine vessel was abandoned to the sea. Her two funnels remained visible until 1919.

Sole French paddle steamers

Under the mail agreement of 1896, it was agreed that the early morning sailing from Dover to Calais should be worked by the French, while the London, Chatham & Dover Railway operated the noon and night departures. Compagnie du Chemin de Fer du Nord chartered the LC&DR's *Invicta* and *Victoria* until it could build its own ships and these emerged as *Le Nord** and *Le Pas de Calais* from the St Nazaire yard of Ateliers & Chantiers de la Loire in summer 1898. Not only were they the only cross-channel paddle steamers built in France, but also they were the largest of their type to sail on the Dover Strait at just over 2,000 grt. Their hulls measured 337.8 x 34.9 ft and their three-crank triple-expansion engines developed 8,000 ihp for a speed of 21.5 knots. Steam was supplied by Lagrafell & d'Allest watertube boilers. Reputed to be good sea boats in rough weather, *Le Pas de Calais* had to remain at sea for twenty-four hours when the port of Calais was closed during the great channel gale of January 1902. On 26 May 1910, the same ship accidentally rammed and sank the French submarine *Pluviose*, which had surfaced unexpectedly in front of her, killing all twenty-seven of her crew. Both ships were reboilered in 1911 with lighter Solignac-Grille units, which used less coal and provided quicker firing as well as an increase in speed. Taken up as auxiliary cruisers in the First World War, they operated in the Second Light Squadron, Channel, but in October 1914 *Le Nord* was loaned to the British Red Cross as a hospital ship. Both were later altered to carry two or three FBA seaplanes; *Le Pas de Calais* was commissioned in July 1915 and based at Cherbourg and *Le Nord* in June 1916 and stationed at Dunkirk. The latter was credited with ramming and sinking a German submarine. They were released in 1917 and were sold in August 1920 to Société Anonyme de Gérance et d'Armement (SAGA), a branch of the Rothschild business empire. They resumed normal channel service but their end came in 1923 – *Le Nord* stranded in May near the South Foreland and became a total loss and her sister was sold in September for demolition.

Last UK cross-channel paddle steamer

The South Eastern Railway ordered its final paddle steamer, *Mabel Grace*, from Laird Bros, Birkenhead just before the railway company merged with its great rival, the London, Chatham & South Coast Railway on 1 January 1899. Built to the maximum dimensions possible for Folkestone Harbour, she measured 1,315 grt on a length of 300 ft and a beam of 36.1 ft. Her engines were similar to those of her immediate predecessors, namely three-cylinder compound diagonal, but six return-tube boilers supplied sufficient steam for an output of 5,500 ihp, giving a mean speed of 20.25 knots on trial runs in Wemyss Bay on 2 September 1899. Differing from earlier SER ships in her distinctly more racy appearance, *Mabel Grace* had well-raked funnels and masts – the former both shorter and wider and lacking the traditional bell tops. Her passenger complement was 730, 500 in saloons and private cabins and the remainder on the promenade deck. She arrived in Folkestone on 19 September, made a trial crossing to Boulogne on the 21st and entered commercial service the following day. At some stage her open bridge was repositioned in front of the forward funnel to improve visibility and a small enclosed wheelhouse added to it. Despite her fine attributes, the arrival of the new turbine steamer *The Queen* in 1903 was the writing on the wall and following the delivery of the fifth of her class, *Empress*, in 1907, *The Queen* and *Onward* were transferred to the Folkestone–Boulogne station, and *Mabel Grace* was placed in reserve. Two years later, only a decade after entering service, she was sold for scrap and although outlived by some of the Belgian and French paddlers, her place in history is assured as the last paddle-driven packet to be built for the English Channel.

Triple-expansion steamers

Mediterranean series

Compagnie Générale Transatlantique obtained the mail contract for Algeria, Oran and Tunis from Compagnie Valéry in 1880 and for which it built eleven new ships in UK yards followed by its first triple-expansion-driven ship, *Ville de Tunis*, from St Nazaire in 1884. The Algiers service became daily in 1886 and with a view to reducing voyage time to 24 hours, four broadly similar ships – *Eugène Péreire*, *Duc de Bragance* (laid down as *Maréchal Bugeaud*), *Maréchal Bugeaud** (launched as *Mogador*) and *Ville d'Alger* were delivered by Chantiers & Ateliers de St Nazaire between 1888 and 1890. A fifth

vessel was laid down in 1891 as *Biarritz* and completed the following February as *Général Chanzy*. They could carry around 200 passengers in three classes and were the first on the route to carry first-class passengers amidships. Triple-expansion engines gave a speed of around 17 knots, allowing a new express service to be inaugurated. Distinguished by a turtle-back poop, the last three to be completed were some 200 tons larger at over 2,200 grt on increased dimensions of 341 × 35.7 ft. *Ville d'Alger* and *Général Chanzy* made some cruises after service frequency was reduced in 1895 and in the winter of 1908–09 all had extra accommodation fitted on the

boat deck while the bridge was moved further forward. On 20 February 1910, during one of the worst Mediterranean storms for forty years, *Général Chanzy* was swept off course and wrecked off Point Llosa on the north-west of Minorca. Only one man survived from the 157 passengers and crew. While moving berth in Marseilles, *Ville d'Alger* struck a mole and sank on 10 June 1921. *Duc de Bragance* was replaced by *Lamorcière* in 1921 and broken up in Italy in summer 1922, *Maréchal Bugeaud* also went to Italian breakers in late 1927 and lead ship *Eugène Péreire* was the last to go, being scrapped in 1929.

Canadian duo

The Yarmouth Steamship Co's 1,452-grt steamer *Yarmouth* was built for the Boston–Yarmouth, Nova Scotia, route by A McMillan & Sons, Dumbarton in 1887. She had a raised forecastle that was faired into the brown-painted superstructure and measured 220.25 × 35 ft on 12.5 ft draught. Propulsion was by means of a single triple-expansion engine supplied with steam by a single boiler and she had a speed of 14 knots. In 1901 she was taken over by the Dominion Atlantic Railway and in 1912 passed to the Canadian Pacific Railway, which disposed of her in 1918 to American Steamship Corp, Yarmouth, which continued to run her to Boston. In November, she was hired by Black Star Line to carry a liquor cargo to Havana, but machinery failure resulted in her being towed to a US port, where she arrived just after the Prohibition Act had become law and her cargo was confiscated. She was broken up by Pittstown Steel Corp, Philadelphia in 1924. Three years after the delivery of *Yarmouth*, Yarmouth Steamship Co received a larger ship, the 1,694-grt *Boston**, from Alexander Stephen, Linthouse. She was a more substantial looking ship, with a flush hull and two

funnels and her accommodation for 1,200 passengers included 300 berths. She measured 245 × 36 ft and her single three-cylinder reciprocating engine developed around 4,400 ihp for a service speed of 15 knots (17 knots on trials). Transferred to the Dominion Atlantic Railway in 1901, *Boston* was leased by the Canadian Pacific

Railway in 1912 for the Bay of Fundy service but was quickly sold to the Eastern Steamship Co. The latter went into liquidation in 1914 and in 1917 she was requisitioned as a potential troop transport. Renamed *Cambridge*, she remained at the Navy Yard, Brooklyn, without ever sailing and was scrapped in Baltimore in 1922.

Channel Islands rivals

In May 1888, the London & South Western Railway Co invited tenders from six shipyards for a new 16-knot steamer for its Channel Islands service. Robert Napier & Sons, Glasgow won the contract with the lowest bid of £32,800, thus breaking the L&SWR Co's long association with Aitken & Mansel. The 741-grt *Dora* took to the water on 2 March 1889. An improved and slightly larger version of the earlier *Hilda*, she measured 240 × 30 ft and was the first of the company's ships to be propelled by a triple-expansion engine and the first to be lit by electricity. Steam was supplied by two double-ended tubular boilers and power output was 2,250 ihp, the latter increased a year after delivery by the installation of forced draught in a futile effort to compete with the Great Western Railway's new twin-screw ships operating from Weymouth. Two classes of passengers were catered for, with berths provided for 140 in first class and sixty in second class. On 17 September 1892, *Dora* struck the Tasse Rock off Guernsey and was out of service for a month during repairs, but the following May hit the Baleine Rock, again off Guernsey, and was towed to St Peter Port by the Great Western Railway's *Lynx*. A noted roller in bad weather, she was unpopular with travellers and after she was replaced by *Vera* in 1898, was sold in July 1901 to the Isle of Man Steam Packet Co when just twelve years old. The latter renamed her *Douglas** after the island's capital and placed her on its Liverpool run. On 6 November 1903, *Douglas* collided with and sank the cargo ship *City of Lisbon* in the Mersey. She briefly returned to the Channel Islands during the First World War to carry Jersey potatoes to Hull but after serving the Isle of Man for twenty years, principally on night service, she was sunk in collision with the *Artemisia* off Liverpool's Herculaneum Dock on 16 August 1923, happily without loss of life.

Following its acquisition of the paddle steamers of the Weymouth & Channel Islands Steam Packet Co, the Great Western Railway ordered three new steel ships from Laird Bros, Birkenhead. Designed by the shipyard, *Lynx*, *Antelope** and *Gazelle* were delivered in 1889 and were the first channel steamers to be propelled by twin screws. They measured 596 grt on dimensions of 235.5 × 27.6 ft and were driven by two triple-expansion engines, supplied with steam by two single-ended boilers, with power output of 1,700 ihp for a service speed of 16 knots. The propellers overlapped, with the starboard screw mounted just forward of the port screw and during the winter iron screws were substituted for the normal bronze. The hull incorporated a turtle-back forecastle and long bridge deck, while two tall raked masts contrasted with a pair of small, closely mounted funnels with horizontal tops. Passenger complement was around 430 persons and after a year in service a new ladies' saloon was added abaft the bridge, requiring the forward pair of boats to be raised and funnels heightened. In 1903 *Lynx* and *Antelope* were transferred to tendering/excursion duties at Plymouth, for which their forward boats were removed, with *Lynx* from July 1906 undertaking a two-month business charter to run excursions in Jersey. *Gazelle* was converted to a cargo ship in 1908 with new hold and kingpost installed between bridge and funnels and *Lynx* was similarly treated in 1912 following a spell on Plymouth–Nantes service. *Antelope*, which had sailed for a while in 1910 between Plymouth and Brest, was sold in August 1913 to Piraeus-based G Yannoulatos Frères, Navigation à Vapeur 'Ionienne', as *Atromitos* (Undaunted). Early in the First World War, the two cargo sisters were taken up by the Admiralty as minesweepers, *Lynx* as HMS *Lynn* to avoid confusion with the destroyer HMS *Lynx*. In March 1915, *Gazelle* switched to minelaying duties from Mudros for six months but both ships were released in early spring 1920 and thereafter maintained sporadic service until broken up in 1925. In 1929 *Atromitos* passed into the ownership of Hellenic Coast Lines and was eventually scrapped in Italy in 1933 after a forty-four-year career.

To meet the competition afforded by the Great Western Railway's new *Lynx* class steamers on the Weymouth–Channel Islands route, the London & South Western Railway Co ordered a trio of faster ships in September 1889 from the lowest bidder, J & G Thomson, Clydebank. *Vera, Lydia* and *Clara* were discussed as possible names but they were completed as *Frederica, Lydia** and *Stella*, the first tried in Stokes Bay near Portsmouth on 21–22 July 1890 reaching nearly 18.75 knots with normal draught and almost 19.5 knots under forced draught. The other two

followed in September and October and the trio marked the final evolution of the yacht-like design introduced by consultant naval architect Professor John Biles and were the first Channel Island ships to exceed 1,000 tons (*Frederica* 1,059 grt). They measured 259 oa x 35.1 ft and were driven by two triple-expansion engines, developing 5,700 ihp for 19 knots. Just ten months after entering service, *Lydia* struck a rock off Guernsey and was out of commission for two weeks. *Frederica* carried the company's directors to the Diamond Jubilee Naval Review at Spithead in June

1897 and was transferred to the Le Havre service on 1 December 1903 in place of the old paddle steamers. *Stella*'s career came to an untimely end on 30 March 1899 when she struck Black Rock off the Casquets to the west of Alderney and foundered with the loss of 105 lives. The new *Vera* and GWR's *Lynx* between them saved 112 persons but the incident ended racing between the two railway companies, which thenceforward agreed to pool their Channel Islands services. *Lydia*'s sale was contemplated due to her poor condition but she was refitted and reboilered by Day Summers in Southampton during winter 1889–90. *Frederica* was similarly treated in 1904 and her funnel heightened but in June 1911 she was sold to Idarei Massousieh of Constantinople and passed to the Administration de Navigation à Vapeur Ottomane in 1912 as *Nilufer*. While acting as a minelayer, she hit a Russian mine off Kilyos near the entrance to the Bosphorous on 22 November 1914 and sank with the loss of sixty-three lives. *Lydia* was sold in December 1919 to James Dredging, Towage & Transport, Southampton, but in 1921 a Captain Yates took her to the Mediterranean for a projected Malta–Syracuse service. Yates was arrested and she was returned to James Dredging, which sold her in September 1922 to Coast Lines for a Preston–Dublin service. The following May she was resold to Greece and as *Ierax* joined her former GWR rival *Antelope* in the fleet of G Yannoulatos Frères, Navigation à Vapeur 'Ionienne'. The latter was absorbed into Hellenic Coast Lines in 1929 and she was eventually scrapped in Savona in 1933.

The Great Western Railway returned to Laird Bros, Birkenhead, for its next channel steamer, the steel 1,160-grt *Ibex* of 1891, which was designed to match the London & South Western Railway Co's *Frederica* trio. She was a larger version of the preceding *Antelope* class, measuring 265 x 32.6 ft, and had taller funnels and a hull featuring a combined forecastle and bridge deck with a separate poop. With two sets of considerably more powerful reciprocating engines, which developed 4,000 ihp for 19 knots in service, she proved more than a match for the rival L&SWR ships, soon beating *Lydia*'s record. Steam was supplied by two double-ended Scotch boilers. On 16 April 1897, she hit the Noirmontaise Rock off Corbiere and was beached in Portelet Bay, subsequent repairs at Barrow taking two months, and on 5 January 1900 she sank outside St Peter Port, Guernsey after hitting another rock. She was not raised until July and underwent extensive repairs at Birkenhead, finally re-entering service in April 1901 with her bridge deck extended to the mainmast. Her funnel cowls were removed in 1910 and an extra pair of boats added on the poop. During the First World War, *Ibex* maintained the Channel Islands service, sinking a submarine, and in 1918–19 was employed on government trooping duties on the Dover–Calais and Weymouth–Le Havre routes. A shelter deck was added during a refit in 1922, but three years later she was broken up at Sharpness on the river Severn.

Newhaven–Dieppe innovations

Completed by Forges et Chantiers de la Mediterranée, Le Havre, in August 1891, the 808-grt *Seine* was the first French-built passenger ship and the first screw-driven steamer on the joint Newhaven–Dieppe service. She was also the world's first channel passenger steamer to have a cruiser type stern and measured 269 × 29.5 ft. Her two triple-expansion engines, fed by six cylindrical return tube boilers, produced 4,000 ihp for a speed of about 19 knots and on her first crossing on 8 August 1891, which lasted three hours and eleven minutes, she burned 1 ton less coal than the paddle steamers. She suffered problems and an improved and more strongly-built sister, *Tamise*, appeared in November 1893. Her new Belleville watertube boilers improved her draught but were prone to breakdown and also used around 4 tons more coal per trip. A third sister, *Manche**, delivered by FCM in 1897, had improved accommodation and crossed in one minute under three hours and *France* (inset) followed in August 1898. Slightly smaller at 264 × 29.5 ft, she had upright masts and funnels. Deck ventilators were replaced by louvres in the funnel houses, but she suffered from overheating problems and on 1 March 1900 an engine-room explosion killed nine stokers and seriously injured another two. In a four-month refit, her copper tubing, unequal to the high pressures developed, was replaced by steel tubing. *Seine* was used for the extra traffic generated by the 1900 Paris Exhibition but was laid up in March 1901 and sold to a Brest scrap merchant in December 1905. In a 1905 refit, *France*'s hull was strengthened and the well between forecastle and superstructure plated in to provide a new second-class smoking room. Replaced

by new turbine steamers in 1911, *Tamise* and *Manche* were laid up in 1912, but war in the Balkans prevented their intended sale to Turkey. *Tamise* was sold to a Dunkirk breaker early in 1914 but was not towed there until after the end of the First World War. *Manche* went to the Gironde in 1914 and maintained a ferry service for the Chamber of Commerce between Bordeaux and Royan as *Le Verdon* until broken up in 1919. *France* was sold to Tourisme Nautique in November 1913 and used

as a white-hulled cruise ship on the French Riviera, but was bought back by her original owner and used as an Admiralty troopship during 1915–19. In October 1920, she was sold to C Seguin of Buenos Aires, who renamed her *Fortuna* and used her to carry gamblers to Mar del Plata. In 1931 she became the Uruguayan *Centenario* but her subsequent history is obscure. She remained in Lloyd's Register book until 1962, but may have been wrecked earlier.

The London, Brighton & South Coast Railway ordered its first screw-driven passenger steamer from Wm Denny & Bros, Dumbarton, in 1893, some two years after the completion of its French partner's very first and similarly propelled packet *Seine*. Denny's testing tank had enabled the yard to come closest to matching John Biles' original specification and thus secure the contract. *Seaford** was completed in July 1894 and made over 20 knots on trials, with her two sets of quadruple-expansion reciprocating engines producing 5,000 ihp, and steam supplied by four single-ended tubular boilers. She measured 997 grt on dimensions of 262.7 × 34 ft and her hull had a short raised forecastle and long bridge deck. She broke with tradition in having a single mast and funnel with horizontal top and could carry a total of 923 passengers with berths supplied for eighty-two in first class and sixty-four in second class. On 22 August 1895, after barely a year in service, she was rammed and sunk in fog about twenty-five miles off Newhaven by the French railway cargo steamer *Lyon*, which rescued all on board and took them to the Sussex port. A replacement was quickly ordered from Denny, and this emerged as *Sussex* in July 1896. Structurally similar to the earlier ship, she was slightly longer to include an extra watertight compartment and her forecastle and bridge deck were combined, raising gross tonnage to 1,117. Her funnel had a normal sloping

top, making her the better looking of the two. In the First World War, she was initially taken up as a troopship but reverted to her normal run in February 1914, albeit with a French crew. Her bows were blown off by a torpedo on 25 March 1916, while *en route* from Folkestone to Dieppe and she was later beached in Boulogne's outer harbour. About eighty people were lost in the explosion,

including all in the first-class saloon. She was later salved and towed to Le Havre for rebuilding after which she was converted to a French naval minesweeper in Rochefort. In 1920, *Sussex* was towed from Toulon to Genoa following her sale to Istanbul-based D Demetriades and was renamed *Aghia Sophia* in 1921. She was broken up in 1922 following a fire.

Screw-driven Isle of Man steamer

The handsome *Tynwald* was only the second screw-driven vessel built by the Isle of Man Steam Packet Co. A two-funnelled steamer with a flush hull, she was built and engined by Fairfield Shipbuilding & Engineering Co in 1891 but was somewhat smaller than the company's large paddle steamers at 940 grt on dimensions of 265 × 34 ft. She was primarily designed for the winter service from Liverpool and in summer usually sailed from Ardrossan, where traffic had increased following the arrival there of the Lancashire & Ayrshire Railway in 1890. Her main machinery comprised two triple-expansion engines producing 535 nhp for a maximum speed of around 19.5 knots and 18 knots in service. During the course of a long career she sailed on most of the Isle of Man services, inaugurating the Whitehaven service from Douglas and Ramsay in 1912, and she helped maintain the Liverpool service during the First World War, carrying the first German POWs to the island for internment in 1914. In 1916 she rushed troops to Dublin to put down the Easter Rebellion and on 9 April 1917 rescued 600 passengers from the liner *New York*, which had struck a mine off the Mersey Bar lightship. During her final year in 1929, she sailed from Blackpool to Morecambe, Douglas and Llandudno and was then laid up. Preparations were under way for her demolition in 1933 but she was sold to Douglas resident Mr Colby Cubbin, who intended to use her as a private yacht named *Western Isles*. Berthed for a while at Greenock and then Shieldhall, she was taken up by the Admiralty in April 1940 for use as an anti-submarine training ship. Commissioned as HMS *Eastern Isles* on 27 October 1941, having swapped her name with the former Batavier Line vessel *Batavier IV*, she became an accommodation ship for

HMS *Eaglet II* in Liverpool for the rest of the war. Handed to the Director of Sea Transport in in April 1946, she was returned to her owner on 5 August 1947, but the cost of refitting was prohibitive and she was eventually towed to La Spezia for demolition in spring 1951 after a career of sixty years.

Irish Sea

The 1,458-grt *Duke of Clarence* was completed by Laird Bros, Birkenhead, in 1892 for the joint Fleetwood–Belfast service of the London & North Western Railway and the Lancashire & Yorkshire Railway. Originally to be named *Birkenhead*, she measured 312.5 × 6.2 ft and was propelled by two triple-expansion engines producing 4,000 ihp for a speed of 19 knots. Of three island design with short well decks at either end of a long bridge deck, she featured two lofty raking masts and a smallish funnel amidships. Her speed enabled the night service to be accelerated and she set the pattern for four more 'Dukes' built during the ensuing decade. In spring 1906, sole ownership passed to the L&YR and she was transferred to the east coast to inaugurate a seasonal service from Hull to Zeebrugge, repainted in the 'soot, blood and suet' colours of the recently-acquired Goole Steam Shipping Co. Her easy schedule involved just two overnight return crossings a week, the passage taking some thirteen hours, but after the first season she was reboilered by her builders and subsequently made three crossings a week following the North Eastern Railway's agreement to take a share in the service. During the winter, she returned to the Irish Sea, sailing on the Liverpool–Drogheda route until 1912, after which she was usually laid up in Fleetwood. Her repositioning voyages were offered as cruises and in the spring she would sail northabout via Stromness and Aberdeen, returning in the autumn via the Isle of Wight and Jersey. The Zeebrugge service was suspended during the First World War and on 6 November 1915, *Duke of Clarence* was requisitioned as an armed boarding steamer, sailing mainly on the Northern Patrol. Released by the Admiralty in February 1920, she resumed service on 15 May and two years later passed to the ownership of the

L&NWR and then in 1923 to the London, Midland & Scottish Railway, with her service renamed the LMS & LNER Joint Express Continental Service. Repositioning cruises were reinstated in the late 1920s but *Duke of Clarence* was withdrawn in autumn 1929 and sold the following May to T W Ward for demolition in Barrow.

Originally to be named *Electric*, the 1,630-grt twin-screw *Magic* was delivered to Belfast Steamship Co by Harland & Wolff in August 1893. She was a handsome two-funnelled ship and a planned sister was never built owing to financial stringency. She measured 311.3 x 38.3 ft and was driven by two triple-expansion engines fed by three single-ended boilers. Service speed was 17 knots for an eight-hour passage, but she could make 19 knots if needed. Overnight berths were provided for 222 persons in saloon class, with no cabin larger than four-berth, and steerage passengers were housed aft. Cattle and horses were carried on the two lower decks. On 22 June 1897, she took part in the Diamond Jubilee Review in the River Mersey and during a refit the following winter was fitted with new propellers to reduce persistent vibration. She was laid up in Belfast in September 1912 but was taken up in November 1914 as a naval hospital ship (pennant number YA14) and transported wounded from the Grand Fleet bases at Scapa Flow and Invergordon and the battle cruiser squadron in the Firth of Forth to south coast ports. In 1916 the suffix *II* was added to her name to avoid confusion with the new destroyer HMS *Magic*. Uncertainty continued and *Magician* was proposed but in June 1918 she became *Classic* and spent the last two months of the war trooping in the English Channel. Her new name was retained on her release in May 1919 and she resumed regular nightly sailings on 10 May 1920. When *Graphic* returned later that summer, she was chartered to the City of Cork Steam Packet Co for Cork–Fishguard/Liverpool services. Reboiled and converted to oil-firing in 1924, she was permanently

transferred to the Cork concern in July and renamed *Killarney*. On 31 December 1931 she was transferred to Coast Lines and in 1932 began running cruises from Liverpool to the Scottish Lochs with yellow funnels and grey hull. During the Second World War, she made two trips to Dunkirk in May 1940 but was otherwise used as a depot and accommodation ship at Rosyth. On 17

March 1947, she was sold to Vergottis' Bury Court Shipping and left Liverpool for Piraeus as *Attiki* on 26 April. Renamed *Adrias* the following year by new owner George Potamianos, she was placed in Epirotiki Steam Navigation Co service to the Aegean islands but was wrecked in heavy weather on the eastern end of Falconera Island on 6 October 1951.

The Barrow Steam Navigation Co was founded in 1867 to run services from Morecambe to Belfast and from Barrow to Douglas, Isle of Man, under the management of J Little & Co. Initially paddle steamers were employed, all but one being second-hand purchases, and it was not until 1893 that the company received its first new screw-driven steamer, *City of Belfast*, from Laird Bros,

Birkenhead. A vessel of 1,055 grt, she measured 260.5 x 32 ft and was propelled by two triple-expansion engines. She was used mainly on the Belfast run with occasional visits to the Isle of Man. Between 1907 and 1922 she was owned by the Midland Railway and passed to the London, Midland & Scottish Railway after the reorganisation of the railways in 1923. In May 1925, she

was sold to Constantinos Togias and renamed *Nicolaos Togias*. Most of the Greek inter-island services, including those of Togias, were consolidated into Hellenic Coast Lines in 1932 and she was renamed *Kefallinia* in 1933. She eventually foundered off northern Egypt on 13 August 1941.

The 1,008-grt *Duke of Fife* was delivered to Dublin & Glasgow Sailing & Steam Packet Co by Ailsa Shipbuilding Co, Troon, in April 1892, and replaced the paddle steamer *Lord Gough*. She measured 244 x 31.8 ft and had a Dunsmuir & Jackson three-cylinder triple-expansion engine, which was supplied with steam by two boilers. Power output was 2,500 ihp and maximum speed 15 knots. Shortly after takeover by G & J Burns in April 1908, she was given the name *Sparrow* but served her new owners for only two years before sale to Panagiotis Pantaleon of Smyrna. As the white-hulled *Arkadia*, she sailed for the Oriental Shipping Co on several routes, which included Italy, North Africa and Turkey as well as Greek coastal services. She was registered to Pantaleon Bros in 1920 and in 1927 was absorbed into the Coast Lines Steamship Co, of Piraeus. In a further reorganisation of Greek coastal shipping, she passed to Hellenic Coast Lines in 1933, and became *Chios* with a yellow funnel with narrow black top. Her end came on 18 April 1941 when she was bombed and sunk by German aircraft at Eretria near Chalkis during the invasion of Greece.

The 1,061-grt *Hound* of 1893 was the first ship in the G & J Burns fleet to measure over 1,000 tons and was the first to be built for Burns by Fairfield Shipbuilding & Engineering Co at Govan. Her length of 250 ft was the same as the *Alligator* trio delivered by Barclay, Curle in 1881 but her beam was 2 ft wider at 32 ft. She was propelled by three-cylinder triple-expansion machinery, which Burns had first employed six years previously in its 771-grt *Hare,* and which developed 2,800 ihp for a speed of 14 knots. She was initially placed on the Ardrossan–Belfast run and quickly became popular. In 1905 she was reboilered and several single-berth cabins were added during extensive renovation of her passenger accommodation. Later, she sailed from Glasgow and also made occasional voyages on the Londonderry route. After serving her owners for thirty-two years, she was sold in 1925 to Greek owner M G A Manuelides and renamed *Mary M.* In 1933 she passed into the Hellenic Coast Lines fleet and was renamed *Lesbos.* Her funnel colours were now yellow with narrow black top and she was one of the very few Greek coastal ships to come through the Second World War unscathed, having changed name yet again to *Korytza* in 1942. She was broken up in 1950.

Completed for the Glasgow & Londonderry Steam Packet Co (Laird Line) by D & W Henderson in 1893, the 1,141-grt *Olive* was constructed of steel and measured 260 x 33 ft. Her main propelling machinery was similar to that in G & J Burns' *Hound*, namely a triple-expansion engine of 369 nhp and gave her a speed in service of around 12.25 knots. She could carry 100 saloon-class passengers and 1,000 deck passengers in addition to cattle on both the main and 'tween decks, which were fan ventilated. Laird's smart funnel colours of broad red and white bands beneath a black top contrasted with the plain black of J & G Burns. *Olive* began her career on the Glasgow–Londonderry service, but in later years switched her UK terminal to Heysham. New boilers were installed in 1911. In 1922 she passed into the combined Burns & Laird fleet and in 1929 briefly held the name *Lairdsbank* when all the ships were renamed with a *Lairds* prefix. She was sold the following year to the North of Scotland & Orkney & Shetland Steam Navigation Co, which needed a replacement for its wrecked *St Sunniva*. Renamed *St Catherine*, she spent her first summer sailing to Stromness and Scalloway, thereafter as the winter steamer on the Aberdeen–Lerwick run until broken up at Rosyth in 1937. (*Bruce Peter collection*)

*Innisfallen** was built for the City of Cork Steam Packet Co's Cork–Milford Haven service by Wigham Richardson & Sons in 1893. A two-funnelled steamer of 1,405 grt, she measured 272 x 35.5 ft and was driven at 16 knots by a triple-expansion engine. Ten years later the same shipyard completed the 1,412-grt *Inniscarra*, which was broadly similar in appearance save for horizontal tops to her funnels. Her hull dimensions were slightly larger at 280.5 x 38.2 ft but she was propelled by similar machinery of 529 nhp. She sailed initially on the Cork–Milford run and transferred her English terminal to Fishguard following completion of the GWR's new harbour in 1906, sailing on alternate nights with a lay-over in Cork on Sunday. *Innisfallen* also sailed to Fishguard on occasion and later switched to the Liverpool service. When Cork-bound and sailing between the Welsh Skerries and the Kish light vessel on 23 May 1918, she was torpedoed without warning by the German submarine *U 64* in position 53 26N 05 21W and sank with the loss of ten lives. *Inniscarra* sailed daily for most of the war years but on 11 May 1918 when westbound with a general cargo was torpedoed by *U 86* some ten miles south-east of Mine Head near Waterford with the loss of twenty-eight of the thirty-three on board. (*British Museums, Galleries & Archives, York 3233*)

CHAPTER

4

Improved Steamers for the Turn of the Century

The final years of the nineteenth century witnessed a flurry of improved steamers entering service along with the last paddle steamers to be built for cross-channel service in Europe, the majority for Dover Strait and southern North Sea operation where ports were still comparatively shallow and unsuited to the deeper draft required by triple-expansion-driven vessels. One exception was the Isle of Man Steam Packet Co's *Empress Queen*, which with the final Belgian and Dutch paddle steamers ranked among the largest and finest examples of their type ever built.

In 1897 the Hon Charles Parsons' diminutive *Turbinia* raced at over 30 knots between the lines of warships anchored at Spithead for Queen Victoria's Diamond Jubilee Fleet Review, demonstrating the superiority of his revolutionary new steam turbine, which would soon prove ideally suited to powering small high-speed steamers and providing a fitting replacement for paddle propulsion.

Among the triple-expansion steamers delivered in the early years of the new century was the first of the Canadian Pacific Railway's famous three-funnelled steamers, *Princess Victoria*, which was soon sweeping all opposition before her and setting new records on the 'Triangle Route' linking Vancouver with Victoria and Seattle.

Note: An asterisk in a caption indicates the vessel shown in the photograph.

New triple-expansion ships for Harwich–Hook

The 1,635-grt *Chelmsford*, built by Earle's, Hull, in 1893, was the first in the Great Eastern Railway fleet to be driven by triple-expansion machinery and her two engines fed by five single-ended boilers provided 17.5 knots service speed. She measured 300.3 x 34.5 ft and berthed 200 first-, sixty-four second- and several third-class passengers. Her entry into service coincided with the opening of the new terminal at the Hook of Holland, where ships paused to allow passengers to join trains heading for the European hinterland before proceeding up the New Waterway to Rotterdam. After this arrangement ceased in 1904, GER steamers terminated at the Hook. *Chelmsford* was a prototype for four similar ships from the same yard; *Amsterdam** and *Berlin* in April 1894, *Vienna* in October 1894 and *Dresden* in 1897. The first three were just 2 ft longer and 1.5 ft broader and the latter 3.5 ft broader but all eight boats were mounted on the boat deck instead of a pair on the poop deckhouse. Power output was 5,000 ihp and speed 18 knots. On 21 February 1907, *Berlin* was swept across the mole at the entrance to the New Waterway in a strong north-westerly gale, losing her bows but the stern section remained fast. Despite heroic efforts, only ten passengers and five crew members were saved, and the loss of 128 lives was one of the worst peacetime disasters. In June 1910, *Chelmsford* was sold to the Great Western Railway and used as *Bretonne* for a cargo service between Plymouth and Nantes. In September the following year, she was resold to the Embiricos-owned National Steam Navigation Co of Greece and employed as *Esperia* on inter-island services. Her named was changed to *Syros* around 1920 but briefly reverted to *Esperia* in the mid-1920s when running for the London subsidiary Byron Steamship Co. The Embiricos fortunes declined in 1933 and she was scrapped a year later. Displaced by new turbine steamers, the other three sometimes ran to Antwerp and *Vienna* seriously damaged Alfred Holt's *Patroclus* in collision in the Scheldt on the night of 19 January 1911. During the First World War, all three became armed boarding steamers, *Vienna* after initial service as an accommodation ship and then, briefly, as one of the first 'Q' ships under her own name and also that of *Antwerp*. *Dresden* was commissioned as HMS *Louvain* but was torpedoed by *UC 22* in the eastern Mediterranean on 20 January 1918. In 1920 *Vienna* was renamed *Roulers* and placed on a new seasonal service to Zeebrugge, sailing on alternate nights. *Amsterdam*, which had been fitted with a raised bridge, was broken up in Blyth in 1929 and *Roulers* followed her in 1930.

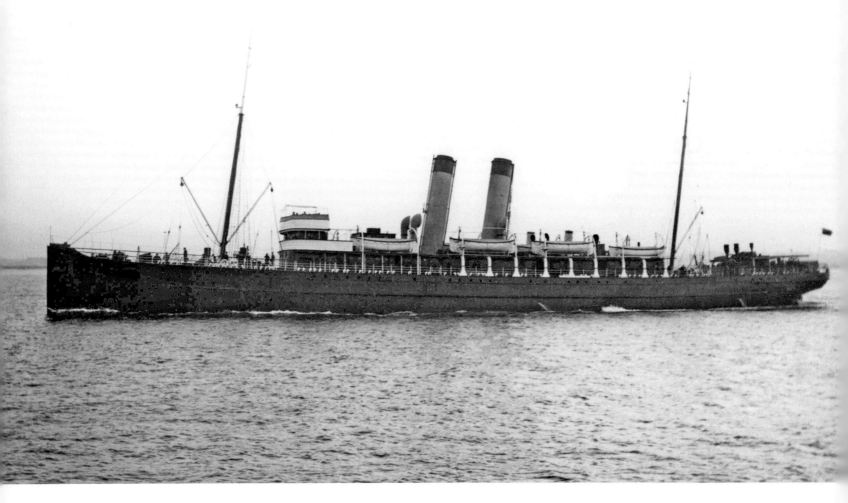

English Channel contrasts

Early in 1894, the London & South Western Railway Co returned to J & G Thomson, Clydebank for two new twin-screw steamers for its Le Havre service. *Columbia** and *Alma* were delivered in Southampton in October and December, allowing *Frederica* to return to the Channel Islands station. They introduced an entirely new and somewhat stiffer profile with two widely spaced funnels and measured 1,145/1,178 grt on dimensions of 270.7 × 34 ft. Two four-cylinder triple-expansion engines were supplied with steam by two Serve vertical tubular boilers for a maximum speed of 19 knots at 3,300 ihp. Designed to fit in with the French Line sailings from Le Havre, they were the first ships in the L&SWR fleet to have private twin-berth cabins in first class and 153 passengers could be berthed in total. Both had minor scrapes, *Alma* colliding with the four-masted sailing ship *Kate Thomas* on 21 March 1895 and *Columbia* with the steamer *Vesuvi* off Calshot on the morning of 17 February 1897. Later that year, *Columbia* attended the Diamond Jubilee Naval Review at Spithead and in a reboilering in 1906 her funnels were placed closer together as a result of the forward stokehold being switched with the first-class cabins aft. *Alma* was reboilered the following year and both had the promenade deck forward end plated over in 1909. Replaced by the new geared turbine steamers *Normannia* and *Hantonia*, they were sold in 1912, *Alma* becoming the

Spanish-registered *Sitges*, owned by Algiers-based Juan J Sitges. In November 1915 she was bought by the French Navy and converted to the auxiliary cruiser *Corse*, but was torpedoed and sunk off La Ciotat on 24 January 1918. Her sister had been sold three weeks after her to E A Cohan and sailed east, and registered to the Eastern Shipping Co of Penang the

following year. In 1917 she passed briefly through the hands of Shanghai resident P N F Heath before resale to M Matsou and U Matsumoto of Nagasaki, who renamed her *Shokiku Maru No 2*. She changed hands yet again in the early 1920s, going to Hongo Ikichiro of Amiro who altered her name to *Shogiku Maru No 2* and was wrecked off Sakhalin Island on 17 June 1924.

The diminutive twin-screw *Channel Queen* was delivered to Onesimus Dorey's Plymouth, Channel Islands & Brittany Steamship Co by Robert Craggs & Sons, Middlesborough in September 1895. She measured 350 grt on dimensions of 177 × 24 ft with a draught of 10.5 ft and was propelled by two triple-expansion engines constructed by Westgarth, English, which developed 800 ihp and enabled her to reach 16 knots on trials in Whitley Bay. Her service speed was nearer to 12 knots. She could carry around one hundred passengers and operated a Plymouth–Guernsey–Jersey–St Brieuc service, making her maiden voyage on 14 September, and the following April was altered during an overhaul, raising gross tonnage to 385. She made several excursions to West Country ports and was chartered to attend Queen Victoria's Diamond Jubilee Naval Review at Spithead on 26 June 1897. Just over seven months later, while *en route* to the Channel Islands, she struck Roque Noire off the northern coast of Guernsey on 1 February 1898 and was wrecked with the loss of twenty-one lives.

New Irish Sea tonnage

The next three new London & North Western Railway Co screw-driven steamers were broadly similar if not exact sisters, the 1,531-grt *Duke of York*, coming from Wm Denny & Bros in 1894, the 1,520-grt *Duke of Lancaster** from the Naval Construction & Armament Co, Barrow in the following year and the 1,540-grt *Duke of Cornwall*, from Barrow in 1898. They measured 310 (*Duke of Cornwall* 315) × 37.1 ft and were driven at around 19 knots by twin three-cylinder triple-expansion engines (*Duke of Cornwall* four-cylinder/5,520 ihp). Dredging at Fleetwood enabled fixed-time sailings to be maintained from 1894 onwards and *Duke of Cornwall* was transferred to the Londonderry service in 1909–10. In March 1911, the first two were sold to the Turkish Patriotic Committee, which had them reboilered by Cammell Laird but failed to take delivery due to the outbreak of the Italo–Turkish war. They were resold in June 1912 to Isle of Man Steam Packet Co, which renamed them *Peel Castle* and *The Ramsey* respectively. In the First World War, all three were taken up as armed boarding steamers and *The Ramsey* (renamed in 1914) was sunk by gunfire and torpedo by the German raider *Meteor* (formerly Currie Line's *Vienna*) about seventy miles off Kinnaird Head on 8 August 1915, losing over fifty crew members. The remaining forty-three were taken prisoner but were released when *Meteor* was scuttled the following day when approached by a warship. After the war, *Peel Castle* returned to the Fleetwood–Isle of Man station and in

1924 was joined by *Duke of Cornwall*, which after a brief spell on the Heysham–Belfast service had also been purchased by the IOMSP Co. Renamed *Rushen Castle*, she underwent a major refit in which her shade deck was extended to the foremast and her accommodation renewed. *Peel Castle* was broken up at Dalmuir in 1939, but *Rushen Castle* continued on

island service throughout the Second World War, at first from Liverpool and then Fleetwood. Back on the Liverpool station in 1946, she stranded overnight on a sandbank in the Mersey and made her last round voyage from Douglas to Fleetwood on 14 September. After a brief lay up in Douglas, she left in tow on 9 January 1947 bound for breakers in Ghent.

In the 1890s, the City of Dublin Steam Packet Co received five sisterships for its secondary Dublin–Liverpool service from Blackwood & Gordon: *Louth** in 1894, *Wicklow*, *Carlow* and *Kerry* in successive years and *Cork* in 1899. They averaged 1,250 grt on dimensions of 260 × 34 ft and were driven at 14 knots by triple-expansion machinery. They accommodated around seventy passengers and were also fitted for the carriage of livestock. Two crossings were offered daily with an eight-hour passage time. *Louth* was present at the Diamond Jubilee Naval Review in the Mersey on 22 June 1897 and during the First World War she was used on the Aberdeen–Bergen run until August 1918. *Wicklow* was taken up for trooping duties in the English Channel under British & Irish Steam Packet Co management and *Cork* was torpedoed nine miles north-east of Point Lynas on 26 January 1918 with the loss of twelve lives. The City of Dublin SP Co's Liverpool and Manchester services were acquired by the British & Irish Steam Packet Co in 1919 and the following year the prefix *Lady* was added to her name. *Lady Louth* was quickly transferred to the City of Cork Steam Packet Co and renamed *Bandon*; *Lady Kerry* was sold for scrap in May 1924, and *Lady*

Carlow was demolished at Troon the following year. *Bandon* was returned in 1931 and renamed *Lady Galway*. By now, well over thirty years old, they were demoted to cargo and cattle carriage and in April 1938 both lost their 'titles' and were broken up later in the year, *Galway* after a brief lay up in Liverpool at Port Glasgow and *Wicklow* in Llanelly. A slightly larger sister, the 154-berth (first class) 1,419-grt *Kilkenny* (296.7 × 36.2 ft) was completed by Clyde

Shipbuilding & Engineering Co, Port Glasgow in April 1903. In September 1917, she was sold to the Great Eastern Railway and renamed *Frinton* in December 1919 for Harwich–Rotterdam service. In May 1926, she was sold to Inglessi Bros and briefly renamed *Samos* before reverting to *Frinton*. She sailed mainly between Piraeus and Brindisi and later made some cruises from Venice and the Ionian Islands. She was bombed and sunk at Megara on 22 April 1941.

The twin-screw 1,065-grt *Rosstrevor** was built by Wm Denny & Bros, Dumbarton in 1895 to speed up the London & North Western Railway's Holyhead–Greenore service. Her steel hull measured 279 oa × 35 ft; draught was limited to 13 ft maximum due to the shallowness of water at both ports. Propulsion was by means of a pair of triple-expansion engines fed by two double-ended return tube boilers and she made 18 knots on trial at an output of 3,848 ihp. Denny & Bros was not satisfied with her speed in service and after tank tests exchanged her four-bladed propellers with three-bladed propellers, which gave an extra half knot. She carried a maximum of 930 passengers and berths were provided for eighty in first class amidships and forty in third class aft. A near-sister, *Connemara*, followed in January 1897, proving about 1 knot faster, and a third slightly longer version the 1,112-grt *Galtee More* was delivered by Denny in August 1898. Her two four-cylinder triple-expansion engines were balanced on the Yarrow-Schlick-Tweedy system and gave a trial speed of over 18.5 knots. Her entry into service saw the last of the old paddle steamers withdrawn and allowed the accelerated schedule to be fully implemented. In 1908 *Rosstrevor* was replaced by

Rathmore and downgraded to cargo carrying and on 3 November 1916, in a strong south-westerly gale, the outbound *Connemara* was struck by the inbound collier *Retriever* near Carlingford Lough bar. Both ships sank, the former with the loss of all eighty-six on board while only one of the collier's crew made it to shore. During the First World War, *Galtee More* spent two weeks on charter to the Great Western Railway for its

Weymouth–Channel Islands service in June 1915 and did a nine-week stint for the London & South Western Railway on its Southampton–Guernsey service during July–September 1921, to make up for a shortage of vessels. The Greenore passenger service was suspended in May 1926 during the General Strike and was not restored. *Galtee More* was broken up at Barrow 1926 and *Rosstrevor* was demolished early the following year.

Long-lived Mediterranean trio

The Italian shipping company Navigazione Generale Italiana was formed in 1881 through a merger of Rubattino and Florio. In 1895 it took delivery of the twin-screw 1,662-grt *Cristoforo Colombo*, first of three fast steamers from N Odero's Sestri Ponente yard near Genoa. Sisters *Marco Polo** and *Galileo Galilei* followed in 1896 but a fourth near-sister, *Ignazio Florio*, completed by Fratelli Orlando, Livorno, was chartered by and then sold to Romania in 1897 and renamed *Principessa Maria*. They were propelled by two triple-expansion engines fed by two double-ended cylindrical boilers mounted athwartships on either side of the engine room and the lead ship attained a speed of 17.25 knots at 4,190 ihp. Designed to serve Sicilian ports from Naples, they were fitted with overnight berths for sixty-one first-, fifty second- and forty-seven third-class passengers. Externally, they featured a raised forecastle and long bridge deck and hull dimensions were 271.7 × 36.7 ft. In 1910 all three were purchased by Spain's Compania Valenciana Vapores Correos de Africa to service a newly-won contract to carry mail to North Africa. Renamed *Antonio Lazaro*, *Vicente Puchol* and *J J Sister* respectively, after the line's founders, and with black hull and funnel, the latter bearing the white superimposed letters CA, they were placed in service from Almeria and Malaga to Melilla. At 4–5 knots faster than the company's other ships, they were nicknamed the 'speedy bicycles'. In 1924, *J J Sister* was re-engined by Fijenoord in Rotterdam with two ten-cylinder four-stroke MAN diesels giving 14 knots in service and *V Puchol* and *A Lazaro* were similarly

treated by Vulcan Yard in Barcelona in 1925–6. Routes varied considerably and in November 1936 *A Lazaro* and *V Puchol* were seized by the Nationalist government and converted to auxiliary cruisers in Cadiz, but were initially used for minelaying. *J J Sister* fell into Republican hands and was used for a while as a prison ship, but was captured at sea by the Nationalist cruiser *Canarias* on 17 September 1937 and armed in Cadiz early in 1938. After the civil war,

A Lazaro and *V Puchol* were refitted and given short motorship-type funnels but in the post-Second World War period the three ships served on many different routes, with the only major incident the grounding of *V Puchol* at Las Galletas on the south coast of Teneriffe. After extremely long and successful lives, *A Lazaro* and *V Puchol* were broken up by in Valencia in 1964 and *J J Sister* in the following year.

Advanced quartets for Holyhead services

The City of Dublin Steam Packet Co retained the mail contract in 1894 after offering a half-hour reduction in passage time and immediately ordered four advanced twin-screw vessels from Laird Bros, Birkenhead. Measuring 2,641 grt on dimensions of 372 oa x 41.5 ft, they were built of mild steel and were designed for the high speed of 23 knots, achieving 24 knots on trials. They took the names of the 1860-built quartet, *Ulster, Leinster* and *Munster** and were launched in June, September and December 1896 respectively, and *Connaught* in September the following year. In terms of design, they retained the long turtle-back forecastle of their earlier namesakes but had a straight stem, two well raked masts and funnels and a counter stern. Propulsion was by twin four-cylinder

triple-expansion engines fed by four double-ended boilers and they were licensed to carry 1,400 passengers in two classes spread over three decks. 'Narrow gutted', they were somewhat heavy rollers which must have made travellers thankful for their fast passages of just under three hours. On her maiden voyage, *Leinster* ran from breakwater to breakwater in a record two hours and twenty-four minutes but later in thick fog she rammed and sank the Kish light vessel on 9 September 1902. The sisters maintained the service throughout the First World War, generally sailing unescorted, but *Connaught* was later requisitioned for trooping service on the South Coast and on 3 March 1917 was torpedoed by *U 48* about thirty miles south of

Selsey Bill with the loss of three crew members. *Munster* was also taken up for trooping duties in December 1917 and between then and April 1918 the three surviving ships were all missed by torpedoes but on 10 October 1918 the Holyhead-bound *Leinster* was torpedoed by *UB 123* seven miles east-south-east of the Kish light vessel with the loss of 176 lives including her master. Two weeks later, *Ulster* was hit by a torpedo that luckily failed to explode. After the war, both surviving ships were in poor condition but ran the service with tonnage chartered from the London & North Western Railway, which finally won the mail contract in 1920. They were laid up after making final trips on 27 November and were broken up in Germany in 1924.

The London & North Western Railway Co ordered the first of a quartet of new steamers for its Holyhead–Dublin service from Wm Denny & Bros, Dumbarton in 1896 to complement a new express rail service from Euston via Crewe and to compete with the City of Dublin Steam Packet Co's new 24-knot *Leinster* quartet then under construction. *Cambria** was the first to be completed in November 1897 followed by *Hibernia* and *Anglia* in January and April 1900 respectively and finally *Scotia* in April 1902. They were typical Denny products with flush hulls, twin raked funnels and elliptical sterns and measured 1,842 grt on dimensions of 329 x 39 ft with a load draught limited to 13.5 ft to permit sailing at any state of the tide. They were propelled by two sets of lightweight four-cylinder reciprocating engines designed by Walther Brock and balanced on the Yarrow-Schlick system. Fed with steam by eight single-ended tubular boilers, they developed a maximum of around 8,000 ihp for a contract speed of 21 knots. Overnight berths were provided for 223 first-class on three decks amidships and 770 third-class passengers on two decks forward and aft. During the First World War, *Anglia* was requisitioned in April 1915 and converted to a 244-berth ambulance carrier for

ferrying wounded across the English Channel; *Cambria* was similarly treated with 158 berths in August. On 17 November, *Anglia* was mined and sunk with the loss of twenty-five lives one mile east of Folkestone Gate, just twelve days after sister *Hibernia* had been torpedoed in the eastern Mediterranean while serving as the armed merchant cruiser HMS *Tara*, sister *Scotia* performing a similar role. *Cambria* was released in January 1919 and the following year she and *Scotia* were renamed *Arvonia* and *Menevia* to free up their names for new turbine ships under

construction. Passing into LMS ownership in 1923 they were employed on various routes, including Heysham–Douglas and Holyhead–Greenore, and carried Lancashire & Yorkshire Railway funnel colours until 1925, when the red band was removed. Both were broken up by T W Ward at Barrow, *Arvonia* in late summer 1925 and in winter 1928–9 *Menevia*, which had briefly been chartered by Isle of Man Steam Packet Co in summer 1925 and made the last London, Midland & Scottish sailing on the Douglas run on 12 September 1927.

The Barrow firm of J Little & Co, operator of the Barrow Steam Navigation Co, received its largest ship to date, *Duchess of Devonshire*, from Naval Construction & Armament Co, Barrow, in 1897. She measured 1,265 grt on dimensions of 300 × 35.1 ft and was propelled by two triple-expansion engines developing 5,200 ihp for a trials speed 18 knots. She was used principally on the Barrow–Douglas, Isle of Man, run but made overnight trips to Belfast during the winter months for which temporary berths were installed. In 1907, Barrow Steam Navigation Co was absorbed into the Midland Railway and the English terminal switched to Heysham. She was laid up in Barrow during the winter and was reboiled in

1910. In the First World War, she was commissioned as an armed boarding steamer and returned to her peacetime route in 1920, running alongside *City of Belfast*. Following the railway regrouping in 1923, she passed to the London, Midland & Scottish Railway and ran on several routes in addition to her normal Isle of Man route, the running of which was handed over to the Isle of Man Steam Packet Co in 1928. That July she was sold to M H Bland & Co of Gibraltar and renamed *Gibel Dersa* made her first trip across the Gibraltar Strait to Tangier on 28 September. Passenger revenue was adversely affected by the worsening economic situation and she was laid up on 15 January 1930, but was back in service for

summer 1932. In 1936, *Gibel Dersa* was attacked by Spanish Republican aircraft on a crossing to Tangier but escaped serious damage. She was requisitioned by the UK government in June 1940 and sent to Casablanca to evacuate 200 Czech and Polish troops from Vichy control, being laid up after her return. In November 1942, the Royal Navy chartered her for use as an accommodation ship, prior to the North Africa landings, and she continued in this role until May 1944. The previous September, she had been sold to Dalhousie Steam & Motor Ship Co of London but was resold to A Benaim of Gibraltar in September 1947 and was eventually broken up in 1949 at Malaga.

North Sea

Det Forenede D/S (United Steamship Co), of Copenhagen, took delivery of the 1,425-grt screw-driven *N J Fjord* for its Esbjerg–Harwich service in 1896. She was built of steel by Lobnitz & Co, which had been responsible for the preceding 1,069 grt, 12-knot paddle steamer *Koldinghus*. Two 1,530-grt sisters, *Ficaria** and *Primula* (provisional name *Saerimner*), followed in the same year and all measured around 271.5 oa × 34 ft with a draught of 17.2 ft. They were propelled by triple-expansion engines fed by two double-ended boilers and the output of 2,500 ihp provided a service speed of 14 knots, which was exceeded by about 1 knot on trials. They could accommodate around seventy first-class passengers and up to 300 emigrants and were distinguished by their very tall masts and single funnel. Fitted with refrigerating machinery, they were the first DFDS ships to have light grey hulls. *N J Fjord* mainly sailed between Esbjerg and Harwich and the other two between Copenhagen and Newcastle, *Primula* shifting to various UK routes after 1903. They were laid up in Denmark following the outbreak of the First World War but were later used for tramping duties. In 1916, *N J Fjord* passed between the opposing fleets just before the Battle of Jutland but on 5 April 1917 was

captured and sunk by explosives about forty miles north of Farne Island by the German submarine *UC 31* while *en route* from Blyth to Odense with a cargo of coal. In 1922 *Primula* inaugurated a new weekly service linking Esbjerg with Antwerp and Dunkirk for which she was refitted by Burmeister & Wain, Copenhagen, to carry seventy-four first- and twenty-six second-class passengers. *Ficaria* was by then sailing

mainly in the Baltic and she was laid up in Copenhagen in September 1931 and sold in November 1934 for demolition in Blyth. In 1935–6, *Primula* sailed for a while between Leith, the Faroe Islands and Iceland but after a final stint on the Esbjerg–Antwerp–Dunkirk run in 1936 was laid up until February 1938, when she was sold for demolition at Dunston-on-Tyne.

The 1,136-grt *Batavier II* and *Batavier III** were completed by Gourlay Bros, Dundee, in 1897 for Wm H Muller & Co, which had acquired the Rotterdam–London service of Nederlandsche Stoomboot Maatschappij two years earlier. Built of steel, they measured 244 × 33.5 ft and were propelled by a four-cylinder triple-expansion engine developing 2,000 ihp for 14 knots in service. They had a short well deck at No 2 hatch forward of the bridge and could accommodate forty-four first-, twenty-seven second- and up to 250 steerage-class passengers. In

1903 they changed their funnel colouring from yellow with a black top to Muller's livery of black with two narrow white bands enclosing a broad red carrying a large white letter M and in 1909–10 they were lengthened by 16 ft and reboiled by Wilton Fijenoord in Rotterdam. At the same time their lifeboats were raised one deck and an extra pair added aft while the forward derrick was replaced by a crane. These alterations raised gross tonnage to 1,335. During the First World War, *Batavier II* was captured by the German submarine *UB 6* on 24 September

1916 and taken to Zeebrugge. While moving to Hamburg as a prize in July the following year she was shelled by the Royal Navy submarine *E 55* one mile north of Molengat buoy off Texel, was abandoned and later sank. Early in 1919 her sister resumed her London service and around ten years later her promenade was partly enclosed. In 1939 she was sold to L P Sclavounos and renamed *El Sonador* under Panamanian flag, but was torpedoed and sunk by *U 61* in position 58N 2E, to the east of the Shetland Islands, on 18 February 1940 with the loss of twenty persons.

Channel Islands

The 1,281-grt *Roebuck* and *Reindeer** were completed for the Great Western Railway by Naval Construction & Armament Co, Barrow-in-Furness, in May and June 1897. Measuring 280 x 34.5 ft, they were designed for a new day service from Weymouth to the Channel Islands and were basically improved versions of *Ibex*, retaining the short well aft disguised by high doors. Competition with the London & South Western Railway was at its height so speed was increased to 20 knots by means of two three-cylinder reciprocating engines developing 5,300 ihp, with steam supplied by a pair of double-ended Scotch boilers. Berths were provided for 150 first- and seventy-six second-class passengers. On her first crossing from Weymouth on 1 July, *Roebuck* reached Guernsey in a record time of just under three and a half hours. *Reindeer* replaced *Ibex* on the day service in August but the latter maintained the winter roster while the newer sisters were laid up in Milford. It was there, during a refit on 26 January 1905, that *Roebuck* caught fire and sank but in a more spectacular incident on 19 July 1911 she impaled herself on Kaines Reef off St Brelades, Jersey, both incidents requiring several months of repair work at Barrow and Southampton respectively. After war broke out in 1914, *Reindeer* was briefly switched to the Fishguard–Rosslare service before requisition by the

Admiralty in October for minesweeping service. At the same time *Roebuck* was converted to an armed merchant cruiser and renamed HMS *Roedean* but she dragged her anchor at Scapa Flow on 13 January 1915 and sank off Langhope after being caught on the bows of HMS *Imperieuse*. *Reindeer* sailed to the Mediterranean and took part in the Gallipoli campaign where she rammed and sank the Great

Central Railway's *Immingham* on 12 June 1916. She returned to peacetime service in February 1920 with new sloping-topped funnels fitted in Southampton and in another refit in 1923 had a shelter deck added. She was placed in reserve following the arrival of the new *St Julien* and *St Helier* in 1925 and made a few day excursions to Guernsey in 1926 before sale for demolition at Briton Ferry in 1928.

The London & South Western Railway ordered a new steamer in late 1897 from Clydebank Engineering & Shipbuilding Co (formerly J & G Thomson). Designed primarily as a spare ship for both the Le Havre and Channel Island services, the 1,193-grt *Vera** was launched in July 1898 and tried in September, reaching 19.5 knots. She marked a return to single funnels but was otherwise an improved *Columbia* with extended superstructure forward and a slightly broader beam, her hull dimensions being 280.5 x 35.5 ft. Main machinery comprised two sets of quadruple expansion engines developing 4,500 ihp and steam was supplied by four single-ended return tube boilers. She had a minor scrape with the P&O liner *Simla* in Southampton Water in March 1901 and in the First World War was credited with shelling and sinking a German submarine off the Isle of Wight. A near-sister, *Alberta* was ordered from the same yard, which had now become John Brown & Co, to replace the loss of *Stella* in March 1899. Just 5 in broader in the beam, she was marginally more powerful with an engine output of 5,000 ihp and initially had her flying bridge mounted ahead of the foremast. Other distinctions included a greater array of ventilators and a different boat arrangement. She was unscathed in the First World War but hit a rock off Guernsey in July 1920. Both ships passed

to the newly formed Southern Railway in 1923 and *Alberta* was withdrawn at the end of 1929, having carried nearly 750,000 passengers in her twenty-eight years. She was sold to Inglessi & Son of Samos in 1930 and the following year began a Lesbos–Chios–Piraeus schedule, being briefly renamed *Mykali* in 1934. Meanwhile, in June 1932, her older sister *Vera* was assigned to the Jersey–St

Malo service, which had been operated by the small French steamer *St Brieuc* since 1919. Replaced by the new *Brittany* in June 1933, she was broken up at Pembroke. As to *Alberta*, efforts to sell her to Canada early in the Second World War failed and she was bombed and sunk at Punta, Salamis Island, during the German invasion on 23 April 1941.

Fast P&O mail steamers

In 1898, the Peninsular & Oriental Steam Navigation Co took delivery of two unusual ships from Caird & Co, Greenock. Akin to cross channel steamers, the 1,728-grt twin-screw *Isis* and *Osiris** were specially designed to convey the overland mail and seventy-eight first-class passengers, who had arrived by train from London, from Brindisi to Port Said where they caught up the mail steamer that had left the UK some two weeks earlier. Their flush-decked hulls measured 300 x 37 ft and they were driven by two four-cylinder triple-expansion engines developing 6,500 ihp for a service speed of 20 knots. While southbound on 1 October 1906, *Isis* shed her starboard screw causing serious damage to both engine and shaft and a starting a leak. Temporary repairs were carried out in Zante but she had to return to Greenock for drydocking. The service was abandoned on the outbreak of war in August 1914 and *Isis* was laid up in Malta. Her sister was requisitioned initially to become an armed merchant cruiser but this was changed to a fleet messenger in October and then again to a depot ship in April 1915. Two months later *Isis* was taken up as a fleet messenger under the name HMS *Isonzo* and in 1916 *Osiris* had the suffix *II* added to her name. Both were released early in 1920 and laid up in

Falmouth. After reverting to their original names, *Isis* was sold in August to M H Bland & Co of Gibraltar and renamed *Gibel Sarsar* while *Osiris* went in July 1922 to John Worthington Bagley of Paris who resold her to German breakers. *Gibel Sarsar* entered service on Bland's Gibraltar–Tangier–Casablanca route in October 1920 and in January 1922 she was

transferred to a new service linking Alicante with Algiers, Oran, Gibraltar, Tangier and Casablanca but lack of success led to her returning to her original service after a year, sailing on a weekly basis. By now in poor condition, she was laid up in January 1923 and three years later was sold to Italian breakers, leaving Gibraltar for Genoa in tow on 17 March.

Canadian sisters

The newly formed Dominion Atlantic Railway's first new ship was the 1,414-grt *Prince Edward* completed by Earle's Shipbuilding & Engineering Co, Hull, in September 1897. Measuring 268 x 38 ft on 12.5 ft draught, she was driven by a pair of triple-expansion engines fed by two double-ended boilers and had a service speed of 16 knots. Too small for the Yarmouth NS–Boston run, she was sold in 1906 to Rederi Aktiebolaget Sverige Tyskland, Malmö, for ferry service between Trelleborg and Sassnitz under the new name of *Prins Gustav Adolph*. Six years later she was sold on to Ivan I Burkoff, who ran her as *Vasilij Velikij* between Archangel and Vardø, Norway, but she was wrecked around 3 March 1916 near Vaidaguba Light. The larger twin-screw 2,194-grt *Prince George** and 2,041-grt *Prince Arthur* were delivered by Earle's in November 1898 and January 1899. They measured 290.5 oa x 38 ft on a draught of 16.5 ft and were driven at 19 knots by two four-cylinder triple-expansion engines, *Prince George* achieving 20.3 knots on trials. Their cowl-topped funnels were painted red with black tops and they bore more than a passing resemblance to the Great Eastern Railway steamers emanating from the same yard. Elegant passenger accommodation was supplied for 314 first and thirty-two second-class passengers with 200 berths and an additional 700 could be carried on deck. They were managed by R C Campbell until 1911, when the Dominion Atlantic

Railway came under the control of Canadian Pacific and on 20 August the following year both ships were sold to the Eastern Steamship Corporation of America but continued to run on the same service under the auspices of the Boston & Yarmouth Steamship Co. In May 1917, they returned to the UK

for use as cross-channel ambulance carriers, for which additional lifeboats and a long after deckhouse were added. Released in 1919, they returned to their peacetime service until 1927 when they were withdrawn. *Prince Arthur* was broken up in Baltimore in 1929 and her sister followed two years later.

New tonnage for North Sea

Completed by Elsinore Shipbuilding & Engineering Co in 1901 for the Det Forenede D/S (United Steamship Co) Esbjerg–Harwich service, the 1,635-grt *J C La Cour* was the first North Sea passenger ship to be built in Denmark. Her steel hull, which measured 270.5 × 36.5 ft, comprised a main deck and awning deck and and she was fitted with a short raised forecastle to make her more sea kindly. She was distinguished by her two very tall, slightly raked masts. A triple-expansion engine developing 3,600 ihp gave her a service speed of 15 knots and she could accommodate 112 berthed passengers of which seventy-six were in first class. The Harwich service was suspended at the start of the First World War and she was laid up in Esbjerg. Following the Armistice in 1918, *J C La Cour* was mainly used for relief sailings interspersed with occasional spells on the Copenhagen–Oslo service. She called at Harwich for the last time in 1931 and following a further period of lay up in Esbjerg was sold to shipbreakers at Blyth in 1933.

Earle's Shipbuilding & Engineering Co, Hull had a full order book after it was saved from bankruptcy by local shipowner Thomas Wilson, so the Great Eastern Railway turned to Gourlay Bros, Dundee for a new steamer to serve Antwerp. Delivered in 1902, *Brussels* followed the pattern established by preceding GER ships but was appreciably smaller, measuring 1,380 grt on dimensions of 285.3 × 34 ft. Her reciprocating engines were similar but with one fewer boiler the reduced output of 3,800 ihp gave a service speed of just 16.5 knots. She could carry 160 first-class

The Rotterdam firm Wm H Muller returned to Gourlay Bros, Dundee, in 1903 for a second pair of larger steamers for its Rotterdam–London service. *Batavier IV* and *Batavier V* measured 1,568 grt and differed from the earlier ships in having their well deck placed aft at No 3 hatch. Hull dimensions were 260.2 × 35 ft on a draught of 15.5 ft and their triple-expansion engines were constructed by Hutson & Sons with steam supplied by two single-ended boilers. Power output was 2,300 ihp and service speed 14.5 knots. Overnight berths were provided for seventy-five first-class and twenty-eight second-class passengers and in addition they could carry up to 325 in steerage. *Batavier IV* grounded in the New Waterway on 8 December 1909 after colliding with and sinking a fishing boat. During the First World War, her sister was captured on 18 March 1915 and taken to Zeebrugge. Later released, she resumed service but on 16 May 1916 hit a mine near the Inner Gabbard light vessel and sank with the loss of four persons. *Batavier IV* had her promenade deck partly enclosed around 1930 and when war came again she assisted in the evacuation of France and the Channel Islands. She was then converted to the training ship *Eastern Isles* and from 14 September 1940 became the HQ ship of the anti-submarine Escort Training Group based at Tobermory. She was renamed *Western Isles* in 1941 and following her release five years later was taken to Rotterdam where her engine was removed and as KNS *Zeearend* (Sea

passengers, mainly in two-berth cabins. During the First World War, she maintained an irregular service between Tilbury and the Hook of Holland and on 28 March 1915 attempted to ram the German submarine *U 33*, which had ordered her to stop some eight miles west of the Maas light vessel. She later used her speed to escape from submarines on three separate occasions and on 20 July was missed by a torpedo about twenty miles east of the South Inner Gabbard buoy. By now the Germans were anxious to capture her and torpedo boats finally achieved this off the Hook of Holland on 23 June 1916 and took her to Zeebrugge. Her crew was imprisoned and the unfortunate Captain Fryatt was tried, found guilty of trying to ram a submarine and shot, leading to an indignant outcry in the UK. The Germans renamed her *Brugge* and used her as a depot ship for flying boats and submarines before sinking her as a blockship on 5 October 1918. Raised by the Belgians in November 1919, she was returned to the British government and put up for sale on the Tyne. Public resentment prevented a foreign sale and in August 1920 she went to a sole bidder acting for Dublin & Lancashire Steamship Co and was rebuilt by Henry Robb in Leith. She emerged with new accommodation and fittings for the carriage of 600 head of cattle and entered Preston–Dublin service on 7 September 1921. In 1922 she was renamed *Lady Brussels* and the following year passed to British & Irish Steam Packet Co. She remained on the same service until April 1929 and was sold to breakers Smith & Co/Port Glasgow the following month.

Eagle) she served as a static ASW base in the Waalhaven. She was moved to the naval base at Den Helder in the early 1960s and when replaced by a shore facility was towed to Bilbao in December 1973 for demolition.

Irish Sea developments

The 1,226-grt *Duke of Rothesay* was completed for the Dublin & Glasgow Sailing & Steam Packet Co by Caledon Shipbuilding & Engineering, Dundee in October 1899. She was some 20 ft longer than the preceding *Duke of Fife*, her hull measuring 265 x 35.2 ft and her single triple-expansion engine had an output of 3,000 ihp. A handsome steamer, she was the first ship on the Clyde–Dublin service to have first-class passenger accommodation positioned amidships and in April 1908 passed to G & J Burns, who renamed her *Puma**. Burns became part of the Coast Lines Group in 1919 and its ships were merged with those of Laird Line in 1922 to form Burns & Laird Lines. In a rationalisation move in 1929, all of the ships in the fleet were given red funnels with a black top and renamed with a 'Laird' prefix, *Puma* becoming *Lairdsford*. She was scrapped by T W Ward at Preston in 1934.

The 1,093-grt *Rose** was built by A & J Inglis and completed in June 1902 for the Glasgow, Dublin & Londonderry Steam Packet Co, for which A A Laird & Co (Laird Line) was manager. Her hull measured 250.5 x 36.1 ft and she was driven at around 15 knots by triple-expansion machinery developing 330 nhp and fed with steam by two double-ended boilers. Her extra beam compared with earlier steamers and the fitting of bilge keels made her a very steady ship and gave added comfort to the 140 first-class passengers housed under her long bridge deck. In addition, some 650 steerage passengers were also catered for. She entered service on the Glasgow–Dublin run but later came to be more associated with the Londonderry service. A flying bridge was later added and during the First World War she was employed as a troopship in the Mediterranean, running between Taranto and Itea from whence troops were taken by rail to Salonika. She returned to her peacetime role in 1919 and in 1922 became part of the newly-merged Burns & Laird Lines. She was renamed *Lairdsrose* in 1929 – the only ship in the former Laird fleet to retain her original name with the addition of the *Laird* prefix. She was broken up at Bo'ness in 1949.

Duke of Connaught was completed for the London & North Western Railway by John Brown, Clydebank, in 1902. Larger than her four predecessors at 1,714 grt, she measured 315 x 38.2 ft and her two four-cylinder triple-expansion engines of 340 nhp and four single-ended boilers gave her the slightly higher speed of 20 knots. Accommodation was arranged on three decks for 490 first-class passengers amidships and a similar number in steerage aft. The first-class dining saloon extended the full width of the upper deck and a smoking room was provided on the promenade deck above. She operated out of Fleetwood, sailing to Belfast, Londonderry and the Isle of Man, and continued to do so during the First World War, surviving a brush with a German submarine on 22 October 1918 by using her speed and a round or two from her defensive armament to escape. Immediately after the war she was loaned to the City of Dublin Steam Packet Co for its Holyhead–Kingstown service and on return in 1921 was sent to Vickers' yard in Barrow for a refit which included fitting four new Babcock & Wilcox watertube boilers. The L&NWR became sole owner in 1922, but on 1 January the following year it became part of the new London, Midland & Scottish Railway following the regrouping of the UK railway companies. *Duke of Connaught* was mainly used on the Heysham–Isle of Man service until 1930, when, with refitted accommodation and repainted in the old Goole Steam Shipping Co colours, she

was transferred to Hull to replace *Duke of Connaught* on the summer Zeebrugge service. Public outcry soon forced her to revert to the old L&NWR's buff with black top as illustrated but after completing only three seasons she was withdrawn and sold to Dutch breakers in 1934.

The twin-screw 1,339-grt sisters *Great Southern** and *Great Western* were completed by Laird Bros, Birkenhead, in April and June 1902 for the Great Western Railway's Milford–Waterford service but transferred to Fishguard in 1906 following the opening of the new harbour. They measured 275.8 × 36.3 ft and were propelled by a pair of four-cylinder triple-expansion engines, fed by two double-ended boilers, which developed 3,250 ihp for a modest 16 knots in service. They could accommodate 246 first- and 439 third-class passengers, with berths for sixty-five in saloon class placed amidships and steerage aft; in addition 500 head of cattle could be carried. They allowed the service to be accelerated and on 9 July

1902 *Great Southern* made a record westward passage of five hours and forty-nine minutes. They continued to sail during the First World War and *Great Southern* was only requisitioned for short periods during 1916–17, between which she made her first appearance at Weymouth for four trips to the Channel Islands in summer 1916 in place of *Ibex*, but she only helped out on this route once more, in 1924. *Great Western* undertook summer relief sailings from Weymouth in 1922 and this became a regular event between 1924 and 1932, after which she was briefly chartered to a Shetland agricultural society at the end of August. *Great Western* was renamed *GWR No 20* in August 1933 to allow her name to pass to a

new ship and she was sold to John Cashmore for scrap in September with work commencing at Newport, Monmouthshire, early in 1934. Her sister followed her shortly afterwards. The similarly dimensioned 1,204-grt *Waterford* was built by Swan, Hunter & Wigham Richardson in 1912 to boost the Fishguard–Waterford service, but was mainly a cargo and cattle carrier with only a few passengers. In September 1924, she was sold to Compania Maritima of Manila and sailed on Philippines coastal services as *Panay* until bombed and sunk by Japanese aircraft at Campomanes Bay, Negros, on 30 December 1941.

The sisters *Colleen Bawn* and *Mellifont* were ordered by the Lancashire & Yorkshire Railway Co from Vickers, Sons & Maxim, Barrow-in-Furness in 1902, following L&YR's acquisition of the Drogheda Steam Packet Co and its services. They were twin-screw vessels with a single funnel and appeared in 1903, replacing the paddlers *Tredagh* and *Kathleen Mavournen*. Gross measurement was 1,204 tons and hull dimensions 260 × 35.7 ft. Two triple-expansion engines of 296 nhp were fed with steam by two boilers for a service speed of 16.5 knots. In 1906, *Mellifont** was transferred to the east coast for a service from Goole to Antwerp, sailing in the 'soot, blood and suet' funnel colours of the L&YR, but returned to the Drogheda service and her original colours in 1912 following the withdrawal of *Iverna*, the last paddle steamer on the route. From 1923, the two ships were part of the London, Midland & Scottish fleet, but continued to sail on the Liverpool–Drogheda route until 1928 when it was taken over by British & Irish Steam Packet Co. *Colleen Bawn* was then transferred to the Holyhead–Greenore service, on which she remained until sold to T W Ward for scrapping at Briton Ferry in October 1930, while *Mellifont* also went to Holyhead for the carriage of cargo and livestock from Dublin North Wall until broken up by T W Ward at Barrow in 1932.

Balearic Islands

Palma-based Sociedad Islena Maritima ordered its first new steamer from Odero, Genoa in 1903. The 1,724-grt *Miramar* was completed in January 1904 and entered service on the Palma–Barcelona route. She had a flush-decked hull with vertical stem and counter stern and a single funnel set between two masts. Her measurements were 269.8 oa × 36.1 ft and she was propelled by a 299-nhp triple-expansion engine, which gave a trial speed of 15 knots using forced draught but 12 knots under normal conditions. She made pilgrim trips to Civitavecchia in June 1910 and July 1912 but during the First World War, when coal became scarce, the Barcelona service was suspended and she was chartered out. With her hull painted black, she loaded coal at Musel on her first voyage, but after leaving Gijon for Cadiz grounded on Carino Rocks at Aguillones Cove near Cape Ortegal on 9 February 1918. Some of her boats tried to seek help, which eventually arrived but not before twelve crew members had perished. Her boiler was later salved and installed in Compania Trasmediterranea's *Romeu* in 1926.

First three-funnelled *Princess* for Canadian Pacific

Canadian Pacific Railway's *Princess Victoria* revolutionised West Coast steamer traffic when she entered service on the seventy-two-mile route between Vancouver and Victoria (Vancouver Island) on 17 August 1903, following a successful day of trials. The first of the famous three-funnelled 'Pacific Princesses', she was a twin-screw steamer of 1,943 grt built in Newcastle by C S Swan & Hunter Ltd and measuring 300 × 40.5 ft. Her main machinery comprised twin four-cylinder triple-expansion units made by Hawthorn Leslie and these produced 5,800 ihp for a speed of 19.5 knots. With shipyard strikes pending, it was thought expedient to sail her on her delivery voyage via the Magellan Strait without her wooden superstructure, which was added along with all interior fittings at Esquimalt after arrival. After her first revenue-earning season, she returned to Esquimalt for final touches to her luxurious accommodation and was back in service in April 1904. A single round trip a day did not press her and in mid-June she started making an overnight voyage to Seattle from Victoria. This resulted in her having to steam 325 miles within twenty-four hours for which two crews were required. Thus was born Canadian Pacific's famous 'Triangle Route'. Her subsequent career was not without incident and she sank two vessels in collision, the tug *Chehalis* in Burrard Inlet on 21 July 1906 and the larger Admiral Line steamer *Admiral Sampson* in fog north of Seattle on 26 August 1914 with the loss of sixteen lives. In 1930 she was taken in hand for alterations which allowed her to carry fifty cars aft. Laid up at Victoria in early September 1950, she was sold to Vancouver-based Tahsis & Co in February 1952 and converted to the bulk hog fuel barge *Tahsis No 3* but the end of 'Old Vic', as she had popularly been known, was nigh and on 10 March 1953 she sank after striking a rock in Welcome Pass, while in tow of the tug *Sea Giant*.

CHAPTER
5

The Turbine Revolution

The first successful commercial applications of Charles Parsons' revolutionary steam turbine propulsion system in the Clyde excursion steamers *King Edward* and *Queen Alexandra* in 1901–2 quickly led to its adoption by two railway companies operating on the English Channel. The South Eastern & Chatham Railway's *The Queen* was completed in early summer 1903 and was closely followed by the London, Brighton & South Coast Railway's slightly smaller *Brighton*. All four were built by William Denny & Bros and *The Queen* was followed by four similar ships within a space of four years. *Brighton* was a virtual sister of the triple-expansion-driven *Arundel* of 1900, which allowed direct comparisons to be made, clearly demonstrating the superiority of the turbine.

Turbine propulsion soon spread to other United Kingdom routes and by 1909 its use had spread to services in Australia (*Loongana*), New Zealand (*Maori*), Japan (*Hirafu Maru* etc) and France (*Charles Roux*). Triple-expansion reciprocating engines generally remained the preferred choice for ships operating overnight services, for which speed was less of a consideration. Paddle propulsion was still employed on the River Plate estuary but here too comparisons were made with triple-expansion engines.

Note: An asterisk in a caption indicates the vessel shown in the photograph.

First turbines for English Channel

The South Eastern & Chatham Railway Co's 1,676-grt triple-screw *The Queen*, delivered by Wm Denny & Bros in June 1903, achieved renown as the first cross channel steamer to be propelled by steam turbines, although the London, Brighton & South Coast Railway had contracted its own turbine packet *Brighton* with the same yard some two months prior to the SE&CR placing its order. Both railway concerns had been impressed by the performance of the pioneering Clyde excursion steamers *King Edward* and *Queen Alexandra*. *The Queen* had a flush hull measuring 318 oa x 40 ft with a straight stem and elegant counter stern, two raked funnels completing a pleasing appearance. Three Parsons direct-drive turbines provided the motive power and steam was supplied by pairs of single-ended and double-ended boilers. The high-pressure turbine drove the centre shaft and exhausted into two low-pressure units which powered the wing shafts and were also used for going astern. During extensive trials in May, mean speeds of 21.75 knots ahead and 13 knots astern were achieved and the ship could be brought to a halt from 19 knots in one minute seven seconds in less than two and a half boat lengths. Two decks were given over to passenger accommodation, first class on the awning deck and second class on the main deck abaft the machinery space. The success of her first year, during which she averaged 21 knots, led the SE&CR to order two more ships which emerged from Denny as *Onward** and *Invicta* in April and July 1905 and they in turn were followed two years later by a second pair, *Victoria* and *Empress*. Although interchangeable, the first two vessels came to be associated with the Folkestone–Boulogne route from 1907 but on 30 May the following year collided head on in patchy fog in mid channel, one lookout being killed. During the First World War, the first four sisters were initially employed as channel troop transports and *The Queen* rescued 2,200 refugees from the torpedoed *Amiral Ganteaume* on 26 October 1914; but on 26 August 1916 she was surprised near the Varne Bank by German destroyers and scuttled. *Empress* meanwhile had been converted to a seaplane carrier with a large hanger aft and operated in West African, Mediterranean and Red Sea waters. On 24 September 1918 *Onward* caught fire at Folkestone and was intentionally scuttled,

resting on her side. An array of five winches and railway engines were used to raise her within a month and she was reconditioned in London before sale to Isle of Man Steam Packet Co, which placed her on the Liverpool–Douglas run in May 1920, renaming her *Mona's Isle* that August. Later she was principally engaged on Irish services. In 1923 *Invicta* and *Empress* were sold to France's SAGA group to replace the paddlers *Le Nord* and *Pas de Calais* and served for another decade until sold for scrap in April 1933. *Victoria* joined the former *Onward* in the Isle of Man SP Co fleet in March 1928 and was placed on the Heysham run; she was converted to oil-firing in 1932. After performing useful military service in several roles during the Second World War, *Mona's Isle* was scrapped by T W Ward at Milford Haven in 1948 but *Victoria* lasted until January 1957, when she was sold to the same breaker and demolished at its Barrow facility.

Encouraged by the success of its *Sussex*, the London, Brighton & South Coast Railway returned to Wm Denny & Bros for an improved vessel capable of making the Newhaven–Dieppe crossing in twelve minutes over three hours. *Arundel* was launched in on 5 April 1900 and handed over on 24 June, her length just 2 ft shorter than *Sussex* on the same beam but she drew some two feet more water on 11.7 ft draught. Her reciprocating engines were the same but she had two double-ended boilers in place of single-ended in the earlier ship. Her trials speed was around 20.75 knots while externally she differed in having two masts and funnels and her upper deck was extended to the stern. Her maximum passenger capacity was around 800 and berthing was supplied for 126 in first class and eighty-seven in second class. Meanwhile, the success of the Denny-built steam turbine-propelled Clyde excursion steamer *Queen Alexandra* had not gone unnoticed by the LB&SCR, which specified turbine propulsion for a sister named *Brighton**. Launched in June 1903 she made trial crossings to Dieppe and back on 27–8 August and proved to be marginally faster than *Arundel* averaging three hours and three minutes and using about 10 per cent less coal. Lack of weight in her engine room, however, made her rather tender, necessitating the addition of permanent concrete ballast. On the morning of 6 November 1910, *Brighton* was run into by the German five-masted *Preussen*, the world's largest sailing ship, and her forward funnel and mainmast were removed by the latter's bowsprit, forcing her to return to Newhaven for repairs. *Preussen*, which had lost her fore topmast and been holed forward in the impact, drifted up Channel in worsening weather and eventually stranded just north of Dover Harbour, becoming a total loss. During the First World War, both ships were employed as a troopships and *Brighton* later became a hospital ship. *Brighton* was sold in October 1930 to Lord Moyne and converted to a

private yacht by Thornycroft at Northam, Southampton. Renamed *Roussalka*, her funnels were shortened and deckhouse extended, while to provide greater range she was converted to oil-firing, her centre shaft was removed and 500-ton fuel tanks installed. A refit two years later saw her turbines replaced by two Polar Atlas diesel engines developing 870 bhp for a speed of 15 knots and her forward funnel was removed. In August 1933, she hit an uncharted rock in fog off Galway and was wrecked. Meanwhile *Arundel*, which had been relegated to running cheap day trips to France from Brighton's Palace Pier, was sold to German breakers in 1934.

The Belgian government was quick to adopt steam turbine propulsion for its 1,747-grt *Princesse Elisabeth*, completed by Société Cockerill's Hoboken yard in 1905. Her engines were built by Parsons of Newcastle and followed the direct drive, triple-screw arrangement used in the English cross-channel steamers. She measured 357 × 40 ft and was among the earliest ships with a cruiser stern, which was embellished with 'gingerbread' decoration. Service speed was 22 knots but she reached 24.75 knots on trials in the Scheldt and later improved on this by recording 26.25 knots in the Clyde, making her the world's fastest merchant ship until the advent of Cunard Line's *Lusitania*. A pair of slightly shorter (348 ft) but broadly similar ships followed from Cockerill in 1909–10, their names *Jan Breydel** and *Pieter de Coninck* temporarily breaking their owner's alternate Flemish and French style of nomenclature. Intended for winter service, their entry into service was timed to coincide with the extra traffic expected from the 1910 Brussels exhibition. Before the First World War, *Princesse Elisabeth*'s bridge was raised one deck and fitted with wing cabs to bring her into line with the newer ships. She was lying in Antwerp with engines partly dismantled at the outbreak of war, but managed to escape from the advancing Germans and complete her refit in London. *Jan Breydel* carried the Belgian queen and her family to safety in England, returning her alone to Antwerp on 7 September, and on 6 October she evacuated most of the Belgian diplomatic corps to Le Havre. All three ships were lent to the Admiralty for use as hospital ships during the war and were returned in 1919. *Princesse Elisabeth* was reboilered in a post-war refit and remained in service until 1930, when she was displaced by new ships, and she was scrapped in 1933. During the 1920s, the other ships had the forward end of the promenade deck plated in

and this was later extended further aft with the addition of windows. The funnels lost their cowls and after 1930 were given deeper black tops. *Pieter de Coninck* was scrapped at Pernis in 1931 but her sister was sold to Victor de H Slama of Tunis for a proposed North Africa coastal service. After conversion she was renamed *Tourist* in 1932, but was seized by creditors when her new owner defaulted. She lay in Antwerp until broken up at Ghent in 1933.

The 1,216-grt *Dieppe* was the second triple-screw turbine steamer ordered by the London, Brighton & South Coast Railway, but because Denny had a full order book she was constructed at Govan by Fairfield Shipbuilding & Engineering Co. Launched on 6 April 1905, she was slightly longer than the preceding *Brighton*, measuring 282 oa × 34.8 ft on a draught of 11.5 ft. Her machinery and boiler outfit was the same as that of *Brighton* but developed 6,500 shp and allowed her to record a marginally faster speed of over 21.5 knots on a trial return crossing to Dieppe. She was stiffer looking than the earlier pair with shorter funnels and masts and was otherwise

distinguished by her solid bulwarks forward. She was licenced to carry 850 passengers but this was later increased to 1,034. During the First World War, she was mainly employed transporting troops, ammunition and stores across the English Channel to France, but spent a short period as a hospital ship. Her superstructure was plated in during the 1920s, but she was not converted to oil-burning. Renamed *Rosaurae*, she was bought by Lord Moyne in September 1933 and converted to a yacht in place of his sunken *Roussalka* (her former consort *Brighton* of 1903). The work was carried out at Thornycroft's Woolston yard and two 1,159-bhp Polar Atlas diesels

were substituted for her turbines. The centre shaft was removed and new short single funnel and navigating bridge fitted. New accommodation included eight *en suite* staterooms and a swimming pool was installed on the after weather deck. Her speed was reduced to 15.5 knots but she had an impressive range of 15,000 miles thanks to extra fuel tanks in her former boiler-room. She was requisitioned early in the Second World War, and acted as an armed boarding vessel in the Mediterranean until mined and sunk off Tobruk on 18 March 1941.

Irish Sea turbines

To meet growing traffic on the Stranraer–Larne service, the Portpatrick & Wigtownshire Railways Joint Committee took the bold step in 1903 of ordering a new steam turbine vessel from Wm Denny & Bros of Dumbarton. The 1,746-grt *Princess Maud** was completed in time for the 1904 summer season and her three-island type hull measured 308 (over the rudder) x 40 ft, the short wells hidden by hinged doors. She was the first turbine ship on the Irish Sea and her engines echoed the direct-drive Parsons units fitted in the Denny-built *The Queen* and *Brighton* the previous year, steam in her case supplied by two double-ended and one single-ended tubular boilers. The contract speed of 20 knots using forced draught between the Cloch and Cumbrae lights was exceeded by almost 1 knot at an output of 7,112 shp, with less than half the power needed to reach over 20.5 knots on the measured mile. Passenger facilities included twenty-eight first-class berths amidships with steerage housed aft and provision was made for large numbers of livestock. Funnel cowls were fitted after her first season and in April 1909 two of her propellers were replaced to reduce vibration. In May 1911, her owners returned to Denny for a second vessel, the 1,687-grt *Princess Victoria* delivered in April 1912, which was generally

similar but provided with greater astern power. Both ships were fitted with bow rudders. During the First World War, *Princess Victoria* was chartered by the Admiralty from October 1914 to the end of December 1919 for messenger, trooping and leave duties across the English Channel under South Eastern & Chatham Railway Co management. Sunday excursions to Bangor were instituted from 1928 and early in June 1931 *Princess Maud* grounded on rocks

at Barr's Point, Island Magee on the approaches to Larne and although later refloated, was deemed beyond repair and sold to T W Ward for scrapping at Preston in January 1932. Her younger sister, which had been refitted by Denny in 1922, was transferred to the Heysham service as reserve ship in December 1931 following the sinking of *Duke of Lancaster*. She made her last sailing on 17 September 1933 and was sold to breakers at Stavanger in February 1934.

After it obtained powers to run its own ships, the Midland Railway Co ordered four steamers for an intended new service from its new port at Heysham to Belfast in competition with the London & North Western Railway Co's Fleetwood service. Four separate builders were chosen to ensure delivery in 1904: John Brown, Clydebank for *Antrim* in May, Wm Denny & Bros, Dumbarton for *Londonderry** in July, Caird & Co, Greenock for *Donegal* in August and Vickers, Sons & Maxim, Barrow for the slightly different *Manxman* (described below) in September. Although designed by Sir John Biles to be powered by four-cylinder reciprocating engines, *Londonderry* (and *Manxman*) was completed with turbine propulsion. They measured 337.8 oa x 42.2 ft and overnight berths were provided for around 174 first- and seventy-six third-class passengers. *Londonderry* opened the new port with a sailing to Douglas on 13 August 1904 and the new Belfast service commenced on 1 September. All three ships were taken up by the Admiralty for trooping in 1914 and the following year *Donegal* was converted to an ambulance carrier, using her speed to escape from an enemy submarine in the English Channel on 1 March 1917. Her luck ran out on 17 April when, returning to Southhampton from Le Havre, she was torpedoed by *UC 21* nineteen miles south of the Dean light vessel, Spithead with the loss of twenty-nine patients and eleven crew. The Midland Railway's Belfast service

was resumed in 1920 and three years later came under the control of the new London, Midland & Scottish Railway. With replacement ships imminent, *Londonderry* was sold in 1927 to the newly-formed Société Anonyme de Navigation Alsace-Lorraine-Angleterre, in which the LMS had an interest, and renamed *Flamand* for a Tilbury–Dunkirk night service.

From 1932 onwards she sailed from Folkestone and was scrapped at Hamburg in 1937. In the meantime, *Antrim* had been sold to Isle of Man Steam Packet Co in 1928 and renamed *Ramsey* and later *RamseyTown* for Fleetwood–Douglas service. She was finally scrapped by T W Ward at Preston in 1936.

The 2,030-grt *Manxman* was completed by Vickers, Sons & Maxim, Barrow in September 1904 for the Midland Railway's new Heysham–Douglas service and intended to compete with the Isle of Man Steam Packet Co. She was the first turbine packet to visit the Island and measured 341 oa x 43.1 ft. Her Parsons direct-drive turbines drove three screws and developed 10,000 shp for a service speed of 22.5 knots. Designed for both day and night services to the Isle of Man, she had fewer cabins and more open saloons than her near sisters and inaugurated the new service in June 1905. On 1 January 1915, she was bought by the Admiralty and converted to a seaplane carrier, serving in the Gallipoli campaign and was later based at Taranto. On her release in 1920, she was bought by IOMSP Co, which had recently acquired the Midland Railway's Isle of Man service, and refitted for Liverpool–Douglas service. Altered to burn oil the following year, she was later moved to the Fleetwood station. Requisitioned shortly after the outbreak of the Second World War, she was placed on trooping duties across the English Channel and then made four visits to Dunkirk in May–June 1940, grounding for several hours on her first trip in the Zuydecoote Pass. She loaded 2,394 soldiers on the first three but failed to find any on the last occasion.

She continued further west and evacuated personnel from Cherbourg and St Malo and from May 1941 was used as the radar training ship HMS *Caduceus* based initially in the Isle of Wight, then at Douglas and later in the Clyde where she was blown ashore early in 1943, returning South again for further trooping duties after repairs. She continued to operate from Dover after VE Day but in February

1946 was switched to the British Army of the Rhine (BAOR) Harwich–Hook of Holland leave service, repainted once again in her original Steam Packet colours. She finally left the Essex port for Barrow on 25 February 1949 and arrived three days later because she was forced to seek shelter from strong winds off Ramsey. In August 1949, she was towed to Preston to be broken up by T W Ward.

The steam turbine was first adopted by the Isle of Man Steam Packet Co for the triple-screw *Viking*, constructed by Armstrong Whitworth & Co, Newcastle in June 1905. A twin-funnelled vessel of 1,951 grt, she measured 361.7 oa x 42 ft and was propelled by three sets of Parsons direct drive turbines developing 10,000 shp for a service speed of 22.5 knots. She was intended primarily for the Fleetwood service to compete with the Midland Railway Co's new turbine steamer *Manxman* which had begun serving the island from Heysham a year earlier. She became a great favourite and in 1907 she set up an unbeaten record of two hours and twenty-two minutes for the crossing. On occasions she also sailed to Liverpool but in March 1915 was requisitioned by the Admiralty and converted to a seaplane carrier. A 64-ft ramp was added forward for flying off two single-seat fighters while a large hangar aft housed five seaplanes which were lifted off and on by two electric cranes. On 3 November, she became the first Royal Navy ship to successfully launch a land plane and was purchased a week later and renamed HMS *Vindex* to avoid confusion with the destroyer HMS *Viking*. She was based at Harwich until moved to Malta in 1918, ending the war on trooping duties out of Tilbury. She resumed her Fleetwood sailings in June 1919 and when war came again was requisitioned for trooping duties and also helped evacuate many children from Guernsey to Weymouth. She ended

the war sailing from Tilbury and took up her Fleetwood service again in June 1945. During winter 1950–51, she was extensively overhauled by Cammell Laird and new blades were fitted to her turbines, reducing both coal consumption and voyage times. After completing four more seasons, she made a final

sailing to the Isle of Man on 14 August 1954 before leaving Douglas for lay up in Barrow two days later. In October she was sold to T W Ward for demolition, having completed fifty years of operation in both peace and two wars.

In February 1906, G & J Burns took delivery of its first turbine steamer, the triple-screw 1,713-grt *Viper* from Fairfield Shipbuilding & Engineering Co, Govan. Designed to replace *Adder* on the daytime Ardrossan–Belfast service, she measured 325 oa × 39.6 ft and was driven by three Parsons steam turbines directly connected to three shafts which developed 9,000 shp for a maximum speed of 22 knots and a knot less in service. She had a handsome, almost racy appearance with two well raked black funnels and could carry 1,700 passengers, almost twice the number of *Adder*. As built she carried a 10-ft golden snake emblem on either side of her spirket plate on the forecastle. The daylight service was suspended during the First World War and *Viper* was initially laid up in Glasgow but was later taken up for troop transport duties in the English Channel. She mainly sailed between Southampton and Le Havre and carried, among many others, the 6th Tank Battalion and a number of US forces that had arrived by sea in Liverpool. She resumed normal service in summer 1919 but political unrest in Ireland was beginning to affect passenger numbers and the following March she was sold to the Isle of Man Steam Packet Co, which needed to replace its war losses. Renamed *Snaefell* in July and swapping her drab black funnel colours for her new owner's crimson, she was employed on several of Isle of Man services, sailing out of both Liverpool and Ardrossan and from 1928 onwards mainly from Heysham. During the Second World War, she maintained the island's lifeline service from Fleetwood with *Rushen Castle*, but post-war her age and poor condition resulted in her sale for scrap. She was towed to the yard of Smith & Houston, Port Glasgow in late 1946, but demolition work not start until 1948. Her fine saloon staircase was saved and currently adorns HQS *Wellington*, the home of the Honourable Company of Master Mariners moored on the Victoria Embankment in London.

In anticipation of the completion of the Great Western Railway Co's new harbour at Fishguard, the Fishguard & Rosslare Railways & Harbours Co ordered three new turbine steamers: *St David* and *St Patrick** from John Brown & Co, Clydebank and *St George* from Cammell Laird, Birkenhead (the yard's first turbine steamer). They were of about 2,530 grt and had dimensions of about 351 × 41 ft. Distinctive vessels with high raised forecastles and two very tall, elliptical funnels, they were delivered between June and September 1906 and inaugurated a new service to Rosslare on 30 August. They carried around 1,000 passengers and berths were supplied amidships for 220 in first class and 100 in second class. Main machinery comprised a centreline high-pressure turbine and two low-pressure wing turbines, each directly connected to a propeller. *St George* attained 22.5 knots on trials in blustery conditions with her engines developing 12,420 shp. The ships operated a double daily service but by the time a fourth sister *St Andrew* was completed at Clydebank in 1908, it had been found that three vessels were sufficient (two in service and one on standby). *St George* was sold to the Canadian Pacific Railway in May 1913 and towed across the Atlantic for Bay of Fundy service between Digby and St John. The GWR ships were immediately requisitioned as ambulance carriers on the outbreak of the First World War and were joined by *St George*, which had been towed back from Canada, in May 1915. *St David* and *St Patrick* were released in January 1919, but *St Andrew* was retained for troop repatriation until May, while *St George* was sold in June to the Great Eastern Railway. Her superstructure was extended forward and her accommodation altered to carry around 500 passengers on the Harwich–Hook of Holland night service. In 1925–6, *St David* and *St Patrick* were re-engined by John Brown with a single geared turbine on each of the three shafts and in 1929 *St George* was replaced by the London & North Eastern Railway's new *Vienna* and sold in October to Hughes Bolckow for demolition at Blyth. *St Patrick* had been withdrawn earlier that year following a serious fire at Fishguard on 7 April and was scrapped at Preston in 1930. Her geared machinery was transferred to *St Andrew* which was renamed *Fishguard* in 1932 to free up her name for a new ship, *St David* becoming *Rosslare* for the same reason. Both were scrapped at Newport in 1933.

First southern hemisphere turbine for Bass Strait

In 1903, the Union Steamship Co of New Zealand obtained the contract to carry mail between Melbourne and the northern Tasmanian port of Launceston and in August it ordered a triple-screw turbine steamer from Wm Denny & Bros. *Loongana* (the Tasmanian word for swift) was the fifth turbine ship to be built at the Dumbarton yard but was the first of her type to operate in the southern hemisphere. After attaining a maximum speed of just over 20 knots on trials (19 knots during a six-hour run using two double-ended boilers) she was delivered on 25 August 1904. Her design was modelled on the Midland Railway Co's *Londonderry* but the addition of a raised forecastle to cope with heavy seas in the notoriously rough Bass Strait made her some 400 tons larger, her gross measurement being 2,448 tons on hull dimensions of 308 ft (over the rudder) × 43.1 ft. Her Parsons propelling machinery followed the pattern set in previous Denny-built ships, namely a high pressure turbine driving a centre shaft and low pressure units driving the two wing shafts. Steam was supplied by two double-ended and two single-ended return tube boilers and maximum power output was just over 6,000 shp, with considerably less required for her 18-knot service speed. Accommodation was provided for 246 passengers in first class and 136 in second class. In October 1912, she raced across the Tasman from Port Philip Heads to Burnie at around 22 knots in twelve hours and forty-six minutes when carrying firefighters to help with the disaster at the Mount Lyell copper mine. She was operated in conjunction with the Australian firm of Huddart, Parker and on

1 January 1922 was transferred to Tasmanian Steamers Pty of Melbourne along with the aged *Oonah*. In her thirty-first year, she made her final crossing on 12 March 1935 and in November 1936 was sold to Japanese breakers and towed to Osaka by the Union Steamship freighter *Kauri*.

First North Sea turbines

The Great Central Railway ran a network of shipping services from Grimsby to northern European ports, but in April 1905 it ordered two fast steamers from Cammell Laird, Birkenhead (*Marylebone*) and Swan, Hunter & Wigham Richardson, Newcastle (*Immingham*) for a new express service to Rotterdam. In a bold move and a first for the North Sea, turbine propulsion was stipulated in the expectation of stealing a march on the competing Great Eastern Railway service out of Harwich. Measuring about 2,000 grt, *Marylebone** and *Immingham* were 282 oa × 41.2 ft with the comparatively deep draught of 18.75 ft. Each was fitted with triple screws and Parsons direct-drive turbines, which were fed with steam by four single-ended boilers and the combined output of 6,500 ihp gave *Immingham* an average speed of 18.25 knots during a six-hour trial on 11 January 1907. An 18-knot service speed reduced passage time from seventeen and a half to just ten and a half hours. They were the only two-funnelled ships in the GCR fleet, theirs initially tall with very deep black tops and prominent cowls but the height was later reduced. The three-island type hull was masked by high bulwark doors providing access to the well deck holds. In another first for the railway company, sixty first-class berths were placed amidships in staterooms on the main deck, while twenty-four second-class passengers were berthed in the poop and 300 emigrants housed in the 'tween decks. Uneconomic to run and faced with increasing competition from

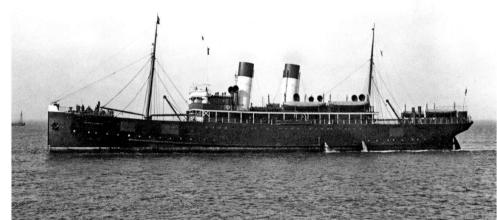

the GER's new turbine steamers, they were sent to Earle's shipyard in Hull in 1911 to be re-engined with a triple-expansion engine driving a single screw. One boiler was removed along with the forward funnel and speed was reduced to 13 knots. During the First World War, *Immingham* was requisitioned as an accommodation ship and later acted as a store carrier on the 'errand boy' run between Imbros and Mudros during the Gallipoli campaign but was lost on 6 June 1915 when rammed at 17 knots by the Great Western Railway's *Reindeer* off Lemnos. After the war,

Marylebone was chartered to the GER in February 1919 for a temporary Tilbury–Antwerp service, but returned to normal Grimsby duties the following year. In 1932 she was sold to Greece and registered to Pandelis N Macris' Tramp Shipping Development Co as *Velos*. Later, this was briefly changed to *Arafat* before reverting to *Velos* and as such she was sold to Italian shipbreakers in 1938, but was not demolished and instead was sunk as a gunnery target off Ostia in May 1938.

The Great Eastern Railway received its first turbine-driven steamer, *Copenhagen*, from John Brown & Co, Clydebank in spring 1908, and she was followed by sisters *Munich** in August and *St Petersburg* in July 1910. Triple-screw steamers of 2,410 grt, they measured 343 oa x 43.2 ft and the first two had flush hulls while the latter had a raised forecastle to improve sea-keeping. They continued the familiar GER twin-funnelled profile, although their stacks were notably tall. First-class accommodation was spread over three decks with 320 berths, 120 in single cabins, and a further 130 in second class on two decks aft. Parsons direct-drive steam turbines developed 10,000 shp for 20 knots and steam was supplied by five single-ended coal-fired boilers fitted with forced draught. Soon after the outbreak of the First World War, *Munich* was requisitioned for use as a 231-bed hospital carrier while *Copenhagen* evacuated Belgian refugees before trooping and in January 1916 also became an ambulance carrier. She was torpedoed without warning on 5 March 1917 eight miles north-east of the North Hinder lightship with the loss of six lives. Political sensibility led to *Munich* and *St Petersburg* being renamed *St Denis* and *Archangel* in 1916 and 1919 respectively. After the war *Archangel* helped to repatriate POWs but the daily service to Holland was not resumed until April 1920. They were replaced by the new *Vienna* and *Prague* in 1929 and thereafter

relieved *Roulers* on the seasonal Zeebrugge service. When war came in 1939 *Archangel* took up trooping duties at Southampton and *St Denis* was sent to Rotterdam in April 1940 to evacuate British civilians but was scuttled on 12 May to avoid falling into German hands. *Archangel* helped evacuate troops from France and was the last ship to leave St Valery, but was bombed on 16 May 1941 while ferrying troops from Kirkwall to Aberdeen. Many were killed including seventeen crew members and although

taken in tow, she was beached seven miles north of her destination and became a total wreck. *St Denis* was raised by the occupying Germans and in 1944 was used as the accommodation ship *Barbara* for a minesweeping squadron in Cuxhaven. Seized by the Allies in October 1945 as auxiliary *Schiff 52*, she was leased back, still in her dazzle paint, to accommodate refugees and later university students. On expiry she was towed back to Sunderland for demolition, which commenced in March 1950.

St Malo Steamer

The London & South Western Railway's 1,203-grt *Princess Ena* was completed by Gourlay Bros, Dundee, in 1906 to replace *Hilda* on the Southampton–St Malo service. Unusual for her owners in being a single ship, she measured 260 oa x 33.3 ft on 14 ft draught and was designed to carry around 600 passengers. Two triple-expansion engines, with an output of 2,700 ihp, gave her a speed of 19 knots on trials and 16 knots in service. On 19 May 1908, she struck the Paternoster Rocks north-west of Jersey in fog, but managed to make St Helier. During the First World War, she was based at Falmouth as a 'Q' ship between April and October 1915, after which she was requisitioned to run a trooping ferry service between Salonika and Mudros during the Dardanelles campaign. She resumed normal service in July 1920 and on 1 January 1923 passed to the new Southern Railway and her funnel was given a black top. On 14 August 1923, she struck the notorious Minquiers rocks between Jersey and St Malo but refloated as the tide rose. Replaced by *Dinard* and *St Briac* in 1924, she sailed to Cherbourg and Caen in summer and later ran excursions between St Malo and the Channel Islands. On the afternoon of 3 August 1935, while returning empty to St Malo, she caught fire about twelve miles south of Jersey. Abandoned by her crew, she was left to burn out and sink.

Irish Sea reciprocators

Graphic and *Heroic* were a pair of twin-screw steamers built for Belfast Steamship Co's overnight Liverpool service by Harland & Wolff in 1906. Handsome ships with single tall funnels, they measured 2,017 grt on dimensions of 320.3 × 41.3 ft and with draught of 16.5 ft. In 1912 they were joined by the 2,254-grt *Patriotic**, which was an improved version, some 5 ft longer with triple-expansion rather than quadruple-expansion engines. Her accommodation was of a particularly high standard including over 150 staterooms, almost half of which had single berths. During the First World War, *Graphic* maintained the Belfast–Liverpool service, at one stage using smoke and speed to escape from a German submarine, but the other two were requisitioned by the Admiralty, *Heroic* for service as an armed merchant cruiser during which she saved 494 persons from the sunken *Britannic* and *Patriotic* for trooping and store carrying duties. With the war over, *Patriotic* carried King George V and Queen Mary to Belfast in 1921 and *Graphic* operated the summer daylight Ardrossan sailing in 1922–3. In June 1923, she sank in Belfast Lough after colliding with the US freighter *Balsam* but was raised and repaired by her builders. In 1929–30, all three were replaced by new motorships and sent for extensive overhauls which

included fitting two new squat funnels with horizontal tops – the after funnel a dummy. Renamed *Lady Munster*, *Lady Connaught* and *Lady Leinster* respectively, they were placed on the Dublin–Liverpool service of the British & Irish Steam Packet Co, also part of the Coast Lines group. When B&I's new motorships *Munster* and *Leinster* joined the service in 1938, *Lady Munster* and *Lady Connaught* were renamed *Louth* and *Longford* (above right), the name *Lady Connaught* passing to the former *Patriotic*. During the Second World War, the latter again sailed to Belfast and in late 1940 struck a mine near the Mersey Bar light vessel but was repaired and sent trooping. After the war, *Louth* returned to the Belfast Steamship Co as *Ulster Duke*, but was withdrawn in 1951 and left Liverpool on 8 March in tow for La Spezia breakers but foundered in the Bay of Biscay a week later. Sister *Longford*, which had sailed on the Dublin route post-war, made her last trip on 31 October 1952. Meanwhile *Lady Connaught* had been transferred to Coast Lines in 1947 and as the single-funnelled *Lady Killarney* operated summer cruises from Liverpool to the Scottish islands, initially with a green hull and buff funnel, but later in Coast Lines' livery. Withdrawn at the end of the 1956 season, she was broken up in Port Glasgow.

In 1906 the 14-knot sisters *Woodcock** and *Partridge* were completed for G & J Burns by John Brown & Co, Clydebank. Intended for the Glasgow–Belfast express service, their speed was insufficient and instead they were placed on the Ardrossan–Belfast overnight run, relieving *Magpie* and *Vulture*. They had berths for 140 saloon-class passengers and had greatly improved steerage accommodation. Total passenger complement was 1,103. They made occasional cruises to Campbeltown and Belfast, but were taken up in the First World War as fleet messengers; *Woodcock* was renamed *Woodnut* to avoid confusion with the General Steam Navigation Co's *Woodcock*. *Partridge* ran between Marseilles and Malta and her sister between Mudros and Constantinople in 1918. They resumed normal peacetime service in 1920 and were later switched to the Dublin service, but 1929 they were renamed *Lairdswood* and *Lairdsloch* respectively in a rationalisation of Burns & Laird Lines nomenclature and given red funnels with black tops. *Lairdswood* was sold to the Aberdeen Steam Navigation Co in November 1930 and as *Lochnagar* placed on the Aberdeen–London coastal service and in October 1936 her sister went to Arnott & Young for scrapping at Dalmuir. *Lochnagar* was sold in 1946 to Panamanian owner Rena Compania de Navegacion SA, beneficially owned by Panos Protopapos, of Athens, and which renamed her *Rena*. She was renamed *Bluestar* in 1951 and in 1952 was broken up at La Spezia after a forty-six year career. *Redbreast*, completed by A & J Inglis in 1908, was very similar in looks but smaller at 1,313 grt on dimensions of 267 × 33.5 ft. Her engine power was

similar but her boilers were double-ended, giving a speed of 16 knots. She replaced *Alligator* on the Glasgow–Belfast service. Requisitioned by the Admiralty in the First World War, she was initially used as an early version of a 'Q' ship but was later employed as a fleet messenger in the eastern Mediterranean. On 15 July 1917, she was torpedoed and sunk by the German submarine *UC 38* while on passage between Skyros and the Doro Channel with the loss of forty-four lives.

The 1,389-grt *Duke of Montrose* was the final ship built for the Dublin & Glasgow Sailing & Steam Packet Co before it was absorbed by G & J Burns. Completed in 1906 by Caledon Shipbuilding & Engineering Co, Dundee, she measured 275 × 36.7 ft and 15.75 ft draught and was propelled by a quadruple-expansion engine developing 3,800 ihp that provided a service speed of 16 knots. She had a Board of Trade certificate for 1,207 passengers. Similar to the preceding *Duke of Rothesay*, she could be distinguished by having five windows at the forward end of the boat deck instead of the earlier ship's four. In 1908 her owner was acquired by G & J Burns and she was renamed *Tiger* to bring her into line with Burns' nomenclature. Burns became part of the Coast Lines group in 1919 and she was used by Langlands to inaugurate seasonal cruises from Liverpool to western Scotland. When these were taken over by *Killarney*, she returned to her normal Dublin run. During the Irish civil war, she was sent south in September 1922 to make extra overnight sailings between Fishguard and Cork and in 1925 she revived the daylight Ardrossan–Belfast summer service which had been withdrawn at the end of the 1920 season due to the political unrest. In 1929 the ships in the Burns &

Laird fleet were renamed with a Laird prefix; *Tiger* became *Lairdsforest* and a year later she was transferred within the Coast Lines group to British & Irish Steam Packet Co. Renamed *Lady Louth*, she was employed as a livestock carrier between Dublin and Liverpool and was broken up in 1934 at Port Glasgow.

Mediterranean developments

In 1904, the 1,284-grt twin-screw *Gallia*, *Corsica*, *Iberia*, *Italia** and *Numidia* were completed by the Sarte shipyard, Nantes, a partner in the newly-formed Compagnie Francaise de Navigation et de Constructions Navales et Sarte Réunis, which had obtained the Corsican mail contract previously held by Compagnie Fraissinet. Their flush hulls measured 260.75 × 28.5 ft with a 14 ft draught and they were distinguished by two funnels that appeared from some angles to be of unequal width. Twin triple-expansion engines fed by two boilers developed 2,600 ihp for a service speed of 17 knots and berths were supplied for 100 passengers in three classes with a further 400 carried in steerage. They originally had black funnels and hulls, the latter with a white upper strake, but their results were disappointing and in 1906 four ships passed to Compagnie Méditerranéene de Navigation and received white hulls and buff funnels. *Gallia* was sold to Compagnie Générale Transatlantique and then Swadeshi Steam Navigation Co of Colombo. After several more changes of owner during 1912–20, she sank at her moorings in Calcutta on 18 June 1921, when owned by the Eastern Peninsula Navigation Co of Calcutta. Meanwhile, Fraissinet had regained the mail contract and in 1907 its Compagnie Marseillaise de Navigation á Vapeur acquired the remaining ships which were given black tops to their funnels and later black hulls. During refits in 1912–13, their twin funnels were replaced with a single stack; taller funnels in the case of *Corsica* and

In anticipation of regaining the mail contract, Fraissinet ordered two new ships from Swan, Hunter & Wigham Richardson, Newcastle, and the 1,380-grt *Golo** and *Liamone* entered service in February and March 1906. Featuring a long raised forecastle and single well-raked funnel, they measured 263 × 34.4 ft on a draught of 17.7 ft and were driven by triple-expansion engines developing 4,200 ihp for a service speed of 17 knots; steam was supplied by four boilers. Overnight berths were provided for forty-four first-, forty-six second- and twenty-four third-class passengers. A third sister, *Corte*, followed in September, but was sold in 1910 to Palma-based Islena Maritima Compania Mallorquina de Vapores and renamed *Rey Jaime II* for Balearic Islands service. The remaining pair was requisitioned early in the First World War, *Golo* becoming a patrol boat/convoy escort and *Liamone* a troop transport and both later took part in the Gallipoli campaign. *Golo* was torpedoed on 22 August 1917 by the German submarine *UC 22* forty-eight miles south-west of Cape Bianco, Corfu while on passage from Malta. The initial explosion set off grenades on board and the subsequent stronger blast sent her to the bottom in three minutes with thirty-eight fatalities. *Liamone* was released in September 1918 and returned to her peacetime duties. In 1932 she was sold to Compagnie Aeropostale, which operated an early airmail service between Paris and Santos but because the planes could not cross the Atlantic, a sea link was needed between Dakar and Natal in Brazil for which she joined other ships as

Iberia. While acting as an army transport during the First World War, *Italia* was torpedoed and sunk by the Austro-Hungarian submarine *U 4* off Santa Maria di Leuca on 30 May 1917. Replaced by new tonnage, *Corsica* and *Iberia* were scrapped at La Spezia and Savona respectively in 1930 and *Numidia*, which had sunk in Marseilles on 31 October 1928 and subsequently been refloated, was sold to George Potamianos in 1931 and registered to the Epirotiki Steamship Co as *Kimon*. In 1937 she passed to S Theofanides, initially as *Leonia* then *Aristone* and finally *Sokratis* in 1938. She was bombed and sunk by the invading Germans at Antikyra in the Gulf of Corinth on 22 April 1941.

Aeropostale V. She was renamed *Air France V* in 1934 after Air France took over the service and was broken up in Germany in 1936–7. Meanwhile, the surviving sister *Rey Jaime II* had been absorbed into the Compania Trasmediterranea fleet in 1923 and lasted into the 1960s. She was sold in 1961 and broken up in Spain in 1963 after a fifty-seven-year career.

Japan and the Americas

The 1,680-grt sisters *Iki Maru* and *Tsushima Maru** were Japan's first international ferries and were built for Sanyo Steamship Co of the private Japanese railway company Nippon Tetsudo Kaisha by Mitsubishi's Nagasaki shipyard in 1905. Designed for the Shimonseki–Busan route across the Korea Strait, they had flush-decked hulls with vertical stem and counter stern and measured 260 × 36 ft. A long deckhouse amidships was topped by a tall, gently raking funnel. Two triple-expansion engines fed by two single-ended boilers developed around 2,400 ihp for a trials speed of just under 15 knots but only 12 knots was required in service for the 166-mile crossing. Passenger capacity was eighteen in first class, sixty-four in second class and 255 in third class. A year after their entry into service, they were taken over by a new national concern, Imperial Government Railways, which gradually absorbed all of Japan's private railway companies. Superseded by new ships in the early 1920s, they were rebuilt in 1923 with raised forecastles and icebreaker bows for the new Chihaku railway service linking Wakkanai Island in northern Hokkaido with Odomari (Korsakov) in

Karafuto (Sakhalin Island), which had been under Japanese control since the end of the Russo–Japanese War in 1905. *Tsushima Maru* was wrecked in a snowstorm near Nosami Light on 17 December 1925 while on passage to Wakkanai and was replaced by the purpose-built two-funnelled icebreaker *Aniwa Maru* in 1927. When the similar but single-funnelled *Soya Maru* was delivered in 1932, *Iki Maru* was sold

to Osaka Shosen Kaisha. Seven years later she was resold to Kita Nippon Kisen KK and renamed *Karafuto Maru* for a Wakkanai–Sakhalin Island service. She reverted to OSK ownership in 1943 and was mainly used for charter work on several routes, including the Seikan across the Tsugaru Strait, after which she was broken up in Japan in 1951. *(Bruce Peter collection)*

Empress was built for the Charlottetown Steam Navigation Co's Charlottetown–Pictou, Prince Edward Island, service by Swan Hunter & Wigham Richardson, Newcastle in 1906. She was a twin-screw steamer with vertical stem, two raked masts and a single funnel and in typical North American fashion her navigating bridge was placed well forward. Her main particulars were 1,158 grt on dimensions of 235 × 34.2 ft and she was driven by a pair of triple-expansion engines of 366 nhp for a service speed of 12 knots. In 1916 she was purchased by the Canadian Pacific Railway to replace the former Dominion Atlantic Railway Co's *Yarmouth* and, following alterations that raised her gross measurement to 1,342 tons, was placed on the Saint John–Digby service running alongside the steamers *Prince Rupert* and *St George*. Following the sale of the former and the requisition of the latter in 1915 for use as a hospital ship back in the UK, she maintained the Bay of Fundy crossing on her own. In May 1926, she was lucky to survive a very severe gale that caused extensive damage to her superstructure as well as to her interior fittings and cargo. Replaced by the new *Princess Helene* in 1930, she suffered a serious fire on 12 June the following year while laid up in West St John and which gutted her accommodation. She was converted to a coal hulk by Dominion Coal Co in 1932.

In 1906 Nicolas Mihanovich took delivery of the triple-screw 2,670-grt *Londres** from Gourlay Bros, Dundee in July and the paddle steamer *Viena* from A & J Inglis, Pointhouse, in October. Initially operated by Navigation à Vapeur Nicolas Mihanovich, they were transferred to Argentina de Navigation (manager Nicolas Mihanovich) in 1910. *Londres* was driven by three quadruple-expansion engines developing 4,320 ihp for a service speed of 15 knots and could carry 408 passengers. The 2376-grt *Viena* – a larger version of the company's *Paris* (1897) – was renamed *Washington* in 1915 as a result of to political sensibilities arising from the First World War. Both passed into the Dodero fleet in 1942 and three years later *Londres* was withdrawn and converted to a cotton lighter named *Minerva*. Shipping was nationalised by the Peron government in 1949 and *Washington* was transferred to Flota Argentina de Navegacion Fluvial (FANF) in 1951 and then Empresa Flota Fluvial del Estado Argentino (EFFEA) in 1958. She was withdrawn in 1960, but later sank in the port area of Buenos Aires known as La Boca. *Washington* was eventually raised and broken up in 1967. *(Histarmar)*

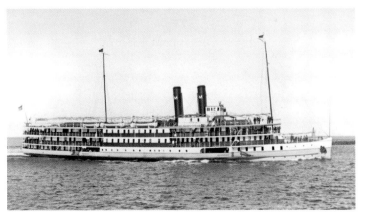

Irish Sea

The London & North Western Railway Co chose John Brown & Co to build the sixth and last of its twin-screw steamers, which since *Duke of Clarence* of 1892 had gradually increased in size but remained remarkably similar in looks. Delivered in 1907, the 2,259-grt *Duke of Albany* was 500 tons larger than her Clydebank-built predecessor *Duke of Connaught* and differed in having solid white-painted bulwarks on her promenade and boat decks. Her accommodation also differed in having thirty-seven single-berth cabins for saloon passengers in addition to the normal two- and four-berth cabins. She employed the same machinery as the earlier vessel but steam was supplied by five rather than four boilers employing forced draught. She was taken up as an armed boarding steamer in the First World War, but while patrolling on 26 August 1916 in company with her former running mate *Duke of Clarence*, she was torpedoed twenty miles east of Pentland Skerries by the German submarine *UB 27*. Struck on her port side abaft the engine room, she went down in seven minutes losing two crew members in the blast and a further twenty-two when depth charges on her stern exploded as she sank.

Laird Line chose Fairfield Shipbuilding & Engineering Co, Govan, a noted builder of fast cross-channel steamers, for its new steamer *Hazel*, completed in May 1907. With a trials speed of around 19 knots, she was designed to complete the summer-only return crossing between Ardrossan and Portrush in daylight, the service having previously required two ships, which had to lay over in port overnight. Calls were also made at some Arran ports. She measured 1,241 grt on dimensions of 260.8 x 36.1 ft and was driven by two four-cylinder triple-expansion engines, fed by four single-ended boilers, and which provided a service speed of 16 knots. Her high superstructure coupled with a shallow draught of 12.8 ft made her rather lively in a seaway. The Portrush service was suspended following the outbreak of the First World War and *Hazel* was requisitioned by the Admiralty as a fleet messenger, serving in the Mediterranean. Returned to Laird Line in 1919, she was quickly sold to the Isle of Man Steam Packet Co and renamed *Mona,* entering service on 9 January 1920 and generally used on secondary and overnight services. On Whit Monday 1922, she ran a one-off excursion from Preston and on 2 July 1930 in dense fog she grounded spectacularly on Conister Rock near the Tower of Refuge in Douglas Bay. Refloated by tugs the following day, she sailed on 6 July for hull repairs in Liverpool. From 1936 she was downgraded to relief and cargo work and was finally broken up by E G Rees at Llanelly in 1938.

Completed by Vickers, Sons & Maxim, Barrow in March 1908, the 1,569-grt twin-screw *Rathmore* was the London & North Western Railway Co's last reciprocating-engined steamer. She measured 299.5 x 40.2 ft and her twin four-cylinder triple-expansion machinery developed 6,300 ihp for a service speed of 20 knots. Her passenger accommodation was much more extensive than that of the preceding ships on the Holyhead–Greenore service and provided for 350 first and 599 second class. During the First World War, she was transferred to the Holyhead–Dublin (North Wall) service but was sunk in collision on 4 March 1918. She was salved and returned to service, passing to the new London, Midland & Scottish Railway at the beginning of 1923. The LMS closed the Greenore service in 1926 and she was sold the following year to the French company Société Anonyme de Navigation Alsace-Lorraine-Angleterre, which, with LMS help, was in the process of setting up a new service between Tilbury and Dunkirk. Renamed *Lorrain* and with her funnels painted black, she sailed until 1932 when, with the Great Depression approaching its height, she was sold to Van Heyghen Frères and was broken up in Ghent.

Second three-funnelled 'Princess' for Canada

In 1908, Fairfield Shipbuilding & Engineering Co, Govan delivered the 3,926-grt twin-screw *Princess Charlotte* to Canadian Pacific Railway. A larger and more substantial-looking version of the *Princess Victoria*, her superstructure was partly built of steel and her three funnels were shorter. She measured 330 × 46.7 ft and her machinery outfit comprised two four-cylinder triple-expansion engines fed by six single-ended boilers with eighteen furnaces. Her service speed was 19.5 knots. She was designed to carry a total of around 1,200 passengers and could also load fifteen cars into her holds. After a delivery voyage via Cape Horn, she arrived in Victoria, British Columbia on the penultimate day of 1908 and entered service on the Vancouver run on 12 January 1909. During the Second World War, *Princess Victoria* was kept busy with local troop movements, sailing in grey livery. Withdrawn in June 1949, she was laid up in Thetis Cove and was sold in December to Typaldos Bros of Piraeus. She left Vancouver for Greece on 17

June 1950 and during a substantial reconstruction was fitted with a single large funnel and a new bridge placed further aft, while changes to her accommodation provided berths for 389 passengers. Renamed *Mediterranean*, she was initially placed on an

express service linking Piraeus, Alexandria and Marseilles and later with a white hull sailed from Venice to Brindisi, Piraeus, Rhodes and Istanbul. She was eventually broken up at Perama in 1965.

First turbine ferries for New Zealand and Japanese waters

The Union Steamship Co of New Zealand returned to Wm Denny & Bros, Dumbarton, in 1906 for another express short-sea passenger steamer, the first to be specially designed for the Wellington–Lyttelton overnight service. The triple-screw turbine *Maori* was delivered on 25 September 1907 and was a ship of 3,399 grt on dimensions of 350.5 × 47.2 ft. Her design featured a long raised forecastle and two closely-spaced funnels and she was fitted with a bow rudder. Cabin accommodation for the overnight service was provided for 423 in first class and 130 in second class, although the latter could be increased

by fifty during busy periods and 32,020 cu ft of space was made available for cargo. Her main machinery and boilers were similar to those installed three years earlier in *Loongana* and developed around 6,500 shp for a maximum 20.5 knots with the bypass open. During her trials off Skelmorlie, she collided with and sank the Campbeltown & Glasgow Steam Packet Co's *Kintyre*, which had failed to keep a straight course as *Maori* overtook her. Just over a month after entering service, she broke the record for the crossing, taking eight hours and twenty-three minutes and averaging nearly 20.75 knots. She was converted

to oil-burning in 1923, but eight years later was placed in reserve and laid up. In June 1946, she was bought by the United Corporation of China and renamed *Hwalien* for a service linking Shanghai with Australia, which was later extended to Tsingtao. In 1950 she was sold to the Chung Lien Steamship Co and laid up in Keelung but she dragged her anchors during a typhoon on 13 January 1951 and sank after driving aground. *Hwalien* was later raised and broken up but part of her double bottom was used as a pontoon for a floating crane.

Impressed by the early turbine-driven excursion and cross-channel steamers built on the Clyde, Japan's Nippon Tetsudo Kaisha ordered two triple-screw turbine vessels, *Hirafu Maru** and *Tamura Maru*, from Wm Denny & Bros. Completed in the last quarter of 1907, they were the first turbine-driven ships in the Japanese merchant fleet and measured 1,484 grt on dimensions of 287.5 (over the rudder) × 35.1 ft on 11.5 ft draught. With flush hulls and single funnels, they were similar in looks to the Denny-built railway steamer *Duke of York* of 1894 and were designed for the new express Seikan service linking Aomori in Honshu with Hakodate in Hokkaido across the Tsuruga Strait. Berths were supplied for fifteen, twenty and 200 passengers in three classes, each having its own separate bathing facilities to meet with Japanese custom, while 23,900 cu ft of space was available for the carriage of cargo in two holds. Main machinery comprised three Parsons direct-drive turbines supplied with steam by two single-ended return tube boilers and the combined output of around 3,000 shp gave trials speeds of just over 19 knots with the bypass open. They entered service in spring 1908, and their 18-knot service speed was sufficient for a three-hour passage on the fifty-nine-mile crossing. *Tamura Maru* was later used on a Wakkanai–Ohaku service and in 1929 was sold to Awanokuni Kyodo KK for Inland Sea service. In the same year *Hirafu Maru* was bought by Osaka Shosen Kaisha, in whose colours she is depicted, but in 1931 was transferred to Setsuyo Shosen Kaisha for Inland Sea service. Both vessels were broken up in Japan in 1933–4.

During the Russo–Japanese War, the Japanese Imperial Marine Association planned to build ten fast vessels for conversion to auxiliary cruisers in time of war and paid for by public donations. Only half of the money needed was forthcoming and as a result only four of the ten ships were actually completed. The first two were the 2,970-grt *Sakura Maru* and 3,272-grt *Umegaka Maru**completed by Mitsubishi, Nagasaki in 1909. The former differed in having a clipper bow, but *Umegaka Maru* is included here because she was leased to the Japanese railway ministry for its Shimonoseki–Busan ferry service. She measured 335 × 42.4 ft and was propelled by three Parsons direct-drive steam turbines producing 9,000 shp, which gave her a trials speed of 21.25 knots. From January 1910, she sailed for a year on the Seikan route between Aomori and Hakodate but while at anchor in the Kanmon Strait in September 1912 was caught in a typhoon, took on water and sank. She was raised by her builders but was deemed not worth repairing and was broken up in 1916.

Isle of Man flyer

The Isle of Man Steam Packet Co's third *Ben-my-Chree* was the longest and most powerful it ever owned and proved to be something of a record breaker. Completed at Barrow by Vickers, Sons & Maxim in July 1908, she had a flush hull measuring 390 oa × 46 ft and her tonnage was 2,651 gross. Two sets of Parsons steam turbines were fed by four cylindrical boilers and developed 14,000 shp for a speed of 24.5 knots. She quickly established herself as a 'flyer' and on 6 July 1909 made a record passage of two hours and fifty-eight minutes from Liverpool Landing Stage to Douglas Head, which was only bettered by the high speed ferry *Seacat Isle of Man* introduced in 1994. She had been in service for just over five years when the First World War began and on 1 January 1915 she was chartered by the Admiralty and converted to a seaplane carrier by Cammell Laird. A large hangar was fitted aft together with a tall kingpost and derrick for lifting seaplanes of which she could carry up to six, usually two large and four smaller. She also had a collapsible ramp forward for launching land planes from trolleys. Initially she operated out of Harwich but was sent to the Mediterranean in May to take part in the Gallipoli campaign where her main duties were spotting and reconnaissance. In August, one of her aircraft became

the first to launch an aerial torpedo at a ship and when the campaign ended she was sent to Port Said where she became the flagship of the East India and Egypt Seaplane Squadron. She made a trip to Aden and saw action in the Red Sea before going to the Dodecanese island of Kastelorizo, which had recently

been captured by French troops. When anchored off the island on 11 January 1917, she was shelled by a secret Turkish battery and caught fire and sank. Although raised in 1920 and taken to Piraeus, she was not considered worth repairing and was broken up in Venice in 1923.

Mediterranean and Midland Railway turbines

Designed for an express service from Marseilles to Algeria, Compagnie Générale Transatlantique's triple-screw 4,104-grt *Charles Roux* was completed by Chantier de l'Atlantique (Penhoët), St Nazaire, in June 1908. Celebrated as the first French merchant ship to be propelled by steam turbines, her three SEM/Parsons direct-drive units were fed by eight boilers and developed 9,500 shp for a speed of 18 knots. She could accommodate 203 first-, sixty-eight second- and forty-nine third-class passengers but these numbers were later revised to 145/135/44. She made an initial cruise to Lisbon, Funchal and Casablanca *en route* to Marseilles but turbine problems delayed her entry into service and she did not make her maiden voyage to Algiers until 2 February 1909. Her white hull was repainted black in June and that autumn her funnels were raised in height to improve draft. In March 1915, she was requisitioned to carry troops to Gallipoli and in July was converted to a hospital ship at Port de Bouc before returning to Mudros in a static role. *Charles Roux* was returned to her owner in March 1916, but was taken up for trooping again in December and ended the war as an auxiliary cruiser. After renovation, she resumed normal service in June 1921 and in July 1928 was switched to a Bone–Philippeville

service. During an eight-month winter refit in 1929–30, her centre shaft was removed and two new oil-fired turbines installed, developing 4,400 shp for 14 knots. Her funnels were shortened at the same time. She made a few cruises in 1933 and early in 1935

spent a few weeks on the Bordeaux–Casablanca run, after which she sailed to Le Havre for a projected service to the Baltic. This never materialised and she was sold to breakers at Dunkirk in November 1936.

Completed by Wm Denny & Bros at Dumbarton in 1909, the 2,052-grt *Duke of Cumberland** and *Duke of Argyll* were the only sister ships owned by the Lancashire & Yorkshire Railway and the London & North Western Railway and the last to be built for their Fleetwood–Belfast service. Unlike their predecessors, they had two funnels and were driven by a set of direct-drive steam turbines with the high pressure turbine driving the centre shaft and the two low pressure turbines the wing shafts. Steam came from five single-ended boilers and power output was higher at 9,000 shp ensuring a service speed of around 21 knots. Dimensions were 340 oa × 41.1 ft on 15.5 ft draught and the three-island type hull, which had wells disguised by hinged doors, was fitted with a bow rudder. Berths were provided for 241 first-class and thirty-seven third-class passengers, while two tiers of temporary overflow berths were provided around the sides of the first-class dining saloon. The total accommodation was for 668 first-class and 576 third-class passengers. With the closure of the Fleetwood service pending, *Duke of Argyll* was sold in April 1927 to Société Anonyme de Navigation Alsace-Lorraine-Angleterre (ALA), a SAGA subsidiary working in cooperation with the London, Midland & Scottish Railway, for a new overnight service linking Tilbury with Dunkirk. Re-christened *Alsacien*, she was joined the following March by her sister under the name *Picard*. Losses forced ALA to close the service in October 1931, but after a new

agreement was reached with the Southern Railway, it moved its English terminal to Folkestone in 1932. A projected sale of both vessels to South Africa in 1935 failed to materialise and they were withdrawn in October 1936 following the start of the new train ferry service from Dover. *Alsacien* went to German breakers along with running mate *Flamand* (the former *Rathmore*). *Picard* was sold to Skenderia Shipping Co of Greece and renamed *Heliopolis* for eastern Mediterranean service, eventually being broken up in Genoa in 1939.

Scottish and Dutch reciprocators

Completed by D & W Henderson in June 1909, *Rowan* was the largest of all Laird Line's ships at 1,493 grt on dimensions of 280.8 × 38.1 ft. Recognised by her large diameter funnel with its distinctive cowl top, she was propelled by a three-cylinder triple-expansion engine supplied with steam by four single-ended boilers and the 525 nhp generated ensured a service speed of 16 knots. Accommodation was provided for 180 first-class passengers. She was requisitioned by the Admiralty in November 1914 and and commissioned as the armed boarding steamer *M 01* with two 12-pounder and one 3-pounder guns. Her duties were to examine ships to ensure that they were not carrying war materials and in 1916 she was sent to the Mediterranean and based at Lemnos for the Gallipoli campaign, operating in both Greek and Bulgarian waters. Her pennant number was changed to *MI 19* in January 1918 and *MI 08* the following June. Released in June 1920, she returned to civilian service but only a year later on 8 October 1921 was run into in thick fog off Corsewall Point by the US freighter *West Camak*. Fifteen minutes later the Clan Line steamer *Clan Malcolm* collided with both ships and *Rowan* sank. (*Bruce Peter collection*)

In 1908 the Dutch government insisted on screw-driven ships when renegotiating the ten-year mail contract with Stoomvaart Maatschappij Zeeland (Zeeland Line) and orders for three new steamers named *Prinses Juliana**, *Oranje Nassau* and *Mecklenburg*, were placed with the faithful Fairfield yard. Completed in 1909, they measured 2,885 grt on dimensions of 364 oa × 42.7 ft and had a raised forecastle and two funnels. Surprisingly, they were fitted with twin four-cylinder triple-expansion engines rather than turbines, but these were balanced on the Yarrow-Schlick-Tweedy system to minimise vibration on the overnight crossing. Steam was supplied by four double-ended boilers and power output was 10,000 ihp, sufficient for 22 knots in normal service, although *Oranje Nassau* averaged over 23.5 knots during a six-hour trial. They were placed on the Flushing–Queenborough night service from April 1910, but transferred to Folkestone the following May because of draught limitations in the river Medway. The shorter route and new through rail services from Flushing led to record passenger numbers in 1913, but war soon brought disruption. On 1 February 1916, *Prinses Juliana* hit a mine laid by the submarine *UC 5* near the Sunk light vessel and was beached near Felixstowe the following day. On 27 February, a mine from *UC 7* sank the Flushing-bound *Mecklenburg* south-east of the Galloper lightship, after which the service, by then operating from Tilbury, was suspended and *Oranje Nassau* was laid up. Just over month later on the night of 28–9 March, the wreck of *Prinses Juliana* broke in two during a storm. *Oranje Nassau* reopened the night service from Folkestone on 23 June 1919 and in 1922 switched to the day service. Five years later, she moved to

a new English terminal at Harwich and was reboilered in 1932. Early in the Second World War, she maintained a thrice-weekly service to Tilbury and escaped to the UK from the advancing German army in May 1940, thereafter used as a depot ship for the Royal Netherlands Navy in various ports. Released in 1946, she partnered the London & North Eastern Railway's *Prague* in a thrice-weekly night service from Harwich to the Hook, switching to day service the following year. She was converted to oil-burning in 1948. The next year she was chartered to Batavier Line for its Rotterdam–Tilbury service, resuming her Harwich day run in 1952. She was sold to breakers at Hendrik-Ido-Ambacht in 1954 after a forty-five-year career.

CHAPTER

6

Geared Turbines and the First World War

Geared turbines were first used commercially in the 19-knot sisters *Normannia* and *Hantonia* built by Fairfield Shipbuilding & Engineering Co in 1912 for the London & South Western Railway's overnight Le Havre service. They had been perfected by Charles Parsons after experiments in the cargo ship *Vespasian* and proved to be more economical and smoother running than the direct drive turbines. They also demonstrated that turbine propulsion could be successfully employed in slower ships but were equally well suited to powering high-speed ships as evidenced a year later by the London, Brighton & South Coast Railway's 25-knot *Paris*. The Isle of Man Steam Packet Co and the Canadian Pacific Railway were two companies quick to adopt the new form of propulsion but war intervened and the latter's two new *Princesses* were destined never to sail on their intended route.

The versatility of the cross-channel and short-sea fleet resulted in many ships being requisitioned for use as troopships, hospital carriers, armed boarding steamers, minelayers and even rudimentary aircraft carriers. The latter initially carried floatplanes but later operated land aircraft by means of temporary bow-mounted launching ramps. Few new ships were built during the conflict and most of these were completed for military purposes.

Note: An asterisk in a caption indicates the vessel shown in the photograph.

Wilson's crack North Sea ship

Thomas Wilson, Sons & Co of Hull was the largest privately-owned shipping company in the world in the early years of the twentieth century and ran numerous services to northern Europe and Scandinavia, among which were regular passenger services to Trondheim, Bergen, Oslo (via Kristiansand), Gothenburg and Copenhagen. With its ships making no more than 13–15 knots, voyages lasted more than twenty-four hours, but this changed in May 1910 when the company received the 3,326-grt twin-funnelled *Eskimo* for its Oslo service from the local yard of Earle's Shipbuilding & Engineering Co. The largest ship yet built for North Sea service, she measured 331 x 45 ft and was driven by a pair of quadruple-expansion engines supplied with steam by four boilers. Total power output was 5,000 shp and she averaged 17.3 knots on an eight-hour trial; 16 knots being sufficient to complete the open sea part of her voyage to Kristiansand in around twenty-two hours. Her design incorporated a raised forecastle and long raised bridge deck and she could carry 150 first- and fifty second-class passengers with a further 500 emigrants in third class, each class having its dining saloon. In June 1911, she was requisitioned by the Admiralty to carry official guests at the Coronation Naval Review and was taken up again in November 1914 and converted to an armed merchant cruiser in Liverpool. Her armament consisted of four 6-in and two 2-pounder guns and she was commissioned into the 10th Cruiser Squadron as HMS *Eskimo*. Her

comparatively small size proved insufficient for patrolling North Atlantic waters in all weathers and she was returned to her owners in July 1915. On 26 July 1916 she was captured off Risør, some fifteen miles south-east of Arendal, by the German auxiliary cruiser *Möwe*, which had followed her down the Oslofjord posing as the neutral steamer *Vineta*. She

was taken to Swinemünde and converted to a naval netlayer, which involved stripping her to the weather deck abaft her second funnel. Returned to her owners in 1919, she was sold in 1921 to Marseilles owner Compagnie de Navigation Paquet and employed as a cargo ship in the North Africa trade until broken up in Germany in 1923.

New Isle of Man design

The Isle of Man Steam Packet Co's twin-screw steamer 1,368-grt *Snaefell* was completed by Cammell Laird & Co, Birkenhead, in August 1910. Unusual for the company in being a single-funnelled passenger ship, she had a flush deck and measured 269.8 x 41.5 ft. She was propelled by two four-cylinder triple-expansion engines of 670 nhp for a speed of 18.5 knots and was designed for year-round service and in particular the winter Liverpool–Douglas run, hence her more enclosed superstructure. During the First World War, she was requisitioned for duties with the Plymouth Patrol and in 1915 was despatched to the eastern Mediterranean as an escort for the monitor HMS *Raglan*. During the Dardanelles campaign she was altered to carry seaplanes to act as spotters for the monitor's guns. She was converted to a troop carrier in Genoa in 1917 and in April 1918 received serious fire damage while refitting at Alexandria. After temporary repairs, she was on her way to Malta when she was torpedoed and sunk by the German submarine *UB 105* on 5 June 1918 about 240 nautical miles east-south-east of her destination.

More English Channel turbines

The 1,499-grt *Caesarea** and *Sarnia* were the London & South Western Railway's first turbine steamers and were completed by Cammell Laird, Birkenhead, in September 1910 and April 1911. They continued the single-funnelled theme of the previous two vessels, more closely resembling *Vera*, but were longer at 284.6 ft on the same beam of 39.1 ft. Their

three sets of Parsons steam turbines were directly connected to three screws, the two low pressure turbines driving the outer screws, and steam was supplied by two double-ended Babcock & Wilcox boilers. Power output was around 6,500 shp for a service speed of 20 knots and accommodation was provided for a total of 980 passengers in two classes.

In November 1914, *Sarnia* was requisitioned as an armed boarding steamer and fitted with two 12-pounder guns. While serving in the northern Aegean during the Gallipoli campaign, she collided with and sank the South Eastern Railway cargo ship *Hythe* off Cape Helles on 28 October 1915, but was herself sunk by torpedo from *U 65* off Alexandria on 12 September 1918, while bound for Port Said. Apart from similar service as an armed boarding ship between November 1914 and December 1915, *Caesarea* remained on her normal run during the First World War. Outward bound from St Helier on 7 July 1932 in thick fog, she struck the Pignonet Rock off Noirmont and while returning to port hit the Oyster Rock, requiring her to be beached near the outer breakwater with a leaking stokehold. Raised and towed to Birkenhead for repairs, she was sold to Isle of Man Steam Packet Co on 27 November to replace the loss of *Douglas* (formerly L&SWR's *Dora*). Converted to oil-firing and renamed *Manx Maid*, she entered Liverpool–Douglas service in 1924 and continued thus until the outbreak of the Second World War when she was again taken up, initially as a fleet messenger then as a troop transport. In October 1941, she was renamed HMS *Bruce* and between December 1942 and March 1946 served as a Fleet Air Arm tender. Returned to her owners without a mainmast, she only sailed at summer weekends and was towed from Douglas to Barrow for demolition in November 1950.

Completed for the South Eastern & Chatham Railway by Wm Denny & Bros in June 1911, the 1,675-grt *Riviera** was followed by sister *Engadine* in September. They were improved versions of the *Victoria/Empress* design but their superstructure ended at the mainmast to give a clear after deck for the carriage of motor cars, which could also be loaded into a hold below. They measured 316 × 41.1 ft and were driven by the usual direct-drive triple-screw turbine arrangement but with steam supplied by six Babcock & Wilcox watertube boilers giving a slightly higher output of 8,100 shp for a trials speed of 23 knots. Cabin accommodation was provided for 105 first- and forty-five second-class passengers and they ran between Dover and Calais until the First World War, when the Admiralty requisitioned them and temporarily altered them to carry three seaplanes at Chatham. In 1915 they were more extensively converted at Liverpool to carry four planes in a large rectangular hangar abaft the funnels. Both served in the North Sea and *Engadine* made history at Jutland when she became the first ship to launch an aircraft during a naval engagement. She then tried to take the damaged cruiser HMS *Warrior* in tow and took off 675 sailors when she sank. Refitted in Chatham after the war, both emerged in 1920 with black funnels and were mainly used on the Folkestone–Boulogne service. After the railways reorganisation of 1923, they adopted the Southern Railway livery of buff funnel with black top and from 1925 were relegated to running summer excursions. In summer 1932, *Engadine* was chartered to Instone Lines and with bright yellow funnels ran day trips from the Pool of London to the Nore light vessel. After winter lay-up in Dover, she was sold in 1933 to Compania Maritima of Manila and renamed *Corregidor* for inter-island service. On 17 December 1941, while evacuating students from Manila, she hit a mine and sank in three minutes. Of the

estimated 1,200 on board, only 282 were saved and seven of these died later. *Riviera* had been sold in 1932 to J B Coupar, acting for HMS *Catherwood*, but was resold to Burns & Laird Lines early in 1933. Converted to oil-firing and renamed *Lairds Isle*, she was put into summer service between Ardrossan and Belfast. Apart from the Second World War years, when she acted in turn as an armed boarding ship, a paravane ranging vessel, an infantry landing ship for the Normandy invasion and finally a troopship, she remained on the seasonal Ardrossan service until 6 August 1957, when she was laid up at Greenock. Two months later she went to Troon to be broken up after a 46-year career.

Under the ownership of Société de Chemin de Fer de l'Etat, the first French turbine steamers for the joint Newhaven–Dieppe service were delivered by Forges & Chantiers de la Méditerranée, Le Havre, in May 1911 and September 1912. *Newhaven** and *Rouen* (planned as *London*) measured 1,556 grt on dimensions of 301.8 oa × 34.6 ft and were driven by three Parsons direct-drive steam turbines fed by four watertube boilers. Maximum output was 13,000 shp, which enabled them to comfortably exceed the contact speed of 21.75 knots, *Newhaven* averaging over 23.75 knots on her official trial return crossing and *Rouen* bettering this with over 24 knots. They could be stopped in their own length from 12 knots and had a passenger capacity of around 1,000. In 1914 both ships were requisitioned as auxiliary channel scouts but *Rouen* lost her bows to a German torpedo on 29 December 1916. Repaired in Cherbourg, she was converted to carry two FBA seaplanes and acted as a convoy escort in the Mediterranean in 1917, later undertaking trooping duties between Taranto and Greece. Meanwhile, her sister had become an Admiralty hospital carrier between Scapa Flow and the south and later a troop carrier. She reentered peacetime service on 5 July 1920,

eleven months after *Newhaven*, which stranded in fog below Berneval cliffs near Dieppe on 5 August 1924. She was towed off on the 14th with superficial damage and repaired. During winter 1929–30, both were extensively altered (*above right*) with plated-in superstructure and improved accommodation, raising gross measurement by 300 tons. In 1932–3 they were converted to oil-firing, given larger single funnels and their mainmasts were repositioned at the end of the boat deck (*Rouen**). These changes were considered less expensive than building new ships in the poor economic climate. Taken up once again in the Second World War, they carried troops to Dunkirk and then evacuated them along with refugees. Both were captured as the Germans advanced south; *Newhaven* became the auxiliary patrol vessel *Skorpion* in 1943, then the depot ship *Skagerrak* and finally the accommodation ship *Barbara*. *Rouen* served as the auxiliary cruiser *Natter* in 1941 and from 1942 as the experimental *Wullenwever*, suffering mine damage in the Baltic on 25 April 1943. Both ships were returned to Dieppe from Kiel in October 1945 and were towed to Le Treport the following August before being broken up in Ghent and Dieppe respectively.

Italian turbine quartet

In 1910, Italian State Railways (Ferrovie dello Stato) took delivery of four large passenger ferries for its Naples–Sicily services. *Città di Catania** (3,262 grt) and *Città di Palermo* completed in June and November by Ansaldo Armstrong, Sestri Ponente and Riuniti, Palermo were driven by three direct-drive turbines, while *Città di Messina* and *Città di Siracusa* (3,497 grt) delivered in June and July by Odero, Sestri Ponente and Odero, Foce, were propelled by two triple-expansion engines driving twin screws. *Città di Catania* had three funnels and the others' two shorter ones, but all shared the same hull dimensions of 363.5 × 42.1 ft on a loaded draught of 18.5 ft. They could steam at 20 knots, the turbine ships developing 13,620 shp and the reciprocating engine vessels 12,000 ihp, steam being supplied in all cases by ten boilers. Designed to be used as auxiliary cruisers in time of war, they had only been in service a short time before being requisitioned in late 1911 for the Italo–Turkish war. All four were taken up again in 1915 and operated mainly in the Adriatic. On 8 January 1916, while sailing from Brindisi to Vlora, *Città di Palermo* struck a mine laid by the Austro-Hungarian submarine *UC 14* and sank six miles north-east of Brindisi with the loss of eighty-seven lives and on 23 June of the same year thirty-three were lost when *Città di Messina* inbound from Vlora was torpedoed by *U 15* twenty miles off Otranto. In 1931 *Città di Siracusa* was requisitioned for a third time and converted to a water distillation ship. She supplied Italian troops at Massawa during the 1935–6 Abyssinian war and was broken up in 1938. Meanwhile *Città di Catania*, which had supported Italo Balbo's

1933 mass Atlantic seaplane flight to Chicago, passed into the Tirrenia fleet. She was taken up as an AMC in 1940 but was also used for trooping and in November 1941 was chartered to Adriatica for a Brindisi–Durres service. Inbound from Durres on 3 August 1943, she was torpedoed eight miles off Brindisi by HMS *Unruffled* and broke in two, sinking almost immediately with the loss of 256 lives.

New Mediterranean tonnage

Compagnie Générale Transatlantique took delivery in August 1910 and November 1911 of two large new passenger ships for its Marseilles–Tunis overnight service. The 5,601-grt *Carthage* and 5,232-grt *Timgad** were completed by Swan Hunter & Co, Newcastle, and Chantiers & Ateliers de Provence, Port de Bouc, respectively and were improved versions of *Charles Roux*. Their hulls featured a raised forecastle and poop and measured 403 × 51.4 ft on a draught of 18.7 ft. Main propulsion marked a reversion to reciprocating engines and their two four-cylinder triple-expansion units developed 9,000 ihp for a maximum of 19 knots and sea speed of 17–18 knots giving a passage time of around twenty-four hours. Accommodation was arranged on three decks for 170 in first class (*Timgad* 205), ninety-four in second class and seventy in third class. On 16 July 1912, during the war between Italy and Turkey, the Tunis-bound *Carthage* was stopped and taken into Cagliari by the Italian cruiser *Agordat* on suspicion that an exhibition aircraft travelling to an air display was destined for Turkey, but she was released after intervention by the French government. Early in the First World War, both were taken up as auxiliary cruisers but in 1915 were altered for trooping duties in connection with the Gallipoli campaign and *Carthage* was torpedoed and sunk on 4 July by the German submarine *U 21* while anchored two miles east of Cape

Helles. *Timgad* was altered to an ambulance transport in June 1917 and resumed peacetime duties in 1919, running to both Tunis and Algiers. Replaced by *Ville d'Alger* in 1935, she was put into reserve with winter lay-ups and was finally broken up at Ghent in 1939.

The 1,706-grt *Corte II* was completed in June 1911 by Swan, Hunter & Wigham Richardson, Newcastle, for Fraissinet & Compagnie's Corsica service. An improved version of the earlier *Golo* class with an extra accommodation deck, she measured 279.8 × 37 ft with an 18.6 ft draught and was propelled at 17.5 knots by a single triple-expansion engine developing 4,200 ihp. Overnight berths were provided for fifty first-, sixty second- and twenty-four third-class passengers and she could carry an additional 873 persons in steerage. Replaced by *Sampiero Corso* in 1936, she was bought by John D Chandris and registered to Chandris Steamship Co, Malta, as *Patris*. She was altered to carry 161 passengers in one class and operated in the eastern Mediterranean, sailing mainly out of Venice. During the German invasion of Greece in 1941, she was bombed in Piraeus harbour on 6 April, caught fire and subsequently sank.

The 2,257-grt *Rey Jaime I* was completed for the Majorcan shipowner Sociedad Islena Maritima by Odero Shipyard, Sestri Ponente, Genoa, in June 1911. She was designed to sail year-round between Palma and Barcelona, making two return trips a week and carrying up to 498 passengers. She measured 304.8 × 37.8 ft with 16.8 ft draught and was driven by two triple-expansion engines developing 4,000 ihp, which produced an average of over 17.5 knots on trials. Her initial voyage was to Valencia to bring the prime minister back to Palma and she entered her scheduled service in early August, replacing *Rey Jaime II*. On 5 July 1913, she made a special trip to Alicante to pick up Isabel of Bourbon and in November 1914 was joined by near-sister *Mallorca**. During a special pilgrimage voyage in July 1923, she grounded on the 23rd off Livorno but was towed off by the company's *Jorge Juan*. She was again used for trooping duties in 1925 and took part in the celebrations following the return of *Plus Ultra*, carrying General Franco from Huelva to Seville. Islena Maritima's ships were absorbed into Compania Trasmediterranea in 1930 and during the Civil War *Rey Jaime I* was initially used as a Nationalist prison ship in Palma, but both were requisitioned in October 1936 for conversion to auxiliary cruisers, proceeding to La Spezia for arming under the false names of *Buccaro* and *Isarco*. *Mallorca* underwent a major refit during 1949–53 and emerged with a short motor ship-type funnel and was converted to oil-firing; her sister was similarly

treated during 1953–5, but retained her normal funnel. New tonnage in 1955–6 saw both relegated to lesser Balearic services and after a final mail run to Palma in October 1967, *Rey Jaime I* was broken up in Valencia after a sixty-five-year career. On 26 June 1969, her sister suffered a fire in her bridge and first-class saloon at Palma but after repairs in Cadiz, lasted until broken up at Burriana in 1974.

Pacific west coast sisters

The Canadian Pacific Railway's near-identical sisters *Princess Adelaide** and *Princess Alice* were built for the overnight service between Vancouver and Victoria. Respective products of Fairfield Shipbuilding & Engineering Co, Govan in 1910 and Swan, Hunter & Wigham Richardson, Newcastle in September 1911, they measured 3,061/3,099 grt on dimensions of 299.8 × 46.1 ft and 13 ft draught and could be distinguished by *Princess Adelaide*'s slightly taller funnel and her sister's larger ventilators. In view of their comparatively easy schedule, they were driven by single four-cylinder triple-expansion engines of 610 nhp for a service speed of 16 knots, which was exceeded by a couple of knots on trials. Their 118 staterooms were fitted with all modern conveniences and overall they could carry up to 1,200 passengers and around five cars. On their delivery voyages, *Princess Adelaide* sailed via the Strait of Magellan, while her sister rounded Cape Horn. Apart from their designed route, they sailed occasionally on the 'Triangle Route' and also to Alaska. In 1949 both ships were sold to Typaldos Bros, Piraeus, and renamed

Angelika and *Aegeon* respectively. Following conversion for Mediterranean service, during which the forward part of the upper deck was plated in and swimming pools fitted on the boat deck, *Angelika* entered regular service between Piraeus and Crete but later came to be associated with the Piraeus–Corfu–Brindisi run, while her sister generally

sailed to Venice. In 1966 *Aegeon* was sold to Italian breakers in Savona but ran ashore near Civitavecchia on 2 December after breaking adrift when in tow and was later broken up. Her sister was sold the following year after a planned restaurant venture in South Africa fell through and she was demolished at Vado Ligure in 1968.

First geared turbines

The London & South Western Railway's twin-screw sisters *Normannia** and *Hantonia* (launched as *Louvima*) completed by Fairfield Shipbuilding & Engineering Co, Govan, in 1912 for the Southampton–Le Havre overnight service, made shipping history as the first new ships to be propelled by Parsons single-reduction geared turbines. They measured 1,567 grt on dimensions of 290.3 × 36.1 ft and were the first of the railway company's ships to have twin funnels since the *Alma/Columbia* pair of 1894, which they replaced on entering service in 1912. Steam was provided by one double-ended boiler and one single-ended boiler and power amounted to 6,000 shp for a contract speed of 19.5 knots. *Normannia* performed faultlessly on trials, reaching 20.5 knots on the Skelmorlie mile and averaging 19.5 knots over six hours, using less coal and water than her direct-drive counterparts. Both ships ran with great reliability on the Le Havre service, which was briefly diverted to St Nazaire early in the First World War, before reduction to three sailings a week. In 1915, the area of the weather deck under the second lifeboat was plated in. In the 1930s both ships covered the winter Jersey–St Malo service with *Lorina*. In the Second World War, *Hantonia* undertook trooping duties between Folkestone and Calais before being moved to the Channel Islands run with her sister and she was the last ship to leave St Malo on 16 June 1940, sailing direct to Southampton with 700 passengers. A fortnight previously, her sister

had been sunk by German aircraft during the Dunkirk evacuation. *Hantonia* ran on the Great Western Railway's Fishguard–Rosslare service from 30 June 1941 to 14 January 1942 and then went to the Clyde under Ministry of War Transport charter to serve as an accommodation ship from May to December

1944. She ended the war as a naval accommodation ship in the Scheldt and following release in 1945, was put on Channel Islands service before resuming her Le Havre run in June 1947. She sailed without a mainmast after the war and when replaced by *Normannia* in 1952 was broken up at Grays, Essex.

The London, Brighton & South Coast Railway ordered its third turbine steamer, the 1,774-grt *Paris*, from Wm Denny & Bros, Dumbarton, in December 1911. After consultation, the shipyard and Parsons Co persuaded the railway company to change her machinery from direct drive to the new geared turbines, which were to be installed by Fairfield in London & South Western Railway's *Normannia*. *Paris* had a more powerful outfit, comprising two sets fed by eight coal-fired Yarrow watertube boilers and developing some 14,000 shp for a mean speed of 24.75 knots on trial, making her the fastest merchant ship of her size in the world. She bettered this by averaging just over 25 knots during a trial return crossing to Dieppe on 14 July 1913. She measured 301 oa × 35.6 ft on loaded draught of 11 ft and was the first British channel steamer to have a cruiser stern. Passenger complement was 968 with sixteen single and fifty-three double first-class cabins and a further 128 second-class berths in an open saloon. When war broke out in 1914, she was requisitioned by the Admiralty and converted into a minelayer, for which her speed and shallow draught made her eminently suitable, although her range was restricted. She sowed mines off Belgium in 1916 and deep water mines in the anti-submarine barriers in the Dover Strait, off the Yorkshire Coast and in the Pentland Firth during 1917–18. Post-war, she resumed normal service until winter 1928–9, when in a major refit the sides of her superstructure were plated in and a new wheelhouse added. Four new Yarrow oil-fired boilers were fitted in March 1932 and 1934 saw her take over *Arundel*'s Tuesday and Thursday day

excursions to Dieppe from Brighton's Palace Pier. Taken up for a second time in 1939, she was used as a troop carrier before conversion to a hospital ship the following January. She made five trips to Dunkirk, evacuating 740 wounded on 29 May, but on her sixth outward voyage on 2 June she was immobilised by German bombers and sunk after further attacks ten miles short of the beaches with the loss of twenty crew members.

Propulsion contrasts on Irish Sea

The 1,877-grt *King Orry*, completed by Cammell Laird & Co, Birkenhead, in July 1913, was Isle of Man Steam Packet Co's first geared-turbine steamer. Her flush hull and single funnel were reminiscent of *Snaefell* (1910), but she was larger at 313 oa × 43.1 ft and her two sets of Parsons single-reduction geared turbines developed considerably more power, giving her an economical speed of 21 knots. She had barely completed a year's service before war broke out and she was taken up by the Admiralty as an armed boarding steamer, becoming a target towing vessel after Jutland and at the end of 1916 the disguised neutral steamer *Viking Orry*. On 21 November 1918, she was second in line behind HMS *Cardiff* which led twenty-one surrendered ships of the German High Seas Fleet to Scapa Flow. She was released in July 1919 and refitted for peacetime service, gaining a reputation as a good sea boat. On 19 August 1921, she stranded near the Rock Lighthouse at New Brighton but was undamaged and in winter 1934–5 was converted to burn oil in a major refit. Shortly after the outbreak of the Second World War she was requisitioned once again as an armed boarding steamer for the Dover Patrol, armed with a 4-in gun. During the the evacuation of Dunkirk she was pressed into service as a personnel carrier and was one of the first ships to enter the French harbour early on 29 May 1940, loading 1,131 men. While returning to Dover, she was hit and damaged by shore batteries near Calais and was hit again more seriously the following day while alongside on her second trip. With her rudder and steering gear out of action, she used her engines to manoeuvre clear of the harbour, but while trying to beach clear of the main entrance channel, suddenly capsized and sank.

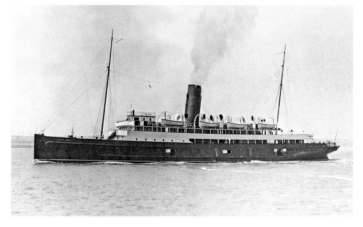

The London & North Western Railway's 1,488-grt *Greenore* was delivered by Cammell Laird, Birkenhead, July 1912 and was the L&NWR's first turbine steamer. Destined for the Holyhead–Greenore service, she was propelled by three sets of Parsons direct-drive units, which gave her a service speed of 20.5 knots. Her two funnels were lower and less closely spaced than *Rathmore*'s and her hull measured 306 × 40.7 ft on 15.5 ft draught. Accommodation was provided for 409 first- and 545 second-class passengers. During the First World War, she was transferred to the Holyhead–Dublin North Wall service while other L&NWR ships were on Admiralty service, and she returned to the Greenore service in 1919. *Greenore* was transferred to the newly-created London, Midland & Scottish Railway in 1923 but was withdrawn in November 1926 following the closure of the Greenore route. After a comparatively short career of only fourteen years, she was sold to T W Ward for demolition in Barrow.

Launched at Govan on 15 June 1912 by Fairfield Shipbuilding & Engineering Co, the twin-screw 1,836-grt *Ermine* was the largest ship ever built for G & J Burns and the largest of all the Clyde-based Irish Sea channel packets. She was the finest ship to serve on the Glasgow–Dublin route, which was previously maintained by *Duke of Rothesay* and *Duke of Montrose*. She measured 311 oa × 40.4 ft and was driven by a pair of four-cylinder reciprocating engines balanced on the Yarrow-Schlick-Tweedy system and developing 3,500 ihp for a speed of 15 knots. Steam was supplied by one single-ended and two double-ended cylindrical boilers. She had accommodation for 170 first-class passengers and a considerable number of cattle. In 1915 she was requisitioned by the Admiralty and in July was commissioned as a fleet messenger. *Ermine* was despatched to the eastern Mediterranean for the Gallipoli campaign and generally sailed between Mudros and Suvla Bay but also carried troops to Salonika. She is reputed to have moved 200,000 troops and 3,000 horses, but on 2 August 1917 she struck a mine laid by the German submarine *UC 23* and sank with the loss of twenty-four lives in position 40 39N 23 34E, some 2.5 miles off Stavros near the mouth of the river Struma. A sad and premature end for a fine ship.

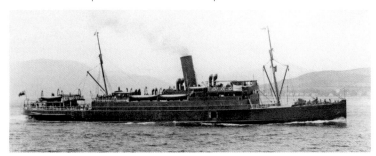

Laird Line's *Maple* was launched at Troon by Ailsa Shipbuilding Co on 26 February 1914 and replaced *Azalea*. Similar to, but smaller than *Rowan*, she had the following main particulars: 1,294 grt, 274.3 oa × 36.2 ft. Her main engine was a triple-expansion unit of 467 nhp, which gave a trial speed of 15.5 knots. She had accommodation for 114 first-class passengers. During the First World War, she partnered her running mate *Rose* on the Taranto–Itea trooping run and was also used for trooping in home waters. After becoming part of the combined Burns & Laird fleet in 1922, she generally operated on the Glasgow–Londonderry run and in 1929 was renamed *Lairdsglen* when the whole fleet was renamed with a 'Laird' prefix. She ran in consort with *Lairdsrose*, *Lairdsgrove*, *Lairdscraig* or *Lairds Loch*. In 1932 the cowl was removed from her funnel. In the following year a glazed observation lounge was added at the forward end of her superstructure and a new bridge fitted above it, while her poop boat deck was extended to the stern. Outbound from the Clyde on 3 December 1939, she collided with Wm Sloan's coastal passenger steamer *Findhorn* off the Cumbrae light; the latter was beached, and she had to return to Glasgow for repairs. *Lairdsglen* was sold in June 1951 to be broken up at Port Glasgow.

New Mediterranean Ships

The 4,452-grt *Duc d'Aumale**, completed in February 1913 by Chantiers & Ateliers de Provence, Port de Bouc, was a shorter version of *Carthage* to make her more manoeuvrable in Oran. Identified by her more closely spaced funnels, she measured 378.8 × 49.3 ft on 15.8 ft draught and was driven by two four-cylinder recipricating engines developing 6,000 ihp for a speed of 18.5 knots. Steam was supplied by four cylindrical coal-fired boilers that were altered to burn oil in 1923. Her original passenger complement was 150/106/56 in three classes. In 1926, she was transferred to French West Indies service but made several voyages to New York during the Second World War. She was broken up at La Spezia in summer 1950. In 1921 Swan, Hunter & Wigham Richardson, Newcastle, completed the improved 4,713-grt *Lamorcière*, which had a 370 × 50 ft hull featuring a raised forecastle and combined bridge and poop. The second turbine ship for Compagnie Générale Transatlantique's Mediterranean services, she had an unusual arrangement of two single-reduction geared turbines and a centreline four-cylinder reciprocating engine, each driving a separate screw. Steam was supplied by six boilers and the output of 8,000 ihp gave her a sea speed of 18 knots. During the Second World War, she continued in service under the Vichy government but on 8 January 1942 got into difficulties in a violent storm while steaming to the aid of the Worms cargo ship *Jumieges*. With an increasing list and engine room flooding, she foundered the following day three miles north of Minorca, only ninety-five of the 372 on board being saved.

More Belgian turbines

After selling two of its old paddle steamers in 1911, the Belgian Marine Administration ordered two more turbine steamers. Although intended to be the fastest yet, common sense prevailed in the poor economic climate at the time and they were completed as smaller, slower ships to maintain the less-patronised winter service. *Stad Antwerpen** (1,384 grt) and *Ville de Liège* (1,366 grt), were delivered by John Cockerill in 1913 and early 1914 and measured 300 × 36 ft. They were driven by three sets of direct-drive turbines and steam was supplied by eight coal-burning Babcock & Wilcox watertube boilers employing forced draught. Power output was 12,000 shp, which gave a maximum speed of 23.5 knots and they could carry up to 900 passengers. More compact looking than the preceding Belgian turbine steamers, they had fuller sterns, which made them difficult to steer when going astern and were inclined

to roll due to the extra weight of a large deckhouse beneath the mainmast. To counter this, anti-rolling tanks were installed but the added weight of 30 tons of water gave rise to fears of greater instability and they were removed. During the First World War, *Ville de Liège* was used as a Belgian army hospital ship in Calais and later both ships were run as troopers and hospital ships by the British Admiralty. After the war they brought the first group of Belgian exiles back to Ostend in January 1919. *Stad Antwerpen* went to Belgian breakers in October 1934 but her sister, in better condition following repairs after grounding and sinking outside Dover's inner harbour in February 1929, was later converted to a car ferry by Cockerill. Her hull was gutted and the forward funnel and two boilers removed; the remaining boilers were converted to oil-firing. Four ramps were fitted to her starboard side at various levels to cope with tidal

range and she could carry one-hundred cars and 200 passengers; speed was reduced to 21.5 knots. She reentered service as *London-Istanbul* in late July with upright masts and short vertical funnel to bring her more into line with the new motor ships. During the Second World War, she acted mainly as a minesweeper depot ship, initially as *Algoma* and then as HMS *Ambitious*, serving at Lyness then at Lerwick as a coastal forces depot ship. She took part in the Normandy landings and finally served as an HQ ship at Terneuzen. *London-Istanbul* reopened the Belgian mail service to Folkestone in 1946 and was laid up in Ostend in 1949 after the delivery of the new purpose-built *Car Ferry* (later *Prinses Josephine H Charlotte*). Chartered by the new British Transport Commission in 1949–50 for Folkestone–Calais service, her boilers failed and she was scrapped in Belgium in 1951. *(World Ship Society)*

Improved Danish North Sea steamer

A P Bernstorff was built by Elsinore Shipbuilding & Engineering Co in 1913. A vessel of 2,316 grt, she measured 291.8 × 41.7 ft and drew 17.3 ft of water. Propulsion was by means of a four-cylinder triple-expansion engine supplied with steam by four boilers and the machinery developed 3,300 ihp for 15.5 knots in service. As built, she had accommodation for 138 first-, and 269 third-class passengers. Externally, she marked a considerable advance from the twelve-year-old *J C La Cour* with a higher forecastle, enlarged superstructure and only a single funnel. Her early success was cut short by the outbreak of the First World War, which also killed plans for a sister ship. With the Harwich service suspended, *A P Bernstorff* sailed to Manchester and other UK west coast ports followed by a period in lay-up and then a spell on the Copenhagen–Oslo service. After the war she underwent a six-week charter to the UK government for the repatriation of POWs and then sailed between Copenhagen and Hull followed by a twice-weekly service from Esbjerg to Grimsby, not returning to her Harwich station until 1919. The following year she was chartered by the Danish government to carry guests to Abenraa Fjord to accompany the king and queen to celebrate the return of southern Jutland. In 1925 she underwent a major overhaul and was fitted with new Howdens forced draft boilers, which gave a 15 per cent saving in coal consumption. In the 1930s, she ran mainly on a weekly Esbjerg–Antwerp–Dunkirk service carrying a reduced number of passengers. She was laid up in Esbjerg in the Second World War, but was seized by Germany in 1943 and later served as the ambulance carrier *Renate*.

Returned after the war, she reentered the Harwich run as a relief ship following a refit. In 1949 she was replaced by *Kronprinsesse Ingrid* and moved to a new weekly Copenhagen–Newcastle service. The Copenhagen Municipal Orchestra used *A P Bernstoff* as a hotel ship off Leith during the Edinburgh Festival in September 1950 and in 1952 she was switched to the Esbjerg–Newcastle service. Finally withdrawn in 1957 after forty years, she was broken up at Hamburg.

Advanced Canadian sisters

Anticipating increased traffic on the Vancouver–Victoria–Seattle 'Triangle Route' as a result of the planned Panama–Pacific Exposition in 1915, Canadian Pacific Railway ordered its largest yet ferries from Wm Denny & Bros in May 1913. These were the 5,934-grt twin-screw *Princess Margaret** and *Princess Irene*, with dimensions of 395 x 54 ft. They continued the three-funnelled profile with vertical stems, but were the first in the railway company's coastal fleet to have cruiser sterns and to be propelled by Parsons geared turbines. Berthing was supplied for around 170 first- and eighty second-class passengers and provision was also made for several cars loaded through side doors. *Princess Margaret* was delivered on 15 November 1914, having achieved just over 23 knots on the measured mile with her engines developing 15,365 shp. By then, war had broken out and in December both she and her unfinished sister were chartered by the Admiralty, which lacked fast vessels suitable for mine laying. Their accommodation was gutted and they were fitted to carry 400 mines (laid through stern doors) and armed with two 4.7-in and several AA guns. After just two minelaying trips to Beachy Head and Borkum Riff, *Princess Irene* was loading her third cargo at a buoy in Saltpan Creek near Sheerness Dockyard on 27 May 1915 when she was totally destroyed in a massive explosion

due to faulty priming of the mines. All but one of her complement of 275 was lost together with seventy-four dock workers. Her sister, however, had a successful war, sowing over 25,000 mines and in March 1919 was purchased by the Admiralty. She saw service against the Bolsheviks in the Baltic and was employed at various times as a minelayer, hospital ship and refugee transport. From December 1921, *Princess Margaret* was used for two years as an Admiralty yacht, carrying guests to the Naval Review in November 1923, but was offered for sale in 1927 and with Canadian Pacific no longer interested in her, was broken up at Blyth in 1929.

River Plate contrasts

In 1913–14, Glasgow shipbuilder A & J Inglis cemented its association with the River Plate estuary by delivering two fine paddle steamers to the Hamburg-South America Line for management by 'La Argentina' Compañia de Navegación (which was controlled by Antonio Delfino). Named *Cabo Santa Maria* and *Cabo Corrientes*, the 2,648/2,627-grt vessels were Argentine-flagged and used for a new overnight service between Buenos Aires and Montevideo. They were handsome two-funnelled ships with registered hull dimensions of 320 x 40.1 ft. Two triple-expansion engines coupled with a low-pressure turbine were fed by two boilers in the first ship and four in the second and developed around 2,500 ihp 14 knots in service. Berths were provided for 238 first- and 180 third-class passengers. The new Linea Nacional al Sud de Delfino was inaugurated on 15 January 1914 under the altered management of La Nueva Argentina Compania

General de Navegacion. On 18 September 1914, *Cabo Santa Maria* had a brush with the north mole in Montevideo but was pulled off by tugs and repaired. In 1921 both were sold to Argentina Compania de Navegacion under the management of A M Delfino & Compania and renamed *General Artigas** and *General Alvear* respectively, but the following year were resold to Nicolas Mihanovich. The latter was operated by Argentine Navigation Co and the former was transferred to Uruguayan flag under Compania Uruguaya de Navegacion management in 1923, but reverted to Argentine registry in 1932. Mihanovich died in 1929, but his fleet was eventually nationalised in the early 1940s under Dodero management, and was restyled Flota Argentina de Navegacion Fluvial (FANF) in 1949. On 24 July 1953, *General*

Alvear stranded in thick fog near Punta Yeguas while *en route* to Montevideo with fifty-seven passengers. She sank five days later during a storm and the wreck was sold for demolition on 23 April 1961. Sister *General Artigas* was sold for scrap in April 1961 and was demolished the following year at Buenos Aires. *(Histamar)*

Ordered just before the outbreak of the First World War, the twin-screw, three-funnelled sisters *Ciudad de Buenos Aires* and *Ciudad de Montevideo** were Nicolas Mihanovich's response to Hamburg-Sud's new Buenos Aires–Montevideo service. Completed by Cammell Laird, Birkenhead, in November 1914 and January 1915, they measured 3,864 grt on dimensions of 364.5 oa x 44.2 ft and 12 ft draught and were propelled at 16 knots by two steam turbines developing 5,825 shp, fed by four boilers. They accommodated 450 first- and 270 third-class passengers and ran initially under the Uruguayan flag for Compania Argentina de Navegacion, but in 1922 *Ciudad de Montevideo* passed to Compania Uruguaya de Navegacion. In 1942 both were transferred to Compania Argentina de Navegacion Dodero and then, following the nationalisation of ferry services in 1949, to Compania de Navegacion Fluvial Argentina SA. A further transfer to Flota Argentina de Navegacion Fluvial (FANF) occurred in 1951 and *Ciudad de Buenos Aires* was moved to Uruguay River service, but while sailing from Buenos Aires to Rosario on 27 August 1957 with 141 passengers and eighty-nine crew on board, she was run down in thick fog by the 7,980-grt US freighter *Mormacsurf* near Km 123 off Juncal Island. She listed violently to starboard and sank in nineteen minutes with the loss of seventy-four including her master. Her sister was broken up in Argentina by TARENA in November 1969.

Geared turbines for Dover and Bass Straits

The 2,495-grt *Biarritz* was ordered by the South Eastern & Chatham Railway Co from Wm Denny & Bros, Dumbarton, just before the outbreak of the First World War and ran trials on 9 March 1915, attaining an average of 23.75 knots on the Skelmorlie mile. She measured 341.2 x 42.1 ft and 12.5 ft draught and was driven by two Parsons single-reduction geared turbines developing 10,000 shp, with steam supplied by six Babcock & Wilcox watertube boilers. Taken up by the Admiralty on completion for minelaying duties, she served initially in the North Sea and later in the Mediterranean, where her mines sank the German cruiser *Breslau* and damaged the battle cruiser *Goeben*. The construction of a sister, *Maid of Orleans**, was delayed and she was taken over by the Admiralty on the stocks and completed as a transport in August 1918. Released in 1920, she took up her intended Dover–Calais run and the following year was joined by her sister after an extensive refit. Converted to oil-burning in winter and spring 1925–6, one boiler was removed, funnels raised and promenade decks almost fully enclosed, after which they switched to the Folkestone–Boulogne service, where they remained until war came again in 1939. Both acted as British Expeditionary Force leave ships until May 1940, but each made a trip to Rotterdam in April to pick up Dutch nationals. During the ensuing Dunkirk evacuation, *Biarritz* was badly damaged in the boiler-room by shellfire and returned to Southampton for repairs but her sister lifted over 5,000 men to safety

before herself being damaged in a collision with a destroyer on 1 June. *Biarritz* then did a stint trooping on the Stranraer–Larne route followed by a short spell as a Fleet Air Arm target ship, but in 1942 both ships were converted to infantry landing ships. During the Normandy invasion, *Maid of Orleans* was mined when returning from the beaches on 28 June 1944

and sank with the loss of six crew members. Her sister continued trooping until the end of 1947 and after refit was mainly engaged in transporting refugees between the Hook of Holland and Harwich. She was laid up in Southampton in August 1948 and in November 1949 was towed to Dover and broken up on the beach.

The Australian firm of Huddart, Parker placed an order with Wm Denny & Bros, Dumbarton, in January 1914 for a geared-turbine steamer for its Melbourne–Launceston service. *Nairana* was launched on 21 June 1915, but work was slowed due to the urgent need to build destroyers for the Royal Navy. When almost complete, she was requisitioned by the Admiralty on 27 February 1917 and converted to carry up to seven aircraft. Land planes were launched over the bow on a sloping 95 ft platform, while seaplanes were handled by a large stern-mounted gantry. In addition three workshops were added to house maintenance personnel and her total complement numbered 278 including ninety air personnel. She joined the Grand Fleet at Scapa Flow and saw action against the Bolsheviks at Archangel in August 1918. In 1920 she was sold back to her original owners and refitted, emerging as originally planned with long raised forecastle and cruiser stern and measuring 3,042 grt on dimensions of 328 oa x 45.5 ft. Main machinery comprised two sets of Parsons geared steam turbines which gave 20.33 knots trials speed on 7,152 shp. Steam was supplied by six Babcock & Wilcox watertube boilers. Passenger complement was 280 in first class and 112 in second class. She sailed from Plymouth on 30 January 1921 and arrived in Melbourne on 27 March, making her first Tasman crossing on 18 April. Service speed was around 15 knots, giving an eighteen-hour passage but she was capable of 19 knots to make up for any delays. On 1 January 1922, she was transferred to Tasmanian Steamers Pty, a new company set up by the two rival concerns on the Bass Strait, Union Steamship Co of New Zealand and Huddart, Parker, along with the latter's *Loongana* and the old Union steamer *Oonah* and her funnels had a red band added beneath the black top. She was twice almost rolled over by freak waves, the first occasion on 24 January 1928 and the second more serious incident on 3 April

1936 when she broached when passing through the notorious 'rip' at the entrance to Port Philip Bay, washing three passengers overboard and crushing another. After the Second World War, *Nairana* served Devonport or Burnie but in February 1948 was laid up in Hobson's Bay. The following January she was sold for scrap, but fate intervened and she was torn from her moorings in a gale on 18 February and driven ashore on Port Melbourne beach. She was broken up where she lay in 1953–4.

Norwegian duo

Det Bergenske D/S (Bergen Line) began a service to Newcastle in 1890. The route was mainly served by 13-knot ships of just over 1,000 tons but in January 1916 the 2,506-grt, 170-passenger *Jupiter** was delivered by Lindholmens Varv, Gothenburg. Measuring 305 x 41.75 ft, she was driven by a 3,000 ihp triple-expansion engine that gave a service speed of 14 knots and allowed her to make the passage in around twenty-six hours. She was laid up in Bergen in 1917 and between November and early 1919 was chartered by the UK government for an Aberdeen–Bergen service under Union-Castle management. An improved version built to the same dimensions but with raked masts and funnel, the 2,519-grt *Leda*, was completed at Armstrong, Whitworth's Walker yard, Newcastle, in 1920. She was the first of the longer distance North Sea passenger steamers to be propelled by geared turbines (Brown-Curtis double reduction), developing 3,300 shp and driving a single screw. Steam was supplied by three single-ended boilers and she had a service speed of around 15–16 knots. Passenger complement was ninety-eight in first class and forty-seven in third class. On 1 October 1923, she grounded near Bergen, suffering a flooded forepeak and extensive bottom damage. In 1931 she was transferred to the Hamburg service when replaced by *Venus*, switching to the Rotterdam service in 1933. In summer 1938, *Jupiter* was replaced by *Vega* and moved to the Rotterdam service, allowing *Leda* to return to the Hamburg run. Seized by the Germans in summer 1940, both were used as accommodation ships or transports and *Leda* was sunk by Russian artillery near Stettin on 25 March

1945, while repatriating refugees to Swinemünde. Her wreck was raised in 1948 and broken up at Bremerhaven. *Jupiter* survived the war and after a refit, reentered service in March 1946. From 1948 she sailed to Antwerp during the summer months and in 1953 moved to the Hurtigrute coastal service when replaced by the new *Leda*. In 1955, she was sold to Epirotiki Steamship Navigation Co 'George Potamianos'

and converted to the 265-passenger cruise ship *Hermes* with a new funnel and superstructure extension forward over the filled-in well deck. She operated mainly in the eastern Mediterranean and Black Sea but caught fire on 4 March 1960 while laid up at Perama and was beached at Salamis. Refloated five days later, she was towed to Split in December for demolition.

Newbuild and conversion for Southampton services

Early in the First World War, the London & South Western Railway ordered two steamers for its Southampton–Channel Islands service, turning for the first time to the well-known builder of channel steamers Wm Denny & Bros, Dumbarton. In the event, only one ship was built due to wartime exigencies and the 1,457-grt *Lorina* was taken by the Admiralty while still on the stocks in 1918 and completed as a troopship. Designed to take the ground at low water, she continued the twin-funnelled theme of the *Normannia* pair but had a less enclosed superstructure and was some 9 feet longer, measuring 299 oa x 36.1 ft and 12.75 ft draught. She could carry a maximum of 1,107 passengers and sleeping accommodation was provided for 148 first- and ninety second-class passengers. Her propelling machinery comprised two sets of Parsons geared turbines fed by one double-ended and one single-ended boiler and she exceeded her contract speed of 19.5 knots during a six-hour trial at an output of 4,830 shp. She entered her intended service some

five years after she was ordered and adopted the livery of the newly-created Southern Railway in 1923. In 1924 she replaced *Caesarea* on the Channel Islands run and in 1928 her promenade deck was partially plated in and solid bulwarks replaced open rails at her stern. After 1932, her employment varied but in 1935 she started a Southampton–Jersey–St

Malo service and in September of the same year suffered considerable hull damage after hitting a rock near St Helier. War again overtook her in 1939 and she was taken up for trooping duties but was sunk by German dive-bombers on 29 May 1940, while involved in the Dunkirk evacuation.

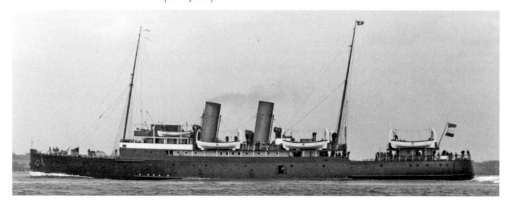

Among several ferries that started out as First World War warships, the London & South Western Railway's *Ardena* was the only example to run on the English Channel. She was originally one of the numerous 'Herbacious Border' class of twin-funnelled escort sloops built on merchant ship lines to replace hastily-converted paddle steamers that had previously performed the task. Named after plants, they numbered seventy-two and were built in five groups. Some became surplus to requirements after the war and the railway company purchased HMS *Peony*. Built in 1915 by A McMillan & Sons, Dumbarton, she was one of the third group known as the 'Arabis' class. *Ardena* replaced the cargo ship *Normandy*, which was lost in the war. Reconstructed at Dundee, her bridge deck was joined to the forecastle and extended almost to her stern and she was renamed *Ardena*. Her gross measurement was 1,092 tons on dimensions of 267 oa × 33.1 ft and 12.8 ft draught. She was propelled by a Rowan four-cylinder triple-expansion engine. Power amounted to 2,400 ihp and she had a speed of 16 knots. *Ardena* made her maiden voyage to St Malo in 1920 and in July reopened the summer service between Southampton and Cherbourg, carrying a maximum of 510 passengers and cargo. The service was switched to Caen in 1925, replacing the former Newhaven cargo service, but was closed in 1931 for commercial

reasons and *Ardena* was laid up until sold in July 1934 to Greek owner E K Togias, who converted her without change of name and ran her in competition with Inglessi's former L&SWR steamer *Alberta*. She became somewhat unstable after her owner sold off

her lead ballast but was credited with making the fastest passage from Piraeus to Lesbos. She was taken over by the Germans in 1941 and was mined off Cephalonia on 27 September 1943; 700 of the 1,000 Italians on board were lost.

First geared turbines for Greenore service

The London & North Western Railway ordered a new geared turbine steamer for its Holyhead–Greenore service from Wm Denny & Bros, Dumbarton, in July 1914. Work was suspended for the duration of the First World War and she was not delivered until 15 October 1919. *Curraghmore* measured 1,587 grt on dimensions of 314 oa × 40.1 ft and 12.1 ft draught and had accommodation for 495 first- and 581 third-class passengers. She was driven by two sets of Parsons single-reduction geared

turbines supplied with steam by five Babcock & Wilcox watertube boilers. The contract speed of 20.5 knots was exceeded by 0.25 knots on trials with her engines developing 6,348 shp at 256 rpm. Like *Rathmore* and *Greenore*, which preceded her on the Greenore run, she had two funnels, but differed in that she had a cruiser stern. In 1930, in order to cope with increased summer traffic on the Heysham–Belfast service engendered by the popularity of its new 'Dukes' and also to act as a

reserve vessel, the London, Midland & Scottish Railway transferred *Curraghmore* and gave her the more appropriate name of *Duke of Abercorn*. She performed her new role for five years but she lacked the following of her newer running mates due to her inferior accommodation and because her crossings took an extra thirty minutes. Displaced in her relief role by the new *Duke of York*, she was broken up by T W Ward in Barrow in 1935.

Final Burns triple-expansion passenger ship

The Glasgow firm of G & J Burns ordered a new steamer in early 1915, but due to war needs, construction did not start until two years later and she was eventually completed in July 1919 as *Killarney* for the City of Cork Steam Packet Co. Following acquisition of both companies by Coast Lines, she was transferred back to Burns in July 1920 and received her originally intended name of *Moorfowl**. She measured 1,578 grt on dimensions of 265 x 36 ft and 15.6 ft draught and was propelled by a triple-expansion engine supplied with steam by two double-ended boilers. The power output was 3,000 ihp and she had a speed of 15 knots. She could carry around 1,000 passengers and sailed on the Glasgow–Belfast service. Her ownership changed to Burns & Laird Lines in 1922 and in 1926 she was converted to burn oil, while at the same time additional superstructure with an observation lounge was added forward. In 1928 she took over the daylight Ardrossan–Belfast service from *Tiger* and on 30 May 1929 she was renamed *Lairdsmoor* when a new form of nomenclature was introduced for the whole fleet. *Lairdscastle* took over the Ardrossan run in 1932 and *Lairdsmoor* moved to the Dublin station. While bound for the Clyde on 7 April 1937, she collided with Shaw Savill's *Taranaki* in thick fog off Black Head and sank with the loss of her master and a fireman.

First French geared turbine channel steamer

The twin-screw steamer *Versailles* was ordered by Chemins de Fer de l'Etat Français for the joint Newhaven service in 1914, but the First World War and subsequent shortages intervened and she was not completed by Forges & Chantiers de la Méditerranée, Le Havre, until July 1921. Named after the peace treaty that ended the war, she was 200 tons larger than the London, Brighton & South Coast Railway's *Paris* at 1,971 grt and her flush hull measured 305.5 x 36.2 ft and 9.8 ft draught. In appearance, she resembled the *Newhaven* pair of 1912 but had a raised bridge and shorter funnels, while initially her stern was ornamented with a large

brass dragon. Her twin Parsons geared turbines were the first to be installed in a French railway steamer and their output of 15,000 shp was 5,000 shp more than the earlier ships to meet a contract speed of 24 knots. On cross-channel trials to Newhaven and back on 1 and 2 August 1921, the first in rough conditions, she averaged 24.3 and 24.75 knots respectively. Capable of carrying around 1,200 passengers, she was converted to oil-firing in 1929 and her promenade deck was plated in early in 1933. Not long afterwards she touched bottom in the trough of a large wave while leaving Newhaven and damaged her rudder but managed to reach shelter in the lee

of Beachy Head and was towed back by the tug *Foremost*. With the nationalisation of the railways in 1938, her owning company became Société Nationale des Chemins de Fer Français (SNCF). *Versailles* was taken up for trooping duties early in the Second World War but was later damaged at Dunkirk and laid up in Brest. She was then moved to Nantes where she was seized by the Germans and used first as a minelayer and later as an accommodation ship. At the end of the war she was found lying in a damaged state in the Danish port of Aalborg and although returned to France, was considered beyond repair and broken up.

Diesel Debut in a Steam World

Post-war reconstruction was dominated by turbine-driven ships and a further refinement included the introduction of double-reduction gearing. Reciprocating engines were still retained for a handful of overnight vessels on the North Sea and the Irish Sea, as well as a single vessel for the South of France–Corsica run but in both types of vessel oil-firing began to replace the use of coal.

The United Kingdom's railway companies were reorganised from 1 January 1923 into four major groups: the London and North Eastern Railway, the London Midland and Scottish Railway, the Southern Railway and the Great Western Railway. Rationalisation was also taking place among some of the private ferry companies with many of the Irish Sea operators coming under the control of the Coast Lines group and its energetic chairman Sir Alfred Read.

Rudolf Diesel's internal combustion engine had been steadily gaining acceptance since its first ocean-going application in 1912 in the Danish cargo/passenger ship *Selandia* but it was not until 1925 that another Danish company, Det Forenede D/S (United Steamship Co), pioneered the use of diesel power in the short-sea field with its North Sea passenger ship *Parkeston*. Three sisters followed and the company never built another steamship but in 1928 the internal combustion engine claimed another first when it was adopted for cross-channel use in the Belfast Steamship Co's *Ulster Monarch*, which set a pattern for many subsequent ships.

Innovations in ship design around this time included the provision of enclosed promenade decks to provide more shelter for passengers and in 1929 a Maierform hull with its distinctive curved bow – designed to improve both efficiency and sea-keeping – was adopted for the new French Corsica service motorship *Cyrnos*.

Note: An asterisk in a caption indicates the vessel shown in the photograph.

Trio for Antwerp service

The Great Eastern Railway prioritised its Antwerp service when it ordered new tonnage after the First World War. John Brown & Co, Clydebank, delivered the 2,957-grt *Antwerp* and *Bruges** in 1920 while a third sister, the 2,969-grt *Malines*, was completed by Armstrong, Whitworth, High Walker, in March 1922 after reaching 21.5 knots on trials. The first geared-turbine steamers in the GER fleet, the war-built *Stockholm* never having sailed for them, they measured 337 oa × 43 ft on draught of 13.3 ft and their Brown-Curtis units developed 12,500 shp. These were fed by five boilers that could burn either coal or oil. Unlike their flush-hulled predecessors, they had long raised forecastles and cruiser sterns. Overnight berths were provided for 263 first- and 100 second-class passengers, but they were certified to carry 430 and 1,250 respectively in addition to 500 tons of cargo. They maintained the British Mail Route to Belgium until 1939, marred only by several collisions in the Scheldt. During the Second World War, *Antwerp* and *Bruges* were used for trooping from Southampton and *Malines* evacuated British civilians from Rotterdam, rescuing the crew of the scuttled *St Denis* before slipping out of the New Waterway without lights. All three assisted in the Dunkirk evacuation, where *Malines* rescued 1,000 troops and naval ratings from the torpedoed destroyer HMS *Grafton*. *Bruges* was bombed off Le Havre on 11 June, her crew escaping

in the company's *Vienna*, and soon afterwards the remaining two sisters helped to evacuate civilians from the Channel Islands. They were later converted to convoy escorts and sent to the Mediterranean via the Cape in October 1941, but *Malines* was torpedoed by aircraft and beached off Port Said on 22 July 1942. Refloated in September 1943, she was used as a Combined Operations training ship at Kabrit in the Suez Canal before return to the Tyne in November 1945 following a lengthy tow, during which she broke adrift several times. Condemned, she was scrapped at

Dunston in 1948. Meanwhile, *Antwerp* had become a Sicily landings headquarters ship in 1943, followed by fighter direction, convoy escort and rescue ship duties before ending the war in the Aegean. Released in April 1945, she was given a large deckhouse beneath her foremast and an extended boat deck and her funnel cowls were removed. She was used as a British Army of the Rhine (BAOR) leave ship on the Hook of Holland–Harwich service but this ceased in 1950 and she was scrapped at Milford Haven the following year.

Fast quartet for Holyhead

The London & North Western Railway ordered four larger steamers from Wm Denny & Bros, Dumbarton, in an attempt to wrest the Holyhead mail contract from the City of Dublin Steam Packet Co. The first two were slated for delivery in 1916 but work was abandoned due to the war. On 11 July 1918, the Admiralty requisitioned both ships for completion as the fast minelayers *Anglesey* and *Sheppey* but the war ended before they were ready. *Anglia* was eventually handed over in May 1920 and *Hibernia* in November, with sisters *Cambria* and *Scotia** following in December 1921. *Cambria*'s delivery was delayed by a joiner's strike and she was partly fitted out in Rouen. At 3,460 grt and measuring 392 oa × 45 ft and 13.75 ft draught, they were the largest and also the most powerful channel steamers in the world – their two sets of Parsons single-reduction geared turbines developed up to 16,000 shp, fed by nine Babcock & Wilcox watertube boilers. The contract speed of 24.5 knots in loaded condition was exceeded by all four, *Scotia* averaging 24.75 knots during a five-hour trial and making over 25 knots on the measured mile. Comfortable accommodation was provided for 936 first- and 478 third-class passengers (486 in the 1921 pair) and public spaces had unusually high headroom of 9 ft. They were fitted with bow rudders for leaving both Holyhead and Kingstown (Dun Laoghaire) astern, eleven watertight bulkheads and ten lifeboats. After just eighteen months in service, *Anglia* was laid up in Barrow and thereafter sailed only intermittently during busy holiday periods until broken up at Troon in 1935. The remaining trio were extensively altered by Denny during winter and spring 1931–2 and given glazed screening on the promenade decks and improved internal accommodation. The cowl tops were removed from the funnels in 1935–6. During the Second World War, *Scotia* was initially used on trooping

service but was bombed and sunk off Calais on 1 June 1940 while returning from her second trip to Dunkirk, losing thirty crew members and around 300 of the 2,000 French troops on board. With their names allocated to new ships, the remaining sisters had the suffix *II* added to their names in May 1948 before being broken up – *Hibernia* at Barrow that autumn and *Cambria* at Milford Haven the following summer.

Batavier war replacements

The 1,573-grt *Batavier II* and *Batavier V** were completed for Wm Muller by Wilton Engineering & Slipway Co in January and June 1921 as replacements for war losses. Virtual repeats of the 1903 Gourlay-built pair, sharing the same dimensions of 260 × 35 ft, they had slightly deeper draught at 16 ft and were distinguished by full height steam pipes on the funnel and different boat davits. As with the earlier ships, they had a combined forecastle and bridge deck and a separate poop, the well deck being hidden by high bulwarks. Overnight berthing was arranged for ninety-eight first- and fifty-three second-class passengers and they were driven by a triple-expansion engine developing 2,250 ihp and fed by a pair of Scotch boilers capable of burning either coal or oil. Their promenade decks were partly enclosed and glazed in the 1930s and first-class accommodation was reduced to seventy. *Batavier V* was seized by invading German forces in in May 1940 and used to supply the Channel Islands. When sailing from Antwerp to Guernsey in November 1941, she was sunk by a Royal Navy motor torpedo boat west of Cap Gris Nez. Her sister, which had evacuated 350 troops from Boulogne to Falmouth on 21 May 1940, became an accommodation ship for Dutch cadets in Falmouth. In July she was moved to Portsmouth house the crew of KNS *Jakob van Heemskerk* during her conversion. At this time, her mainmast was removed and her grey livery was relieved by a white funnel top. Released in April 1941, she was used for UK

coasting and in January 1946 sailed between Rotterdam and Harwich before reverting to her normal London run in June 1947 with a new short mainmast. She was partnered by Zeeland Line's *Koningen Emma* in summer 1948 and by *Oranje Nassau* during 1949–51, after which she provided a lone service carrying around fifty first-class passengers. Boiler trouble led to her withdrawal after a final departure from London on 12 April 1958, bringing the 128-year old link to a close. In autumn the following year she was sold for scrap and was demolished in 1960.

Irish Sea steamers

The City of Cork Steam Packet Co received the 1,679/1,675-grt sister ships *Ardmore* and *Kenmare** from Ardrossan Dockyard in 1921 for its Cork–Liverpool service. They measured 285.4 oa × 37.9 ft and 17 ft draught, and were driven by four-cylinder triple-expansion engines giving 14 knots. They could accommodate about sixty saloon-class passengers and considerably more in steerage class. *Ardmore* was the first on the Irish Sea to have oil-fired boilers but was transferred to the British & Irish Steam Packet Co and renamed *Lady Longford* for its Dublin–Liverpool service. In 1930, she transferred to Burns & Laird Lines and changed her name to *Lairdshill* for the Glasgow–Dublin run. She reverted to *Lady Longford* in June 1936 and had her masts reduced for passage of the Manchester Ship Canal but became *Lairdshill* again in May of the following year and was put on the Clyde–Belfast run. Her sister passed to the British & Irish Steam Packet Co (1936) Ltd in 1936 and during the Second World War was employed on a cargo-only service between Cork and Fishguard. She reopened the passenger service in August 1945 and after being replaced by the new *Munster*, she reopened her old Liverpool service in February 1948. *Kenmare* made her last sailing to Liverpool on 12 May 1956 and was broken up at Passage West that summer. *Lairdshill* was scrapped in Dublin a year later.

The British & Irish Steam Packet Co acquired the Liverpool service of City of Dublin Steam Packet Co in 1919 together with the five steamers employed on the service. Because of their limited passenger accommodation, the company commissioned Ardrossan Dockyard to build two new ships, which were completed as *Lady Louth** and *Lady Limerick* in 1923 and 1924. Measuring 1,870/1,945 grt on dimensions of 276.6 × 37.6 ft, they were slightly larger versions of the City of Cork Steam Packet Co's 1,679-grt *Ardmore* and *Kenmare* but were more severe looking with vertical funnels and masts. Propelled by four-cylinder triple-expansion engines, they had a sea speed of 14 knots. In 1929–30, they were transferred to Burns & Laird Lines for Glasgow–Belfast overnight service under the new names of *Lairdsburn* and *Lairdscastle*. Replaced by new motorships in 1936, they were moved to the Glasgow–Dublin route. They reverted to the Belfast run during the Second World War and *Lairdscastle* sank in tow following collision with the Reardon Smith steamer *Vernon City* on 4 September 1940. *Lairdsburn* collided with the excursion

steamer *King Edward* off Gourock on 21 October 1941 and after the war sailed on the Londonderry service until broken up at Port Glasgow in 1953.

Mediterranean and US developments

Following the First World War, French shipping companies had insufficient funds to replace lost tonnage and in 1920 the government ordered eight 'Gouverneur Général' class ships in two batches – four of 4,500 grt/18 knots and four of 3,500 grt/16 knots. The first of the larger vessels *Gouverneur Général Grévy* was completed by the Brest Arsenal in February 1922, followed by *Gouverneur Général Chanzy** (with higher bridge) from Cammell Laird, Birkenhead, in April and *Gouverneur Général de Gueydon* by Ateliers & Chantiers de Provence, Port de Bouc, in December. A second ship from Brest, *Gouverneur Général Jonnart*, was delivered in April 1923, she and her sister having been launched as *PA 1* and *PA 2*. Assigned to Compagnie Générale Transatlantique for its North Africa services, they had two closely-spaced funnels and measured 362.75 × 53.5 ft on 17.75 ft draught. Two sets of Parsons double-reduction geared turbines fed by six cylindrical boilers developed 6,600 shp for 17 knots (7,200 shp maximum 19.5 knots at 7,200 shp). *de Gueydon* was seized by German troops in Bizerta on 8 December 1942 and handed over to Italy on 22 January 1943 but was scuttled in the Bizerta channel by evacuating Germans on 7 May. *Grévy* and *Chanzy* were also seized by the Germans in Marseilles in 1943 and handed to Italy, which renamed them *Avezzano* and *Nicastro*. When Italy capitulated in 1944, they were taken back and became the hospital ships *Göttingen* and *Giessen* along with *Jonnart*, which became *Greifswald*. During the invasion of southern France, the Germans scuttled *Göttingen* and *Greifswald* in Marseilles in August 1944 and the wrecks were raised in 1946 and 1945 respectively and scrapped – the latter in Savona in 1949 after use to house Italians restoring the damage to Marseilles harbour. Although damaged in drydock at La Ciotat, *Giessen* was repaired and reentered Algiers service in 1945, being restored

Compagnie Fraissinet of Marseilles took delivery of the 2,796-grt *Général Bonaparte* from Chantiers & Ateliers de Provence, Port de Bouc, in April 1923. Measuring 315 × 45 ft and 18 ft draught, she bore a strong resemblance to *Corte II* and had a long raised forecastle and raised poop. Oil-fired, her four-cylinder triple-expansion engine developed 6,000 ihp and provided a service speed of 17 knots. Overnight passenger berths were arranged for forty-six in first, seventy in second and twenty-six in third class and in addition she could also accommodate 600 in steerage. *Général Bonaparte* came under the control of the Vichy government in 1940 and after the German occupation of southern France in November 1942 was one of the few ships that was allowed to continue on her normal run. On 19 May 1943, when she was torpedoed by the submarine HMS *Sportsman* some forty miles off Nice with the loss of thirteen lives.

The Peninsular & Occidental Steamship Co was formed by the merger of two railway-owned companies: the Florida East Coast Line and the Plant Steamship Line. It operated a thrice-weekly service from Port Tampa and Key West to Havana in Cuba. In March 1921, the company took delivery of the 2,479-grt *Cuba** from William Cramp & Sons, Philadelphia. She measured 325 × 47.2 ft and was driven by two triple-expansion engines developing 3,600 ihp, which gave her a speed of 16 knots. During 1942–6 she was chartered as a US Army transport for conveying troops in the Caribbean area and in 1947 was sold to Ignazio Messina of Genoa, who renamed her *Pace* (Peace). She emerged from a major conversion with a white hull with new raked stem, a more modern funnel and her former holds were refitted with dormitory accommodation. From 1948, she ran an express service from Marseilles to Alexandria and Beirut via Genoa and Naples and also made occasional summer cruises. Later she sailed to Haifa via Piraeus and Limassol and in 1960 was renamed *Sassari* after a province in Sardinia. In her forty-second year, 1962, she was broken up at La Spezia. The 4,923-grt twin-screw turbine *Florida* was delivered to Peninsular & Occidental by Newport News Shipbuilding & Dry Dock Co in 1931 for the Key West–Havana service, but after a hurricane destroyed the terminal and rail connection at Key West in 1934, she sailed from Miami instead. She was also used by the US Army during 1942–6 and

to her original name a year later. Apart from a year on the Bordeaux–Casablanca run in 1956, she remained in the Mediterranean until broken up at La Spezia in 1963. The 4,866-grt *President Dal Piaz* was deliverd to CGT by Swan Hunter & Wigham Richardson in 1929. Measuring 363 × 52.8 ft, she was driven by two sets of Parsons single-reduction geared turbines developing 4,800 shp for 17 knots. She could be described as an improved version of the larger 'Gouverneur Général' quartet, with the forward well deck plated in and a more enclosed superstructure. Overnight berths were provided for 125 first-, 164 second- and ninety-four third-class passengers with an additional 300 in steerage. She made her maiden voyage from Marseilles to Algiers on 25 May and after the start of the Second World War was seized by Italy in July 1940 and renamed *Melfi* for use as a troop transport. She was returned to France early in 1943 but was seized again, by the Germans, in Marseilles on 22 February. The Germans returned her to French control on 15 February 1944, but she was taken over once more by the Italians and renamed *Amalfi*. She was scuttled at Cassis on 26 June and became a total loss.

then became a one-class ship, sailing to Havana three times a week until 1960, when Fidel Castro closed down the service in the wake of the Cuban revolution. Latterly she sailed on short three-day cruises to Nassau with a white hull and under Liberian flag for Blue Steamship Co and in 1967 was sold to Montreal interests for use as the floating hotel *Le Palais Flottant* during Expo 67. In 1968 she was towed to Santander for demolition.

Propulsion contrasts for Low Countries

The Stoomvaart Maatschappij Zeeland (Zeeland Line) 2,908-grt *Prinses Juliana**
and *Mecklenburg* replaced their namesakes lost during the First World War, but
because Fairfield Shipbuilding had a full order book they were constructed in
Holland by de Schelde, Flushing. Built to the same design and dimensions as the
earlier ships, they were delivered in 1920 and 1922 but differed externally in
having their steam pipes hidden within the funnels, which now bore thin red, white
and blue bands beneath the black top. The lead ship entered the
Flushing–Folkestone overnight service on 15 August 1920, but a new daytime
service was inaugurated in July 1922 following the arrival of *Mecklenburg*. From
January 1927, Harwich was substituted for Folkestone and soon afterwards both
ships had their boat decks extended further aft and the first-class promenade deck
was largely plated in and glazed. *Prinses Juliana* was damaged in collision with the
Danish motor vessel *Esbjerg* off Harwich on 29 June 1935, and was out of service
for six weeks. On 21 November 1937, she grounded in fog fifteen miles south-
west of Flushing but was soon refloated. Both ships were laid up in Flushing on the
outbreak of war, but while carrying troops to Ijmuiden on 12 May 1940, *Prinses
Juliana* was bombed by German aircraft one mile north of the Hook of Holland
and beached on Terheyden Bank, later breaking in two. Her sister escaped to
England and became a Netherlands Navy accommodation ship but was converted
to an infantry landing ship minus her mainmast in 1943 and took part in the
Normandy landings. Released in 1946, she was converted to oil-firing and fitted
with a new stump mast aft, entering day service from the Hook to Harwich on 14
June 1947 because Flushing was still unusable. On 7 July 1949, she revived the
Flushing–Folkestone day service with twice-weekly summer sailings but made her
last trip on 8 September 1952, thereafter becoming a relief ship for the
Hook–Harwich service. Withdrawn on 25 October 1959, *Prinses Juliana* was sold
the following year and broken up in Ghent.

Completed by Société Cockerill in 1923, *Princesse Marie-José* was the first Belgian
channel steamer to be propelled by geared turbines. Measuring 1,767 grt on
dimensions of 348 × 40 ft, she could be described as an amalgam of the earlier
designs but was readily distinguishable by her elevated bridge front. Her eight
boilers were converted to oil-burning in 1931 and her funnels were given black
tops and had cowls removed. On 9 August 1937, she had to be beached in
Dunkirk outer harbour after she was rammed in fog by the British cargo steamer
Clan Macneil, which had holed her on the port side just abaft the bridge. During
the Second World War, she initially ran to Folkestone but sailed to Southampton in
May 1940 and was used to evacuate troops from Le Havre, Cherbourg and St
Malo. She then went to the Clyde, where her mainmast was removed and she was
refitted as the anti-submarine training ship *Southern Isles*. Commissioned on 3
March 1941, she was renamed HMS *Nemesis* and based at Campbeltown until
March 1943. The poor state of her machinery precluded her conversion to an
infantry landing ship and in September she sailed for Iceland to take up a base-ship
role as HMS *Baldur*. Renamed *Nemesis* once more, she was towed back to the
Clyde in June 1945 and handed back to Belgium. She finished her days in Ostend,
acting as a floating barracks for Belgian marines, and was broken up in 1947.

Japanese geared turbine steamers

Named after imperial gardens in Korea, the 3,620-grt trio *Keifuku Maru**, *Tokuju Maru* and *Shokei Maru* were delivered to Japan's Imperial Government Railways by Mitsubishi's Kobe yard in 1921–3. Designed for the 166-mile Kampu route between Shimonoseki and Pusan, which formed the sea section of the Tokyo–Keijo (Seoul) rail connection, they were larger two-funnelled versions of the 3,102-grt, 16-knot *Shiragi Maru* completed by Kawasaki's Kobe shipyard in 1913, continuing the same hull design with a raised forecastle but differing with cruiser sterns. They bore a resemblance to the Zeeland Line ships on the Flushing–Folkestone service and propulsion was by means of a pair of coal-fired single-reduction geared steam turbines giving a service speed of 17.5 knots, although all reached nearly 20 knots on trials. They accommodated just over forty first-, 235 second- and 700–800 third-class passengers and to minimise rolling were fitted with Motora stabilising gear. In May 1936, *Keifuku Maru* had the honour of carrying the Emperor. In 1943 they were transferred to the new Hakpu route between Hakata in Kyushu and Pusan and although the Second World War devastated

much of the Japanese merchant fleet, all three survived in damaged states and eventually resumed sporadic sailings to Korea from small ports in the Japan Sea, the former Kampu and Hakpu routes having been suspended in June 1945. They sailed for a

further fifteen or so years, with *Tokuju Maru* working at times on the Aomori–Hakodate service, and lead ship *Keifuku Maru* was hulked in 1958 and scrapped soon afterwards. Her sisters *Tokuju Maru* and *Shokei Maru* were both broken up in 1961.

Nippon Yusen Kaisha's twin-screw turbine steamer *Nagasaki Maru** inaugurated a new express passenger and mail service between Nagasaki and Shanghai on 11 February 1923. A product of Wm Denny & Bros, Dumbarton, she was joined by sister *Shanghai Maru* on 25 March. Their profile was fairly typical of the Denny cross-channel steamers of the period but like Huddart, Parker's *Nairana* and Japanese National Railway's contemporary *Keifuku Maru* trio, they had raised forecastles, but unlike the latter retained counter sterns. Their schedule involved two voyages per week on the 540-mile route, which they completed in around twenty-six hours (at 18 knots) and in May 1924 the service was extended to Kobe. Their main particulars were 5,306/5,293 grt and 403 (waterline) × 54.2 ft; draught was just under 20 ft. Ten boilers employing Howdens forced draught supplied steam to two sets of Parsons single-reduction geared turbines, which produced around 9,700 shp for twenty-four-hour trials speeds of around 20 knots – 1.5 knots in excess of contract. Their luxurious accommodation included a veranda tea room and overnight berths were supplied for some 155 in first and 200 in third classes. In the aftermath of the Great Kanto earthquake in September 1923, NYK suspended its Shanghai service and the pair were used for relief work, sailing every other day for around two months between Shinagawa (Tokyo), Yokohama and Kobe. As built, they carried NYK's traditional all-black funnels but in 1929 adopted the company's new livery of black with a broad white band containing two thin red bands.

Both ships were transferred to Toa Kaiun Kaisha in August 1939 and continued to operate during the war, but *Nagasaki Maru* sank on 13 May 1942 after hitting a Japanese-laid mine off Nagasaki. Her sister

was lost in October the following year after colliding about seventy-five miles north-east of Shanghai with NYK's 7,126-grt freighter *Sakito Maru*, which was sailing at the time under army control.

New railway tonnage for English Channel

The twin-screw turbine steamers *Dinard** and *St Briac* (2,291 grt), were delivered to the new Southern Railway by Wm Denny & Bros in July and September 1924 after exceeding their contract speed of 19.5 knots on trials. Designed for the Southampton–St Malo run, they measured 325 oa × 41.1 ft and 12.5 ft draught and had an enclosed superstructure along the lines of *Normannia* and an extra pair of lifeboats in addition to double-bottomed hulls. Maximum passenger capacity was around 1,340 and overnight cabin accommodation was provided for 234 in first class with 118 second class, sleeping in saloons. In the 1930s, *St Briac* inaugurated cruising to French ports, including Rouen, but the St Malo service was withdrawn on 6 September 1939 following the outbreak of war. *Dinard* was quickly converted to a hospital ship and successfully evacuated many stretcher cases from Dunkirk. There followed a period at Scapa Flow acting as a floating hospital for merchant seamen, during which time sister *St Briac* was sunk by mine off Aberdeen on 13 March 1942 while acting as a Fleet Air Arm target ship. In 1943 *Dinard* took part in the Sicily landings and carried some 7,600 patients in the course of steaming 30,000 miles and visiting thirty ports. On 7 June 1944, while returning wounded from the D-Day beaches, she hit a mine and was towed to Southampton for repairs. In May 1945, *Dinard* was refitted to repatriate troops and POWs from Calais and Dieppe and then sailed to the Tyne for conversion to a seventy-capacity car ferry, emerging with a new profile in June 1947. Cars were crane-loaded until a hinged stern door was fitted in 1952. Withdrawn in October 1958, she was sold early next year to Viking Line of Mariehamn, which renamed her *Viking* and increased her car-carrying capacity. On 1 June, she inaugurated the first roll-on/roll-off car ferry service to the Åland Islands, running between Korpo in Finland and Graddö in Sweden; the latter

was changed to Kapellskar in 1960 and the Finnish terminal to Pargas two years later. At the end of 1965, her ownership changed to Rederi A/B Solstad and the windows at the forward end of her boat deck were plated over. Two years later, her hull colour was changed from pale blue to red and funnels from buff to white with a red top, while Naantali became her Finnish terminal. By now forty-six-years old, she made her last trip in August 1970 and after a period of lay-up was towed to Helsinki in 1973 for demolition.

To replenish its ageing Channel Islands fleet, the Great Western Railway turned to John Brown & Co, Clydebank, for its first turbine steamers, *St Julien* and *St Helier**, which were completed in May and June 1925 for an accelerated summer service. At 1,885 grt, 291.5 oa × 40 ft and 13.4 ft draught, they were substantially larger than the *Roebuck* pair of 1897 and their design featured a short raised forecastle, more widely spaced funnels, glazed forward part of the promenade deck, large deckhouse with docking bridge aft and a cruiser stern. Propelling machinery comprised twin Parsons single-reduction geared turbines, fed with steam by four single-ended oil-fired boilers. However, the racing days with the old London & South Western Railway were over and service speed was a more economical 18 knots at 4,350 shp. Maximum passenger complement in two classes was 1,004, 140 of whom could be berthed. Early in 1928, the dummy after funnels were removed to reduce windage together with the docking bridges and in 1937 the remaining funnels were lowered by 5 ft and fitted with cowls; the forward glazing

was plated over at the same time. Both performed useful war service, *St Julien* as a hospital ship, and they assisted in the Dunkirk evacuation where *St Helier* lifted 10,000 persons in four trips. After carrying POWs from the Clyde to the Isle of Man, she was taken up by the Admiralty in November 1940 and used as a coastal forces depot ship at Dartmouth before conversion in summer 1942 to a 180-troop infantry landing ship with six LCAs. *St Julien* spent most of 1943 in the Mediterranean, participating in the Anzio landings, but returned to join her sister for the Normandy landings, only to suffer mine damage on 7 June 1944. They returned to peacetime service in 1946 and passed to the nationalised British Transport Commission in 1948. At the end of the 1959 summer season, the boat trains from Paddington to Weymouth were withdrawn and after a final season, both were laid up in September 1960. The sisters were towed to Belgium for demolition; *St Helier* in December to Antwerp and her sister the following April to Ghent.

The newly-created Southern Railway, formed by a merger of four separate railway companies in 1923, ordered its first Dover Strait steamers from the Denny yard in 1924. The 2,701-grt *Isle of Thanet** and *Maid of Kent* were launched at Dumbarton in April and August 1925 and entered service in July (Dover–Calais) and November (Folkestone–Boulogne), respectively. Developments of *Biarritz/Maid of Orleans*, they measured 342 oa x 45.1 ft and 11.5 ft draught, but had single funnels, Denny-type cruiser sterns and an enclosed promenade deck. Two Parsons single-reduction steam turbines, fed by five oil-burning Babcock & Wilcox watertube boilers, produced 8,500 shp for a service speed of 22 knots. They were designed to carry 1,000 first- and 400 second-class passengers, the latter benefiting from the extra covered deck space. In summer 1939, *Isle of Thanet* ran from Southampton to St Malo but both were requisitioned soon after war broke out and after a few trooping runs were converted to hospital ships in Southampton. *Maid of Kent* was bombed and sunk in Dieppe on 21 May 1940, losing seventeen crew members, but her sister survived the Dunkirk evacuation and sailed to Preston to act as a Fleet Air Arm target ship. Early in 1943, she was converted to an infantry landing ship (hand hoist), and became the headquarters ship of Force J1, which was based at Cowes, Isle of Wight, and later landed troops at Juno

Beach during the Normandy landings. Towards the end of the war, she returned refugees to Ostend and Dieppe from Southampton and Newhaven respectively. Released and refitted in 1945, she spent a year on the Newhaven service before returning to the Dover Strait in February 1947 and spending the rest of her career sailing from Folkestone to Calais or Boulogne apart from a ten-month stint on the Dover–Boulogne run from July 1947. She also made

occasional summer weekend round-trips from Southampton to the Channel Islands in 1949 and again during 1952–8. In her later years, she was reduced to operating summer day trips only and made her final crossing in September 1963 before going into lay-up in Dover. She was sold the following spring to breakers and after a useful career of thirty-eight years was towed to Blyth in June.

Pioneer North Sea motor ships

Completed for Det Forenede D/S (United Steamship Co; DFDS) by Elsinore Shipbuilding & Engineering Co in 1925, the 2,762-grt *Parkeston** was the world's first short-sea passenger ship to be propelled by diesel engines, in her case two six-cylinder B & W units developing 3,800 bhp for a service speed of 16 knots. Her daily oil consumption was 18 tons, compared with the preceding *A P Bernstorff*'s 55 tons of coal. She measured 323.7 oa x 44.2 ft on 17.8 ft draught and could accommodate 124 first- and eighty-eight third-class passengers in addition to twenty crane-loaded cars. A development of *A P Bernstorff*, she had a smaller 'motorship' funnel and made her maiden voyage from Esbjerg to Harwich on 8 October 1925, taking around twenty-four hours and averaging 16.5 knots. She was followed by three sisters: *Jylland* (1926), *Esbjerg* (1929) and *England* (1932). Between June and September 1935, *Parkeston* made several voyages on the Esbjerg–Antwerp/Dunkirk service, but a projected service from Copenhagen to Iceland via Leith was cancelled due to the outbreak of the Second World War, which saw all four ships laid up in Danish ports. In January 1944, they were seized by the Kriegsmarine and taken to Germany for target ship/barrack duties. *England* as *Grenadier* was sunk by Allied aircraft at Kiel on 27 August and *Jylland* as *Musketier* off Travemünde on 10 May 1945 with the loss of some 800 refugees. *Parkeston* as *Pionier* and

Esbjerg as *Kürassier* were seized by the Allies at Lübeck in 1945 and left for Denmark, but the latter was mined and sunk near Stevns Light on 25 July 1945, while *en route* to Copenhagen. *England* had been raised and towed to Flensburg in June 1950 for engine removal and thence to Odense for demolition. *Esbjerg* was also raised, in August 1946, and sold to Compania Trasmediterranea in July. Rebuilt as *Ciudad de Ibiza* (3,059 grt/405 passengers) for Barcelona–Ibiza and later Barcelona–Menorca service, she was sold for scrap in Valencia in 1957. *Parkeston*, meanwhile, had reopened the

Esbjerg–Harwich service on a weekly basis in December 1945 with a funnel extension and extra accommodation aft. In May 1947, her stern was damaged by a mine while sailing back to Esbjerg from Elsinore after drydocking and in 1952 she switched to the Esbjerg–Newcastle service. She returned to the Harwich run for a few months in June 1953 to replace the fire-damaged *Kronprins Frederik*, with sailings reduced to five per week. In September 1964, she was sold to Akers shipyard in Oslo as the worker accommodation ship *Aker II* and in her fiftieth year in 1975 was sold for demolition at Masnedø.

Cook Strait Steamer

Swan, Hunter & Wigham Richardson, Newcastle, completed the 1,989-grt *Tamahine* for the Union Steamship Co of New Zealand's thrice-weekly Wellington–Picton inter-island service in 1925. Her hull dimensions were 274 oa × 40.2 ft and 13.6 ft draught and she was propelled by a pair of four-cylinder triple-expansion engines that provided a service speed of 16.5 knots. The overall passage lasted less than four hours and only one hour and thirty minutes of this was in open water, but the Cook Strait is notoriously one of the roughest areas in the world. Accommodation was provided for a total of 637 passengers, of which 117 could be berthed. Through most of her career, 'Tam', as she was affectionately known, was plagued by an almost permanent list to port. During the Second World War, she sometimes sailed to Lyttelton and afterwards made occasional extra daytime crossings during the height of the summer season in addition to making weekend excursions to Milford and other southern sounds. She was replaced by the government-owned car ferry *Aramoana* in 1962 and made her owner's final departure for Picton on 11 August. She sailed for Hong Kong on 5 January 1963

and was renamed *Kowloon Star* by Hong Kong Shipping Co (Panama). Her ownership changed to

Compania de Navegacion Sunlite in 1967 and she was broken up in Hong Kong the following year.

West and east coasts of America

In the first quarter of 1925, the Canadian Pacific Railway took delivery of the twin-screw sister ships *Princess Kathleen* and *Princess Marguerite** from John Brown & Co, Clydebank. Built for the 'Triangle Route' from Vancouver to Victoria and Seattle, they continued the three-funnelled pattern, but unlike the *Princess Margaret* pair reverted to counter sterns, their design more closely resembling *Princess Charlotte*. They measured 5,875 grt on hull dimensions of 350.1 × 60.1 ft and 15.3 ft draught and their main machinery comprised a pair of single-reduction steam turbines, which gave *Princess Kathleen* a speed of 22.5 knots on the measured mile and better than 21.5 knots in the course of a six-hour trial. Overnight berths were supplied for 600 in addition to 900 deck passengers and garage space could accommodate thirty cars. On 29 May 1939, shortly before the outbreak of the Second World War, *Princess Marguerite* had the honour of carrying King George VI and Queen Elizabeth from Vancouver to Victoria. During the war, both were used for trooping duties but on 17 August 1942, while sailing from Port Said to Famagusta, *Princess Marguerite* was torpedoed by *U 83* with the loss of forty-nine of the 1,000 or so persons on board. Her sister was the first troopship to reach Greece and two days after VE Day transported the German commandant and his staff as POWs from Rhodes. She continued to serve

in the eastern Mediterranean, mainly ferrying troops ashore from larger ships, and did not resume her peacetime duties until June 1947 following a refit that raised passenger capacity to 1,800 and trial speed to 24 knots. In June 1949, she was transferred to the Alaska run and on 30 August 1951 survived a collision with Canadian National Railway's *Prince*

Rupert. Just over a year later, on 7 September 1952, she grounded during a gale on Lena Point in the Favourite Channel to the north of Juneau. All on board were safely taken off but as she had struck at low water, the rising tide swamped her stern and she slid off the ledge on which she was impaled and sank in deep water.

The 5,043-grt twin-screw sisters *Yarmouth* and *Evangeline** were built for Eastern Steamship Lines' subsidiary Nova Scotia Steamship Corp by W R Cramp & Sons, Philadelphia, in 1927. Designed by Theodore Ferris, they were among the last ships to be completed by the famous Philadelphia yard and were intended for overnight service between Boston, Massachusetts, and Yarmouth, Nova Scotia. Their profile incorporated a vertical stem and cruiser stern and the extensive superstructure was topped by a single large cowl-topped funnel set between two tall taking masts. Hull dimensions were 378 oa × 55.7 ft on a draught of 20 ft and they were driven at 16 knots by two sets of double-reduction geared turbines producing 7,500 shp. During the Second World War, *Evangeline* was initially chartered by the US government for use in the Caribbean but in 1942 both ships were converted for trooping duties. They returned to their peacetime service in February 1946 and in 1954 were sold to Frank Leslie Fraser (for McCormick Shipping Corp, Panama) and placed on cruises from Miami and Washington, *Yarmouth* briefly as *Yarmouth Castle* and then *Queen of Nassau*. In 1957 she reverted to *Yarmouth Castle* and just *Yarmouth* a year later. In 1961 *Evangeline* was bought back by Eastern Steamship and operated by the Evangeline Steamship Co on cruises from Miami to the Caribbean, later running to Nassau. In 1962 *Yarmouth* was bought by Canadian Stanley B McDonald, for Yarmouth Steamship Co, and used on the West Coast for ten-day cruises from San Francisco to the Seattle World Fair before returning

to Miami-Nassau run alongside her sister. In 1964–5, *Evangeline* was sold to Charade Steamship Co and renamed *Yarmouth Castle* once more but her condition deteriorated and on 13 November she caught fire off Great Stirrup Key, Bahamas, and sank

with the loss of ninety lives. Her sister was briefly renamed *San Andres* in 1966 before being sold to Greece and moved to Piraeus as *Elizabeth A* the following year. She never sailed again and was and broken up in winter 1977–8. (*Miami Herald*)

The 2,125-grt, triple-screw *Princess Elaine* replaced the ageing *Princess Patricia*, originally the world's second turbine ship *Queen Alexandra*, on the Vancouver–Nanaimo day service across the Georgia Strait on 7 May 1928. A product of John Brown, Clydebank, she measured 299 oa × 48.1 ft with 11.5

ft draught and was propelled by three single-reduction geared steam turbines that provided a maximum of just over 19.5 knots on the measured mile at an output of around 7,000 shp. Her normal speed of 16 knots allowed her to complete the forty-mile passage in two hours and fifteen minutes. She

was a steel two-deck vessel with vertical stem and counter stern and although having the customary CPR three funnels, she differed from the larger steamers in her profile with a glazed promenade deck. She left the Clyde on her delivery voyage via Panama on 17 March 1928 and arrived in Victoria on 25 April. She could carry 1,200 passengers but was also designed with motor transport in mind for which she was fitted with a sixty-car garage on the main deck, which had almost 10 ft headroom and was accessed through side doors. She had a few minor scrapes: colliding with the barge *VT 25* at the entrance to Vancouver Harbour on 13 October 1955 and hitting the cargo ship *Alaska Prince* on 11 January 1960. At the end of summer 1951, she was replaced by *Princess of Nanaimo* and the following April was switched to the Gulf Island route in place of *Princess Mary*, but her larger size made manoeuvring difficult in some of the smaller island ports and her lack of success led to withdrawal on 1 October 1962 after a final summer season. On 30 December 1963 she was towed to Blaine, Washington to become a floating restaurant but this failed and in December 1967 she was bought by a Mrs T Rogers and moved to Seattle for similar purposes. This also proved unsuccessful and she was broken up in 1977.

New turbine ships for Irish Sea

The name *Ben-my-Chree* was resurrected by the Isle of Man Steam Packet Co for the third time for its first new ship to be built after the First World War and the largest since her speedy namesake of 1908. Completed in June 1927 by Cammell Laird, Birkenhead, she introduced a new profile with a single large funnel topped by a distinctive cowl and glazed promenade decks. She had a gross measurement of 2,586 tons on hull dimensions of 355 × 46.1 ft and 13.5 ft load draught and was driven at 22.5 knots by two sets of single-reduction steam turbines. In 1932 she was repainted white with green boot-topping for a Roman Catholic charter to Dublin, but this never materialised and her owners decided to keep the livery, which was later applied to *Lady of Man* and *Mona's Queen*. In 1937 she often sailed on the Fleetwood run and was quickly requisitioned as a transport following the outbreak of the Second World War. Moved south to the English Channel, she made several trips to Dunkirk, evacuating 4,095 troops, but after sailing from Folkestone on 2 June with a new naval crew was severely damaged in collision and took no further part. Following repairs, she ran from Scottish ports to the Shetlands, Faroes and Iceland until converted on the Tyne early in 1944 to an infantry landing ship for the Normandy

invasion, where she acted as HQ ship for the 514th Assault Flotilla, putting her US troops ashore at Omaha Beach. She later returned to trooping service in the Dover Strait before release in 1946. Her funnel was shortened in a major overhaul that winter and

the cowl top removed in 1950. At the end of the 1965 season, with her name already assigned to the IOMSP Co's second new car ferry, she was laid up in Liverpool and in December was towed to Bruges to be broken up.

The London, Midland & Scottish Railway ordered three new twin-screw turbine steamers from Wm Denny & Bros, Dumbarton, in October 1926 and *Duke of Lancaster**, *Duke of Argyll* and *Duke of Rothesay* were duly completed in April, May and June 1928, replacing the former Midland Railway steamers on the Heysham–Belfast service. Although the LMS discontinued its Fleetwood–Belfast service when they entered service, they nevertheless perpetuated that run's traditional 'Duke' nomenclature. Quite large ships at just over 3,600 grt, they measured 360 oa × 53.1 ft and featured a three island type hull with a long bridge deck, two raked funnels and masts and a cruiser stern. Two-stage single-reduction geared turbines drove them at 21.5 knots on trials, steam being supplied by six Babcock & Wilcox coal-fired watertube boilers, two of which had automatic stokers. Designed for overnight service, they could berth 307 first-class passengers, the majority in single cabins spread over four decks amidships, and 104 in second class on three decks aft. Total passenger complement was 1,500 and provision was made for the carriage of eight horses and 296 head of cattle. In November 1931, *Duke of Lancaster* caught fire and sank in Heysham Harbour but was raised two months later and rebuilt by Denny between February and June 1932. *Duke of Argyll* and *Duke of Rothesay* had their funnel cowls removed in 1935 and *Duke of Lancaster* two years later. All three were refitted early

in 1936 and third-class accommodation alterations increased tonnage to 3,814 gross. During the Second World War, *Duke of Lancaster* and *Duke of Argyll* became 400-patient hospital ships (Nos 56 and 65) in 1939 and 1941 respectively and in 1942 *Duke of Lancaster* and *Duke of Rothesay* were converted to hand-hoist infantry landing ships, carrying ten LCAs for the Normandy invasion, where they landed some

500 troops at Juno Beach. They returned to service in 1945–6 and in 1955 had the suffix *II* added to their names to allow their original names to pass to three new 'Dukes' under construction. *Duke of Lancaster* was scrapped at Briton Ferry and *Duke of Argyll* at Troon in 1956 and *Duke of Rothesay* at Milford Haven in 1957.

New English Channel tonnage

The 2,288-grt *Worthing**, delivered by Wm Denny & Bros, Dumbarton, on 30 August 1928, was the first steamer ordered for the Newhaven–Dieppe service by the new Southern Railway. In some respects she was a smaller version of the *Isle of Thanet* pair delivered by Denny for the Dover Strait crossing in 1925, and measuring 306 oa × 38.7 ft, her narrower beam was necessary to obtain the higher speed of 24 knots. Her passenger complement was 1,040 persons

in three classes and the accommodation was a great improvement on the earlier *Paris*. Twin sets of Parsons single-reduction turbines provided 16,400 shp on trials and 14,500 shp in service and steam was supplied by four Yarrow oil-fired watertube boilers working on the closed stokehold principle. A near-sister with slightly less draught was ordered as the fifth *Brighton* (inset) early in 1932. Completed the following March, she averaged just under 24.75 knots

during a trial return crossing to Dieppe. She could be distinguished from *Worthing* by bulwarks on her foredeck and an extended bridge house, while the six rear lifeboats were mounted in gravity davits. Both ships were requisitioned in the Second World War, initially as troop transports and then as hospital ships, but *Brighton* was set on fire by a blazing tanker moored nearby in Dieppe on 24 May 1940 and was later bombed and sunk, happily without loss of life. Her sister made five trips to Dunkirk to evacuate the remnants of the British Expeditionary Force and in September was commissioned as HMS *Brigadier*, serving initially as a Fleet Air Arm target ship in 1941 and the following year was converted to an infantry landing ship carrying six LCAs and 180 troops. She took part in the Normandy landings and returned to the Newhaven station after a post-war refit, performing a further decade of service before sale to John S Latsis for use as an inter-island ferry. Painted white with an all-buff funnel, she performed a weekly 17-knot schedule between Piraeus, Samos, Paros, Naxos and Crete, but the hoped-for economies from her lower running speed did not materialise and she was laid up in 1960 and broken up four years later.

Designed to provide the sea link for a new Golden Arrow/Fleche d'Or first-class Pullman train service between London and Paris, the 2,912-grt *Canterbury** was delivered to the Southern Railway by Wm Denny & Bros, Dumbarton, in March 1929. Similar, although slightly beamier than *Isle of Thanet*, of which she was a development, she measured 341.5 oa × 47.1 ft, but her foremast was stepped on the upper deck in front of the superstructure and lifeboats raised in gravity davits. She was driven by two sets of Parsons single-reduction steam turbines fed by four Babcock & Wilcox watertube boilers and on trials averaged just over 22 knots at 8,850 shp during a four-hour run. Initially, she carried just 300 passengers in luxurious accommodation, which included an observation lounge, a 100-seat dining saloon and a palm court. Although a first-class ship, provision was made for second-class passengers (hence her certification for 1,700 persons) and due to the Depression these were carried from 1932 following an extensive refit that raised gross tonnage to 3,071. She attended King George V's Jubilee Review at Spithead in 1935. During the Second World War, she initially served as a troop transport, from December 1940 to April 1942, and had made five trips to Dunkirk during the evacuation in May 1940. She was then briefly employed as a Fleet Air Arm target ship before taking up the Stranraer–Larne service in July 1941. In June 1942, she was withdrawn for conversion to a hand-hoist infantry landing ship, emerging the following February minus her mainmast and with six LCA's slung outboard from

davits. She was based at Cowes with Force J and was at the Normandy landings. A final stint as a military leave ship in the Dover Strait was followed by a peacetime refit by Vickers-Armstrongs, Newcastle, during which she became the first channel steamer to be fitted with radar. She returned to the Golden Arrow service on 15 April 1946, but was replaced by

Invicta in October and was moved to the Folkestone–Calais service, where she remained, apart from a six-month spell from January 1947 on her old Dover route, until switched in summer 1948 to seasonal Folkestone–Boulogne sailings. She was laid up in Dover after making a final crossing on 27 September 1964 and in July 1965 went to Belgium for scrapping.

North Sea

Swedish Lloyd set new standards for North Sea ferry traffic with its 4,342-grt turbine sisters *Suecia** and *Britannia*, completed in 1929 by Swan, Hunter & Wigham Richardson, Newcastle, for the Gothenburg–London run. They were elegant ships with a raised forecastle, long superstructure topped by a tall raked funnel and a counter stern and their ice-strengthened hulls measured 376.3 oa × 50.1 ft on a draught of 20.3 ft. Propulsion was by means of three sets of Parsons single-reduction turbines geared to a single shaft and producing 5,700 shp for a service speed of 17.5 knots. Steam was supplied by four coal-fired, single-ended boilers. Internally, the decor of both ships reflected the countries after which they were named and they could accommodate 220 first-class passengers in cabins amidships and forty-five in second class aft. They were soon found to be prone to rolling and bilge keels were fitted to modify this. In summer they sailed three times a week in both directions reducing to once a week in winter. Tilbury Landing Stage was used for passengers, while cargo was handled up river in Millwall Dock. In 1937 they were converted to oil-firing in Gothenburg but while in the yard, *Suecia* was sunk in March by the newly-launched tanker *Kollbjorg* when it was shifting berth. She was raised and reentered service in June. Sweden was neutral during the Second World War, and both ships were laid up in Gothenburg, but were allowed to make one safe conduct voyage each. In March 1945, they were taken up by the British government for trooping and refugee duties, sailing between Tilbury and Antwerp and Hull and Cuxhaven, but were released in February 1946. After a short refit they resumed their normal service but sailed with white-painted

hulls in 1947. Around 1950 their forecastles were extended to the superstructure and the kingpost forward of the funnel removed and subsequent internal alterations included a new third-class smoking-room aft in 1953 and revised berthing arrangements in 1956; 127 in first-class and 124 in tourist class plus summer dormitory berthing for ninety-two. After a further decade they were both sold in 1966 to Hellenic Mediterranean Lines, renamed *Isthmia* and *Cynthia* and placed in service between Marseilles and Beirut with intermediate calls at Genoa, Piraeus, Alexandria and Port Said. *Isthmia* was laid up at Kynosura in 1970 and sold to Turkish breakers two years later. *Cynthia* was broken up at Savona in 1974.

Ordered by the London & North Eastern Railway from John Brown & Co, Clydebank, for the Harwich–Hook of Holland night service, the 4,218-grt sisters *Vienna**, *Prague* and *Amsterdam* were delivered in 1929–30. Measuring 366 oa × 50.1 ft on a load draught of 15.25 ft, they were the largest UK cross-channel ships yet and their hull design incorporated a long combined forecastle and bridge and a cruiser stern. Two sets of Brown-Curtis turbines fed by five single-ended coal-fired boilers provided a speed of 21 knots. Maximum passenger capacity was 1,500 with overnight berths for 444 in first class, mainly in single cabins amidships, and 104 second class aft in two-berth and four-berth cabins, all fitted with hot and cold running water. The provision of several shops was an innovation and several cars could be carried in the 'tween decks aft. Between 1932 and 1939, *Vienna* made summer weekend cruises to continental ports between Amsterdam and Rouen, for which she was given extra lounge space and an extended promenade deck and she also attended the Jubilee Naval Review at Spithead in July 1935. Early in the Second World War, all three moved to Southampton for trooping duties. *Prague* and *Amsterdam* took part in the Dunkirk evacuation, where the former, laden with about 3,000 French troops, was holed aft and disabled by a near miss on 1 June 1940, but was towed to Deal and beached. Salvaged and fitted with a new stern, she joined *Amsterdam* trooping between Aberdeen and Orkney, but suffered further bomb damage. *Vienna* was requisitioned by the Admiralty on 21 August 1941 and commissioned the following March as a coastal

forces depot ship, serving initially at Alexandria and later at Bizerta, Bone, Malta, Augusta, Taranto and Brindisi. *Amsterdam* was converted to a hospital ship (No 64/430 patients) in 1942 and then to an infantry assault ship in 1943, and was assigned to the US beaches at the Normandy landings, where she worked alongside *Prague* (Hospital Ship No 61). *Amsterdam* was reconverted to a hospital ship but was mined about five miles off Arromanches on 7 August 1944 with the loss of 106 lives. The surviving sisters returned to Harwich in 1945, but while

refitting at Clydebank *Prague* caught fire in March 1948 and sank. Although later raised, she was scrapped at Barrow that autumn. Back from the Mediterranean, *Vienna* acted as troopship but in 1947 was refitted as a British Army of the Rhine (BAOR) leave ship with 1,048 berths; her initial livery of black hull and grey upperworks was later changed to grey hull with blue 'trooping' band and plain yellow funnels. She was withdrawn in July 1960 and towed to Ghent in September for demolition.

First cross-channel motorships

The Belfast Steamship Co, part of the Coast Lines group since 1919, received its first motorship, *Ulster Monarch**, from Harland & Wolff, Belfast, in 1929. Built for the overnight Belfast–Liverpool service, she was also the first large cross-channel steamer to be propelled by a diesel engine and set the pattern for many subsequent Irish Sea ferries. Her design comprised a three-island type hull with long bridge deck and high side-doors in the wells while her two squat funnels with horizontal tops instigated an entirely new profile for cross-channel ships. Her gross tonnage was 3,735 on dimensions of 358.8 oa × 46.2 ft and she was propelled by two Harland & Wolff/B & W single-acting ten-cylinder diesels developing a maximum of 7,500 bhp at 160 rpm for 18 knots. Only 5,000 bhp was required for the nine and a half hour crossing at 16.5–17 knots. Berths were provided for 418 first- and eighty-six third-class passengers and provision was made for 700 tons of cargo. Sisters *Ulster Queen* and *Ulster Prince* were launched in quick succession in March–April but delivery was delayed until 1930 due to industrial action. The trio operated successfully until the outbreak of the Second World War, after which only *Ulster Queen* remained on her route but she was driven ashore in Ramsey Bay in February 1940. The other two were quickly taken up as military transports, *Ulster Monarch* circumnavigating Africa and serving in all the major European theatres but *Ulster Prince* grounded at Nauplion during the evacuation of Greece in April 1941 and was subsequently bombed and burnt out. Meanwhile, *Ulster Queen* had been refloated and converted to an assault landing ship and later acted as a fighter direction ship armed with six 4-in guns. After the war she was laid up but due to

the high cost of reconstruction was broken up in Belgium in 1948. *Ulster Monarch* had returned to the Liverpool–Belfast run in autumn 1946 and the following year was joined by British & Irish's former *Leinster*, which was renamed *Ulster Prince*. Both were withdrawn in October 1966 and after a very successful career of thirty-seven years, *Ulster Monarch* arrived in Ghent on 8 December for demolition.

Mediterranean packets

Completed by Forges & Chantiers de la Méditerranee, La Seyne, in 1928, the 4,654-grt *El Biar* marked a step forward for Compagnie de Navigation Mixte of Marseilles and was loosely based on Compagnie Générale Transatlantique's larger 'Gouverneur Général' class ships. Her two reciprocating engines developed 5,000 ihp for a service speed of 16 knots. Accommodation was provided for sixty-eight first-, 108 second-, and eighty third-class passengers. Considered somewhat old-fashioned and lacking in speed compared with the newer *Els*, she was rebuilt in 1934 with a lengthened hull, shorter funnels and masts, while a Bauer-Wach low pressure turbine was added to her existing machinery, increasing speed to 18 knots. In November 1942, she was found by the Allies in North Africa and put into service. On 20 April 1944, she left Algiers under escort but at dusk the following day was torpedoed and sunk by an enemy aircraft. At the end of August 1929, the La Seyne yard delivered an improved *El Biar* in the shape of the 4,840-grt *El Golea**, instantly recognisable by her two uneven height funnels and cruiser stern. She was the first ship to wear the new Mixte funnel colours of black with two thin red bands surrounding a broad white band bearing the letters CM in black. She measured 370 × 52.6 ft and was propelled by two sets of Parsons double-reduction steam turbines developing 7,000 shp, which gave her a service speed of 18 knots and allowed her to complete the Port Vendres–Algiers

service in twenty-eight hours, some four hours quicker than *El Biar*. Her passenger accommodation provided berths for 91/138/100 in first, second and third classes respectively. In 1930 the enclosed part of her promenade deck and solid bulwark were extended aft to the first lifeboat but on 25 May the following year, while *en route* from Port Vendres to

Algiers, she ran aground in thick fog one mile west of Cap Freu, Majorca. Efforts by *El Biar* to tow her off were unsuccessful but during a strong swell a few days later she refloated herself only to ground again. On 15 June, in a strong mistral, she broke in two between bridge and forward funnel and became a total loss.

The sisters *Cap Corse* and *Ville d'Ajaccio** were delivered to Compagnie Fraissinet, Marseilles, by Ateliers & Chantiers de Bretagne, Nantes, and Chantiers & Ateliers de Provence, Port de Bouc, in March 1929, as the first part of a fleet renewal programme following the retention of the Corsican mail contract for a further twenty years from 1927. Measuring 2,543/2,444 grt on hull dimensions of 269 × 41 ft, they were smaller versions of *Général Bonaparte* with a shorter forecastle and longer raised poop extending from the aft end of the superstructure. Main propulsion comprised a triple-expansion engine with an output of 3,200 ihp for a service speed of 15 knots. Berths were provided for thirty-four first-, sixty-second and thirty-one third-class passengers and in addition they could carry around 250 deck passengers. They served on the Marseilles–Corsica route until taken up as armed patrol boats *P 5* and *P 4* following the outbreak of the Second World War but were returned to Fraissinet in July 1940 and resumed Corsica sailings. *Ville d'Ajaccio* was torpedoed in February 1943 off Saint Tropez but did not sink and managed to reach Ajaccio. *Cap Corse* was not seized by the occupying German forces and survived two torpedo attacks in 1943, but was scuttled at the entrance to the old port in Marseilles on 21 August 1944 as the Germans retreated. Her

sister was used by the Allies until the end of the war but was sold to Compagnie Générale Transatlantique in 1948 and changed her funnel colour from white to red. She was laid up in 1960 following the arrival of the new car ferry *Napoleon* and was sold in September to Far East Corporation of Panama, which renamed her *East Wind* and scrapped her in Hong Kong the following year.

The 1,553-grt *Knight of Malta* was completed by Swan Hunter & Wigham Richardson, Walker-on-Tyne, in December 1929 for Cassar Co of Malta, to operate a mail and passenger service between Valletta and the Sicilian port of Syracuse. She was an elegant two-funnelled ship built on the three-island principle with vertical stem and counter stern and measured 270 oa × 37.3 ft on 16 ft draught. A 328-nhp triple-expansion engine drove a single screw and steam was supplied by three single-ended tubular boilers. Service speed was 15 knots. Accommodation was provided for sixty-three first-class passengers in single and double cabins and thirty second class in four-berth cabins aft. In addition, sixteen emigrants could be housed forward and she could carry around 2,000 tons of cargo. Her funnel colours were originally white with black top but the white was later changed to red to avoid confusion

with the Italian Tirrenia ships, which called at Valletta. During the Second World War, she was taken over by the Ministry of War Transport, placed under the management of the London firm of Harris & Dixon,

and used initially as an armed boarding vessel. She later saw service as a naval stores carrier, but she was wrecked two miles from Raz Azzaz in Libya on 2 March 1941.

War reparation motorship for Corsica service

The 2,406-grt *Cyrnos*, completed in 1929 by Deshimag's AG Weser yard in Bremen for the French government as part of First World War reparations, was assigned to Compagnie Fraissinet for the Corsican mail service. She was the first French ship to have a maierform hull with its distinctive curved bow and also double-acting MAN diesel engines. A two-deck ship, she measured 309.5 oa × 41.1 ft on 17 ft draught and her hull incorporated a raised forecastle and poop and a cruiser stern. She was designed for overnight service and sleeping berths were provided for sixty-two first-class and sixty-six second-class passengers, the latter below first on the main and lower decks, while twenty-four third class were housed on the lower deck forward. Her twin six-cylinder engines had a combined output of 3,700 bhp, giving 16.5 knots on half loaded trials but only 3,300 bhp was required for a loaded service speed of 15 knots. On the outbreak of the Second World War, she was requisitioned as the armed patrol boat *P 2* with five 100-mm guns but was seized by German forces in January 1943 becoming patrol boat *SG 13*. She was torpedoed by an allied aircraft but after repair became a minelayer. On 21 August 1944, she was scuttled in Marseilles by the retreating Germans but was refloated in 1945 and subjected to a major reconstruction that saw her forecastle extended and passenger complement raised to 151 in first, ninety-nine in third and 350 on deck. When almost ready she sank during a violent storm at La Ciotat on 26 September 1947. She was raised, but before final completion was transferred in

May 1948 to the ownership of Compagnie Générale Transatlantique, which had taken over the Corsican ferry services. She suffered machinery problems and was re-engined during winter 1952–3. She was broken up at La Seyne in 1966.

Spanish and Italian motorships

In a fleet reconstruction programme, Compania Trasmediterránea ordered three ships from Cantiere Navale Triestino, Monfalcone. The largest and first to be completed was *Infanta Cristina* (4602 grt) destined for the Canary Islands run, but sisters *Infante Don Jaime** and *Principe Alfonso* delivered in 1929 and 1930 were intended to maintain the Barcelona–Balearic Islands service. They measured 3,946/3,959 grt respectively on dimensions of 332 oa × 49 ft with a maximum draught of just over 21 ft and were propelled by twin eight-cylinder four-stroke single-acting B & W diesels with a maximum output of 6,300 bhp, which gave a service speed of around 17 knots. Passenger capacity was ninety-four, seventy-eight and ninety-two in three classes. Following the creation of the Second Republic in 1931, they were renamed *Ciudad de Barcelona* and *Ciudad de Palma* respectively and transferred to a Barcelona–Cadiz–Canaries service. They were soon caught up in the Civil War and on 30 May 1937, *Ciudad de Barcelona* was torpedoed and sunk off Malgrat near Tordera by the Nationalist submarine *General Sanjurjo*, purchased from the Italian navy. Of the 312 passengers on board, 187 were lost along with four crew members. *Ciudad de Cadiz*, the former *Infante Cristina*, was also torpedoed, in the Aegean on 15 August, but *Ciudad de Palma* survived after acting as a Nationalist armed merchant cruiser and hospital ship. She also came through the Second World War unscathed and resumed the Canaries service with occasional stints

on the Barcelona–Palma run. She grounded at Cape Cala Figuera near Palma on 1 April 1953, but was refloated after five days and repaired in Valencia by UN di Levante. In later years she served on the

Seville–Canaries run before its termination and then ran from Barcelona to Mahon, Ibiza and Valencia as well as from Alicante to Ibiza before broken up in Villanueva y Geltrú in 1968.

In 1929 Ansaldo, Sestri Ponente, completed three 3,000-grt motor ferries for Compagnia Italiana Transatlantica for a daily government subsidised service between Civitavecchia and the Sardinian port of Terranova (old name for Olbia). *Caralis*, *Attilio Deffenu** and *Olbia* had flush hulls and single funnels and measured 324 × 43.8 on 16.3ft draught. *Caralis* was driven by two Tosi six-cylinder diesels and the other two by two MAN three-cylinder double-acting diesels, all three developing 3,000 bhp for a trials speed of over 15.5 knots and around 14 knots in service. Passenger capacity was seventy-six in first-, eighty-two in second- and eighty in third-class accommodation while four holds, two forward and two aft, provided space for around 1,000 tons of cargo. Their owner was one of several companies nationalised and absorbed into Tirrenia SA di Navigazione in December 1936. All three were lost in the course of the Second World War while acting as armed merchant cruisers. *Attilio Deffenu* was the first to go when torpedoed by the British submarine HMS *Thrasher* some twenty miles east of Brindisi in 40 37N 18 27E on 25 November 1941. *Caralis* was damaged during an air raid on Leghorn on 15 May 1943 and was sunk in a further attack on the 28th. The wreck

was later salvaged and broken up. *Olbia* suffered a similar fate to *Attilio Deffenu* at the hands of HMS

United on 20 June 1943 at 37 35N 16 05E, about twenty miles south of Cape Spartivento.

CHAPTER
8
The 1930s – Depression and More Motorships

The 1930s was a somewhat turbulent decade that opened in the aftermath of the Wall Street Crash, suffered from the lengthy economic crisis of the Great Depression and ended with Europe once again embroiled in war. Despite this, the development of cross-channel and short-sea passenger ships continued apace with over fifty vessels completed during the period. Maierform hulls were employed in a second Corsican ferry and to a less marked extent in the Southern Railway's *Isle of Sark*, which also pioneered the use of gyro-controlled, retractable stabilising fins developed jointly by Wm Denny & Bros of Dumbarton and Brown Bros of Edinburgh.

Turbo-electric drive was adopted by Union Steamship Co of New Zealand for its inter-island ferry *Rangatira* and France built several advanced ships for North African service. Diesel power continued to win new converts and just a few years apart Bergen Line's *Venus* of 1931 and the Belgian government's *Prince Baudouin* of 1934 held the title of the world's fastest motorship, the latters' trial speed of over 25 knots causing a sensation and proving that the diesel engine was also suited to the propulsion of small, high-speed vessels. Second-generation motor vessels appeared on both the Irish Sea and the North Sea and in 1939 Zeeland Line introduced its advanced diesel-driven *Koningin Emma* pair, having switched directly from reciprocating engines without ever owning a turbine-driven ship. As a portent of things to come, the same year saw the completion of the Denny-built *Princess Victoria*, the United Kingdom's first stern-loading car ferry and first railway-owned cross-channel motorship.

Note: An asterisk in a caption indicates the vessel shown in the photograph.

New turbines for the English Channel and Irish Sea

In 1928, the Belgian government ordered two new turbine steamers from Société Cockerill to cope with extra traffic arising from the Antwerp and Liege exhibitions scheduled for 1930. The 3,088-grt *Prinses Astrid* and *Prince Leopold** were delivered early in 1930 and a repeat order led to *Prince Charles* and *Prinses Josephine Charlotte* following later that year. Identical sisters, they were the largest Belgian channel ships yet, measuring 347 oa (360 × 48) × 46.2 ft and were propelled by two sets of single-reduction geared turbines developing 15,400 shp for a contract speed of 23.5 knots. Steam was supplied by six Babcock & Wilcox oil-fired boilers with a high working pressure, which, coupled with superheating, made for very economical operation. Beamier than preceding ships, they had a four-deck-high terraced front to their superstructure and carried their boats in gravity davits that combined to make their two short funnels even more unobtrusive. Passenger capacity was around 1,400. *Prince Charles* visited the Pool of London with members of the Ligue Maritime Belge in 1931 and all performed successfully until the outbreak of war in 1939, when Dover was closed and a single daily service to Folkestone substituted. Soon all four were sent to Southampton and used for evacuation duties from north-west France and the Channel Islands; *Prinses Josephine Charlotte* after transporting internees from Liverpool to the Isle of Man. They were then converted to infantry landing ships (small); *Prince Charles* and *Prince Leopold* in Devonport and the

others in Falmouth, and were commissioned into the Royal Navy in March and May 1941 respectively. They carried eight infantry landing craft mounted in large hand-operated gravity davits and were sent north to Inverary for Combined Operations training. Thereafter, despite frequent mechanical problems, they performed invaluable service landing troops at Vaagso Island, Dieppe, Gela and Licata (Sicily), Salerno (Italy) and Normandy (Gold, Sword and Omaha beaches). During the follow-up to the latter operation, *Prince Leopold* was torpedoed on 29 July 1944 by *U 621* and capsized under tow south-east of the Nab Tower. The surviving three ended the war on trooping duties, with

Prinses Josephine Charlotte helping with the liberation of the Channel Islands, and were released in 1946. On 22 June 1949, *Prinses Josephine Charlotte* hit a mine about four miles off Dunkirk and sank on an even keel with just her masts and funnels protruding above the surface. Five lives were lost in the explosion and salvage attempts were abandoned on 20 July after her keel had broken in two. She was sold to L Engelen for scrap and towed to Boom, where she arrived on 10 January 1951. *Prince Charles*, by then the last steamship in the Belgian Marine fleet, served for a further decade and was broken up at Hoboken in 1960–61.

Rothschild-owned Société Anonyme de Gérance et d'Armement (SAGA) ordered its first new steamers from Forges & Chantiers de la Méditerranée, Le Havre, in 1929. Named after two well-known holiday destinations, the flush-hulled 3,047-grt *Cote d'Azur** was completed in 1930 and sister *Cote d'Argent* in 1932, making her first crossing between Calais and Dover on 3 April. Remarkably similar in design and looks to the Southern Railway's *Isle of Thanet* pair, the only difference lay in the many more large windows on the main passenger deck and a smaller bridge deck resulting in all eight lifeboats at the same level. Although having the same 45 ft beam as the British pair, they were somewhat shorter in length at just under 326 ft. Main machinery was also similar, but steam was supplied by four oil-fired watertube boilers by Rauber & Luquet. Power output however was considerably greater at around 14,000 shp for a speed of 23 knots. They could be distinguished from one another by *Cote d'Azur* having a taller funnel with deeper black top separated from the white lower portion by a small blue metal band, while that of her sister was silver in colour. Passenger complement was 900 persons in first class and a further 500 in second class. During the height of the Great Depression, their owners tried to sell them

to the UK's Southern Railway but this was vetoed by the French Ministry of Merchant Marine for reasons of national prestige. In May 1940, *Cote d'Azur* was requisitioned to evacuate troops and refugees from Flushing and Ostend, but while performing a similar task at Dunkirk, was bombed and sunk on the 27th. She was raised by the occupying Germans in 1941 and converted to the minelayer *Ostmark*, operating in the

Baltic minus her mainmast. On the night of 21 April 1945, she was surprised by RAF Mosquitos west of Anholt and sunk. Meanwhile, her sister had also been converted to a minelayer at St Nazaire after seizure in a damaged state by the advancing Germans while assisting in the evacuation of La Pallice in 1940. Under the name *Elsass* she was mined and sunk off Namsos on 3 June 1944.

The Southern Railway's 2,143-grt *Isle of Jersey** and *Isle of Guernsey* were delivered by Wm Denny & Bros in January and March 1930, having comfortably reached their contract speed of 19.5 knots during five- and six-hour trial runs. Designed to meet increasing demand for both day and night service they measured 306 oa × 42.1 ft and 12.5 ft draught and were similar to *Dinard* and *St Briac*, but differed in having extended bulwarks aft and the second and third pairs of boats carried in raised davits. Main engines were the familiar Parsons geared turbines but they had three single-ended return-tube Scotch boilers. Their success in service led to the delivery in January 1932 of third sister, *Isle of Sark*, distinguished by longer forward bulwarks and the first UK example of a curved maierform stem. At Denny's suggestion, she had a different boiler arrangement and two years later she made history as the first vessel to successfully demonstrate the new Denny-Brown stabilising fins. The two earlier ships were quickly converted to hospital ships in the Second World War; *Isle of Jersey* was based at Scapa Flow and *Isle of Guernsey* assisted in the Dunkirk evacuation until forced out by damage on 30 May 1940. After briefly serving as a Fleet Air Arm target ship, she was converted to a small infantry assault ship in 1943, rejoining her sister at the Normandy landings. *Isle of Sark* maintained the Channel Islands run until 28 June 1940 and was moored in St Peter Port during the air raid prior to the German occupation. After a spell on the Irish Sea, she became a radar training ship and finally an anti-aircraft ship. After the war *Isle of Guernsey* reopened

the Newhaven–Dieppe service and then the Channel Islands service on 25 June 1945. In 1959 *Isle of Jersey* was sold to Mohammed Senussi Giabor and left the Tyne for Tripoli as *Libda* on 29 April, but a hoped-for Hadj pilgrim contract went to John Latsis instead and she was eventually scrapped at La Spezia in 1963. *Isle of Sark* was withdrawn in November 1960 and sold to be broken up at Ghent. The British Transport Commission closed the Southampton service on 12 May 1969 and *Isle of Guernsey* was moved to Weymouth, where she made a few day excursions to Guernsey including some from Torquay. She made her last sailing on 16 June and followed her sister to Ghent.

The Great Western Railway commissioned Alexander Stephen & Sons, Linthouse to build a new *St Patrick* to replace a namesake destroyed by fire in April 1929. Registered to the Fishguard & Rosslare Railways & Harbours Co and wearing its funnel colours of red with a black top, she was intended to operate on both the Fishguard and Weymouth stations. She measured 1,922 grt on dimensions of 281.3 × 41.1 ft and 14 ft draught and was propelled by two sets of single-reduction geared steam turbines developing 4,720 shp for a maximum of 22 knots and 19 knots in service; steam was supplied by four single-ended boilers. Externally, she differed from the earlier *St Julien* pair in having her forecastle extended to the superstructure and a shorter, broader single funnel while, internally, she had an extra watertight bulkhead, making eleven in all, and also diesel generators. Accommodation was arranged for a maximum of 913 passengers with 216 berths in first class and 116 in third class. She made her first departure from Weymouth on 18 April 1930, following a three-week delay due to rudder damage incurred during her initial berthing at the port, but on 5 April 1932 in thick fog she struck the Frouquie Rock on Kaines Reef near Corbière on the south-west corner of Jersey and flooded her engine room. She was towed to St Aubins Bay by *St Julien* and then to St Helier the following day by *Princess Ena* and was later repaired at Birkenhead. Soon after war broke out in 1939, she was briefly used for English

Channel trooping duties before returning to her Irish Sea service, but when approaching Fishguard on 13 June 1941 was dive bombed by enemy aircraft and broke in two, sinking with the loss of thirty lives including her master.

Motor vessel for the Irish Republic

The City of Cork Steam Packet Co's new motor vessel *Innisfallen* was completed at Belfast by Harland & Wolff in June 1930. At 3,019 grt she was smaller than the Belfast Steamship Co's trio, but was similar in design apart from her mainmast placed in the after well as opposed to the aft end of the bridge deck. Her hull measurements were 321 × 45.7 ft, but she had the same engines as the Belfast ships and a similar speed of 18 knots. She replaced *Killarney* on the Cork–Fishguard service and in February 1936 sailed for a few weeks in Burns & Laird colours on its Belfast–Glasgow overnight service in order to familiarise that company's crew members with motor vessel operation prior to the arrival of the new *Royal Ulsterman* and *Royal Scotsman*. In 1937 she was transferred to the newly-established British & Irish SP Co (1936) Ltd. The Fishguard service was suspended following the outbreak of the Second World War and *Innisfallen* was transferred to the Liverpool run. Inbound to the Mersey during an air raid on 21 December 1940 she hit a mine and sank off the entrance to Canada Dock. All 143 passengers were saved, but two crew members and two cattlemen were lost.

Isle of Man centenary ship

Delivered in the year that the Isle of Man Steam Packet Co celebrated its 100th anniversary, *Lady of Mann* was built by Vickers-Armstrongs, Barrow and launched by the Duchess of Atholl on 3 March 1930. At 3,104 grt, she eclipsed *Ben-my-Chree* of 1908 to become the largest steamer by tonnage built for the company, but her dimensions of 371 oa × 50.2 ft on 13 ft draught were less than those of *Ben-my-Chree*. During trials on the Arran measured mile on 13 June, her two sets of single-reduction steam turbines developed 11,500 shp for a speed of 22.8 knots although this was often exceeded in service. She replaced *Viking* on the Douglas–Fleetwood station and her hull was repainted white for the 1933 season. Soon after the outbreak of war she was requisitioned in autumn 1939 and sent south for trooping duties. During the evacuation of Dunkirk in May–June 1940, she rescued 4,262 persons, many of them casualties, before continuing her evacuation duties further west, sailing to Le Havre, Cherbourg and Brest. In August she steamed north to undertake ferry duties between Scottish ports and the Northern Isles, including the Faroes. In preparation for the Normandy landings, she was converted in April 1944 to an infantry landing ship with six hand-hoisted LCAs and her mainmast removed. On D-Day she acted as HQ ship for the 521st Assault Flotilla in the Juno sector. Her war ended where it began, with Dover Strait trooping duties. *Lady of Mann* was released in March 1946 and reconditioned by Cammell Laird; she reentered service in mid-June. After serving the island for over forty-one years, this much-loved ship left Douglas for the last time on 17 August 1971 bound for lay-up in Barrow, from where she was towed to Dalmuir at the end of December for scrapping.

New Mediterranean tonnage

The elegant 2,600-grt *Ile de Beauté** was the second war reparation ship built for service with Compagnie Fraissinet, Marseilles, at the AG Weser yard in Bremen. Completed in 1930, she measured 335 oa × 43.3 ft, and like *Cyrnos* also featured a maierform bow but differed in having a white flush-decked hull, which gave a yacht-like appearance, and the forward part of her promenade deck enclosed. Her main propulsion was also different comprising two steam turbines with a combined output of 5,500 shp, which provided a service speed of 20 knots. Overnight accommodation was arranged for forty first- and thirty-two second-class passengers and an additional 400 were carried in deck class. Just before the start of the Second World War, she formed part of a large heavily-escorted convoy of French ferries that sailed from Marseilles to Oran on 3 September 1939. She was seized by the Germans on 18 January 1943 and converted into the Kriegsmarine's first night fighter direction ship, *Kreta*. Her mainmast was removed and a large Freya 303 radar scanner put in its place and she also had a smaller Würzburg 213 dish scanner mounted on a platform behind her funnel. Her formast was shortened and supported by a reinforcing strut and her armament consisted of four 105-mm and two 75-mm guns. *Kreta* was only in service for a short while and when engaged in evacuating German personnel from Sardinia, was torpedoed and sunk on 21 September by HMS *Unseen* about seven miles north-east of the island of Capraia.

In 1930 Florio Società Italiana di Navigazione took delivery of the 5,400-grt motor ferries, *Città di Napoli** and *Città di Tunisi* from Cantieri del Tirreno/Riva Trigoso in January and May, and *Città di Genova* and *Città di Palermo* from C N Riuniti/Palermo in August and December. Heavily subsidised, they were designed for a Naples-Palermo express service extending once a week to Tunis and Tripoli. Distinctive ships, they measured 388 × 51 ft and were driven by the first Tosi two-stroke diesels comprising twin six-cylinder units developing 8,000 bhp for a service speed of 17 knots. Passenger capacity was 600 in three classes. In March 1932 Florio merged with Compagnia Italiana Transatlantica to form Tirrenia Flotta Riunite Florio-Citras which became Tirrenia Societa Anonima di Navigazione in 1936. In 1938 *Città di Napoli* was part of a convoy carrying troops to Libya and during the Second World War all four were requisitioned as auxiliary cruisers (D1-D4). They were engaged in escorting North Africa convoys and on 27 November 1942 *Città di Tunisi* rammed and sank the destroyer escort *Circe* north of Sicily. On her return trip two days later she was mined off Cape San Vito, north-west Sicily, and sank off the Aeolian Islands. On 5 January 1942 *Citta di Palermo* was torpedoed with the loss of 921 lives by HM Submarine *Proteus* northwest of Cape Ducato and on 21 January 1943 *Città di Genova* met a similar fate with the loss of 173 lives at the hands of HMS *Tigris* about 25 miles west of Saseno. *Città di Tunisi* was seized by the Germans after Italy capitulated in 1943 and renamed *Heidelberg* but was found abandoned at San Rocco in 1945. She re-entered commercial service in 1947 and in 1951–52 was rebuilt with two eight-cylinder Ansaldo diesels (8,000 bhp, 15 knots), passenger capacity being reduced to 486 in four classes. She continued to run mainly to Sicilian ports, latterly as a three-class ship, and finally left Naples in November 1971 for scrapping in Trieste.

Canadian developments

Bay of Fundy

Increasing the traffic levels led Canadian Pacific Railway to order a new vessel for its Bay of Fundy service in 1929. Once again the company turned to Wm Denny & Bros, Dumbarton, and the 4,035-grt *Princess Helene* took to the water on 12 May 1930, ran trials on 5 August, when she averaged nearly 19.5 knots over eight hours and arrived at St John, New Brunswick on the 22nd, entering service five days later. To reduce noise and vibration to a minimum, two Parsons three-stage single-reduction steam turbines were chosen, with steam supplied by three Yarrow watertube boilers but one of these was soon replaced by one of a new design by CPR's superintendent engineer. She was licensed to carry 1,000 passengers and up to forty-five cars in summer, ten fewer in winter. Public rooms included an observation lounge forward, dining saloon and large smoking room aft while forty-four first-class staterooms, including two suites, were provided to allow passengers to spend the night aboard before the early morning departure from St John. She made two return trips daily with an extra sailing on summer Sundays and the passage to Digby lasted around three hours. In 1950 she underwent a major overhaul, which included interior refurbishment and the installation of an automatic fire-fighting sprinkler system. After thirty-two years' service, she was withdrawn in February 1963 and replaced by the west coast car ferry *Princess of Nanaimo*. Three months later she was bought by the Chandris

subsidiary Marivic Navigation Co and left St John on 11 July for the Mediterranean as *Helene*. Following two years' idleness, during which plans to run her as a car ferry between Piraeus and Venice were considered, she was rebuilt at Perama as the cruise ship *Carina II* with a new curved stem, a single streamlined mast and larger funnel. She sailed

between Piraeus and Venice and in November 1967 the *II* suffix was dropped when Chandris' *Carina* (the former *Mona's Queen*) was renamed *Fiesta*. She was transferred within the Chandris group to International Cruises SA and continued to operate until autumn 1972, when she was laid up in Eleusis Bay. She was broken up at Perama 1977.

West Coast rivals

In 1930, the Canadian Pacific Railway took delivery of its final pair of three-funnelled coastal steamers from Fairfield Shipbuilding & Engineering Co. The 5,251-grt *Princess Elizabeth** and *Princess Joan* measured 366 oa × 52.1 ft and, designed for the Vancouver–Victoria overnight service, were fitted with quiet running reciprocating machinery in the form of two quadruple-expansion engines that developed a maximum of 3,600 ihp. The seven-hour night crossing only required around 12 knots but on trials both ships made 16–17 knots. They sailed from the Clyde via the Panama Canal and arrived in Victoria thirteen days apart in May. They could carry 1,000 passengers and forty-eight cars, which were driven on and off through side doors while cargo lifts were also installed. On 24 February 1959, *Princess Joan* closed the night run that had lasted nearly fifty years and following a period of lay-up both ships were sold to Epirotiki Steamship Co of Piraeus in December 1960. After sailing to Greece, they were renamed *Pegasus* and *Hermes* respectively and rebuilt with a curved stem and single large funnel. They were placed in a seasonal service carrying up to 700 passengers between Venice and Piraeus via Patras

and the Corinth Canal. The route was later extended southwards to Haifa and they were also used for occasional cruises. In 1970 *Hermes* was sold to the Nigerian government for use as a floating hotel in Lagos, changing her location in October 1973 to Nigg Bay, Cromarty Firth for new owners L Dupes & Associates of Cyprus to house oil-platform construction workers. There she was reunited with

her sister, which had been chartered for the same purpose earlier in the year by Brown & Root and renamed *Highland Queen*. In 1974 *Princess Joan* was sold to Loima Shipping and broken up at Inverkeithing and the following year her sister was bought by Highland Shipping Co and was towed from the Tees in March 1976 for demolition in Bruges.

Canadian National Railway's fast and expensive sisters *Prince Robert*, *Prince David** and *Prince Henry* were completed in 1930 by Cammell Laird, Birkenhead, to compete with Canadian Pacific's 'Princesses' on the Vancouver–Seattle–Victoria run and also between Vancouver and Alaska. Measuring 6,893 grt on dimensions of 366.4 x 57.1 ft, they also had three funnels but an extra deck combined with a vertical stem, short forecastle and cruiser stern gave them a somewhat dumpy appearance. They were driven by six Parson's single-reduction geared turbines, fed by six Yarrow watertube boilers, which developed 19,000 shp for a trial speed 23 knots – 16,500 shp sufficient for 20 knots in service. They could carry 334 first-class passengers and seventy deck passengers and several cars. Their debut coincided with the start of the Depression and this combined with high running costs and strong Canadian Pacific Railway retaliation led to their withdrawal and layup in Vancouver in 1931. The following year *Prince David* and *Prince Henry* were moved to the east coast and with white hulls were used for cruises from Canada to the Caribbean and *Prince Henry* later ran between Boston and Bermuda, where she grounded heavily at St George's on 13 March 1934. In 1937 she was chartered by Clarke Steamships of Quebec, which bought her the following year and refitted her to carry 335 cruise passengers. With yellow funnel with four narrow blue bands, she cruised from Miami to the Caribbean during the winter and from New York to Montreal in summer. *Prince David* returned to the west coast and *Prince David* was laid up in Halifax in 1937. Early in the Second World War, all three were requisitioned by the Royal Canadian Navy and converted to armed merchant cruisers. Additional bulkheads and a new naval type bridge were installed and the two forward funnels trunked into a single larger funnel. Initially based in Bermuda for Caribbean patrols, they returned to the west coast and *Prince Robert* captured the German freighter *Weser* off Manzanillo on 25 September 1940. In preparation for the Normandy landings, *Prince Robert* and

Prince David were converted to 550-troop landing ships, carrying six LCAs and two LCMs. On D-Day they landed Canadian troops at Juno Beach and later took part in the invasion of southern France. *Prince Henry* was altered to an anti-aircraft ship in 1943, serving in the Atlantic and Mediterranean and later visiting Australasia before repatriating Canadian troops from Hong Kong after VJ Day. She was bought by the UK government in 1946 and renamed *Empire Parkeston* (inset) for the Harwich–Hook of Holland leave service, sailing initially with black hull and funnels and grey upperworks. Her funnels were later fitted with Thornycroft tops and she adopted troopship colours of grey hull with blue band and yellow funnels after taking part in the ill-fated Suez invasion in 1956. Withdrawn in September 1961 when troop movements were transferred to aircraft, she was broken up at La Spezia in 1962. *Prince Robert* and *Prince David* were sold in 1947 to Chandris subsidiary Charlton Steam Shipping Co and converted to emigrant ships for the International Refugee Organization. Refitted to carry 750 passengers in austere, mainly dormitory, accommodation, they emerged in 1948 with ten lifeboats in gravity davits as *Charlton Sovereign* and *Charlton Monarch*. The latter's engine was sabotaged on 11 June 1948 on her first voyage to South America and she was towed back to the Clyde. She was scrapped at Briton Ferry in 1951–2 after lying in Barry for three years. *Charlton Sovereign* sailed from the UK to Australia and South America and then ran between Naples and the Americas. She switched to Panama registry in 1951 and even carried Hadj pilgrims from North Africa to Jeddah before sale to Fratelli Grimaldi, who rebuilt her as *Lucania* for a Genoa–Central America emigrant service. She was given a new raked stem, which increased her length by 50 ft, and extra superstructure topped by two new blue funnels with white bands. She sailed for Grimaldi's Sicula Oceanica for sixteen years before scrapping at Vado Ligure in 1962.
(Main photograph Edward Radcliffe)

Irish Sea turbines

The London, Midland & Scottish Railway twin-screw channel steamer *Princess Margaret* replaced the old *Princess Maud* on the Stranraer–Larne service when delivered by Wm Denny in March 1931. A ship of 2,838 grt, she measured 324 oa × 47.1 ft and had a flush-decked hull with vertical stem and cruiser stern topped by two raked masts and a long midships deckhouse mounting a large single funnel. She was propelled by two sets of Parsons two-stage single-reduction geared turbines and steam was supplied by four Babcock & Wilcox coal-burning watertube boilers. On trials, she exceeded the 20-knot contract speed by just over half a knot with her engines producing 7,462 shp at 269 rpm and reached a maximum of just under 21 knots. She could carry

668 first-class passengers (107 berthed) on four decks amidships and 553 third-class passengers aft in addition to 236 cattle, thirty-seven horses and 37,850 cu ft of cargo. The advent of the new car ferry *Princess Victoria* in 1939 saw her transferred to the Heysham–Belfast service to supplement the 'Dukes' at weekends but she reverted to the Stranraer station when *Princess Victoria* was requisitioned on the outbreak of war. In 1944 she made several trips to the Normandy beaches as an assault landing ship. During a refit by D & W Henderson in winter 1950–1, she was modernised and converted to oil-burning and another modernisation occurred in 1956. In mid-1960 she was placed under the management of Caledonian Steam Packet Co (Irish services).

Following the arrival of the car ferry *Caledonian Princess*, she was sold in March 1962 to Shun Tak Shipping Co, Hong Kong, and upon refit was given a new funnel and renamed *Macao*. She sailed on the Hong Kong–Macao ferry service, but was laid up with damage sustained in a typhoon in August 1971 and was scrapped locally in 1974.

The Great Western Railway ordered two larger versions of *St Patrick* from Cammell Laird & Co, Birkenhead, and these were completed as *St Andrew** and *St David* in 1932. Their gross measurement was 2,702 tons on dimensions of 338.5 oa × 46.7 ft and they were intended to operate on the Fishguard–Rosslare service, being registered to and bearing the red funnel colours of the Fishguard & Rosslare Railways & Harbours Co. Two sets of oil-fired geared turbines gave them a speed of 21 knots and they could carry a maximum of 1,050 passengers. Both were requisitioned early in the Second World War for conversion to hospital carriers Nos 24 and 27 with 267 beds for patients and accommodation for fifty-eight medical staff. They were initially based at Newhaven and took part in the evacuation of Dunkirk but in June 1943 were sent to the Mediterranean and based at Malta. While assisting at the Anzio landings, they were bombed some twenty-five miles off the beachhead during the night of 24 January 1944, despite correct lighting and *St David* was sunk by a guided bomb with the loss of fifty-five lives and *St Andrew* damaged along with *Leinster*. *St Andrew* later moved to the Adriatic, sailing between Bari and Ancona but hit a mine in September and was towed to Taranto. She returned to her builders in February 1945 and reopened the Fishguard–Rosslare service in May 1947. During an extensive refit in 1955, her original masts were replaced by light tripod masts abaft the bridge and at the end of the boat deck to allow more cars to be loaded; gross tonnage was raised to

3,035. In winter 1963–4, *St Andrew* was altered to enable cars to be driven on through side doors in Fishguard instead of crane loaded, which continued at Rosslare until June 1965. The white letters FR were added to her funnel and, alternating with *St David*, she introduced a new day service complementing the traditional overnight service. She adopted Sealink's blue hull in 1965 and made her final regular sailing on 30 December 1966. She was then placed in reserve. With *Duke of Rothesay* scheduled to replace her, *St Andrew* was laid up in Holyhead in early 1967 and three months later was sold for demolition in Antwerp.

Completed by Wm Denny & Bros for the London, Midland & Scottish Railway in February 1933, *Princess Maud* was an improved version of running mate *Princess Margaret*. Her dimensions were marginally greater at 330 oa × 49.1 ft, giving a gross tonnage of 2,886. The main external differences were foredeck bulwarks extended to the foremast, a more enclosed superstructure with extended bridge deck and six rather than eight lifeboats while internally she was fitted with automatic stokers, which had been successfully fitted to *Duke of Lancaster* the previous year. Her fire precautions were also more extensive than any previous Denny ship and included an automatic sprinkler system. Passenger capacity was 1,250 with 223 berths catering for both classes. Early in 1939, she was refitted by Denny and played a part in the Dunkirk evacuation, being the second last ship to leave. Thereafter trooping duties occupied her until November 1943. She was then converted to an infantry assault ship with six hand-hoisted LCAs, and as such took part in the Normandy landings in June 1944. In 1946 she was converted to oil-firing and resumed sailings on 1 August, but the following year was transferred to the LMS Holyhead–Dun Laoghaire service when the ageing *Cambria* and *Hibernia* were laid up due to coal shortages; she was then permanently based at the Anglesey port as reserve ship. In summer 1951, *Princess Maud* sailed on the Southampton–Guernsey service for two months and apart from reserve duties on the Holyhead and Stranraer runs, also relieved *Great Western* on the Fishguard–Waterford service. Replaced by the new

car ferry *Holyhead Ferry 1* in 1965, she was sold to Lefkosia Compania Naviera SA of Cyprus. Refitted with side doors for loading cars and renamed *Venus*, she sailed under the management of Cyprus Sea Cruises (Limassol) on a weekly schedule linking Brindisi, Piraeus, Limassol and Haifa. In summer 1969, she was sold to Burmeister & Wain for use as an accommodation ship under the name *Nybo* and was towed to Bilbao for demolition in January 1973.

First motorship for Bergen Line

The 5,406-grt *Venus* was Bergen Line's response to competition from Swedish Lloyd's *Suecia* and *Britannia* on the Gothenburg–London service, which provided a fast rail connection to Oslo. Delivered by Elsinore Shipbuilding & Engineering Co in spring 1931, she was the first motorship on the Bergen–Newcastle service and measured 412 oa x 54.2 ft on a draught of 20 ft. Her twin ten-cylinder B & W diesels developed 10,250 bhp for a service speed of over 19 knots and on the Hveen measured mile in the Oslofjord she reached 20.5 knots at 11,000 bhp, making her briefly the fastest motorship in the world. She was the largest packet in regular North Sea service and introduced a two funnelled profile to the nineteen-hour route, sailing twice a week in both directions with up to 201 first- and seventy-six second-class passengers. In January 1937, she rescued the crew of the Norwegian tramp *Trym* in a gale and on the return trip helped her running mate *Jupiter* to save the crew of the Haugesund-registered *Veni*. Laid up early in the Second World War due to excessive war risk insurance demand, she was seized by the Germans in 1940 and in March 1941 handed to the Kriegsmarine for conversion to a submarine depot/target ship based in the Baltic. On 15 April, she was sunk during an Allied air raid on Hamburg but was raised in 1945 and towed

to Elsinore for rebuilding (*above right*). A new bow section with raked stem and an extra deck were fitted in the German-built drydock at Aarhus and she was given larger funnels and new overnight accommodation for 135 first- and 278 tourist-class passengers. Garage space for thirty cars was also provided. She reentered service in May 1948 and that December inaugurated a regular series of winter cruises from Plymouth to Madeira and Teneriffe carrying 260 passengers in one class. In November 1950 she undertook two fourteen-day private charter cruises from Liverpool and Dublin to the Mediterranean and three years later was fitted with stabilisers. On 23 March 1955, she was blown onto rocks in Plymouth in a gale but was refloated three days later. Her cruise terminal was changed to Southampton and she was repainted white with yellow funnels in spring 1965, running a twice weekly summer service from Newcastle to Stavanger with a hydrofoil connection to Bergen. In summer 1966, she was replaced by the new car ferry *Jupiter* and transferred to a weekly Bergen–Rotterdam service and also made winter weekend shopping trips to Newcastle. Withdrawn in autumn 1968 after a final cruise from Southampton, *Venus* arrived at Faslane on 19 October for demolition.

Turbo-electric steamer for Cook Strait

The Union Steamship Co of New Zealand's 6,152-grt twin-screw *Rangatira* was complated by Vickers-Armstrongs, Barrow, in August 1931 to replace the ageing *Maori* on the Wellington–Lyttelton express service and entered service on 3 November. A handsome two-funnelled ship with a flush hull and pleasing sheerline, she measured 419 oa x 58.2 ft on loaded draught of 17 ft, and was the first USSNZ ship to be propelled by turbo-electric machinery. Steam was supplied by six watertube boilers and on trials she attained a maximum speed of 22 knots, although her schedule required only a more modest 16.5 knots. Berths were supplied for 720 first-class and 236 second-class passengers but she was licensed to carry up to 2,300 on day trips. She quickly became established as a popular ship, if a little accident prone. On 2 February 1936, she ran aground off Sinclair Head, Cook Strait, in heavy weather but on 6 April 1939 broke the record for the passage from Lyttelton to Wellington, averaging just under 21.5 knots and covering the 174 miles in eight hours and eight minutes. On 28 December 1940, she grounded again, this time in fog, at the entrance to Pigeon Bay on Banks Peninsula while following the swept channel to Lyttelton. During the Second World War, she was armed with single 4-in and 12-pounder guns and made several trooping runs to the Pacific islands as well as run to Sydney. After the war, she carried 520 first- and 274 second-class passengers and was later converted to a one-class ship. After 1953 she became the stand-by ship and also relieved *Tamahine* on the Wellington–Picton run during the summer season. She stranded in the Tory Channel on Christmas Day 1959 but was refloated just over twenty-four hours

later. After a career of thirty-four years she was laid up in Wellington on 16 December 1965 and on 26 May 1967 was bought by John Manners & Co of Hong Kong who resold her to Fortune & Co. She left Wellington on 25 October in tow arrived in Hong Kong on 27 November for demolition.

US East Coast sisters

The last ships built for Eastern Steamship Lines were the 6,185-grt *Saint John** and *Acadia*, which were delivered by Newport News Shipbuilding & Dry Dock Co in April and June 1932. Designed by Theodore Ferris, they were improved versions of *Yarmouth* (1927) and measured 403 oa × 61.2 ft and were driven at 20 knots by two steam turbines. During the summer, *Saint John* ran between Boston and St John NB and her sister between New York and Yarmouth/Newfoundland, but in winter they sailed on the old Metropolitan Line service between New York and Boston, switching to New York–Bermuda and Nassau in 1938–40. In March 1941, both were briefly chartered to Alcoa Steamship Co for Caribbean cruises but *Saint John* was quickly commissioned as the submarine tender USS *Antaeus* (AS 21). *Acadia* was chartered by the US Maritime Commission as an army transport (AG 67). In April 1942 and after returning US diplomats from South America, she was sent to Boston for conversion to a joint troopship/hospital ship. She sailed to Casablanca and in mid-1943 was converted to America's first full-time hospital ship with berths for 788 wounded. She served in the Mediterranean in the North African and Italian campaigns and was decommissioned in February 1946, after which she transported US military dependants back from Europe. The charter agreement provided for her to be restored to her pre-war state but failure to reach agreement

between her owners and the Maritime Commission led to a long court case, during which she was laid up in the James River. She was eventually sold for breaking up at Bruges in 1955. *Saint John* had also become a hospital ship – the 792-bed *Rescue* (AH 18) – in January 1945, and served off Japan during the final stages of the Second World War. Decommissioned in June 1946, she was laid up at Olympia, Washington, and while being broken up at Ballard in Seattle in 1959 was destroyed by fire.

New Mediterranean turbine steamers

The 3,378-grt *Pascal Paoli* was delivered to Compagnie Fraissinet by Ateliers & Chantiers de la Méditerranée, Port de Bouc in May 1932 and was the third new vessel for the Corsican mail services. She measuerd 313.3 × 47.6 ft on 17.8 ft draught and was driven by two steam turbines developing 5,500 shp, which provided a maximum of 19 knots and 16 knots in normal service. Overnight berths were provided for seventy-four in first-class, seventy-two in second class and twenty-eight in third class and she also carried a number of deck passengers. In 1939 she became a French navy patrol ship (P 7), but after seizure by German forces on 7 January 1943 was transferred to Italy and renamed *Altamura*. She was scuttled at La Spezia on 10 September shortly after Italy capitulated but was later raised by the Germans and converted to the anti-aircraft ship *SG 5*. She was finally sunk by Allied aircraft in September 1944.

*El Kantara** was built to replace *El Golea* on Compagnie de Navigation Mixte's Port Vendres–Algiers service and was the first of three improved vessels. Completed in April 1932 at Low Walker on the Tyne by Swan Hunter & Wigham Richardson, she measured 5,079 grt on dimensions of 396 oa x 53.8 ft and was more powerful than her predecessor with her six Parsons single-reduction geared turbines, fed by five Prudhon Capus boilers, developing 8,500 shp for a service speed of 20 knots and 21.5 knots on trials. Berths were provided for 106/154/102 passengers in three classes with a further 680 on deck. She had two squat funnels on a larger superstructure and a cruiser stern. On 20 June 1936, she grounded near Palamos but was towed off by the company's *El Mansour* and *Djebel Antar*. On the outbreak of the Second World War, she was taken up as an auxiliary cruiser under the pennant number X 16 and took part in the Norway campaign, after which she helped move part of France's gold reserves to Dakar. She was unscathed in the British attack on that port on 23 September but was later released and in 1941 handed back to her owners, who was unable to run her due to insufficient coal stocks. She was seized by Italy on 9 January 1943 and renamed *Acquino*, but sank on

23 April after she was bombed and set on fire in a North African bound convoy some thirty-four nautical miles north-west of Marettimo in the Aegadian Islands.

Compagnie de Navigation Mixte's *El Mansour* and *El Djezair** were improved versions of *El Kantara* with raked bow and broader funnels. Completed by Forges & Chantiers de la Méditerranée, La Seyne, in 1932–3 they measured 390/387 x 54 ft and their machinery comprised six Parsons single-reduction geared steam turbines developing 12,000 shp for 20 knots. *El Mansour* achieved over 22.5 knots on trials. Berths were provided for 113/142/126 passengers in three classes and they also carried 580 deck passengers. In refits during winter 1937–8 and the following spring, both ships had the dummy after funnel removed and the forward funnel heightened. Requisitioned as auxiliary cruisers (X 6 and X 17) after the outbreak of war, they took part in the Norway campaign in April 1940, landing troops and then evacuating them from Namsos. In June and July, they were among several ships used to transport French gold reserves to safety in Dakar. Seized by the Germans in January 1943, they were assigned to Italy and renamed *Amagni* and *Cassino* respectively but were taken back by the Germans in September 1943 following Italy's capitulation. The latter was bombed and sunk by the RAF near Sète on 25 June 1944 and her sister was scuttled in Marseilles on 22 August. Both were raised after the war, but *El Djezair* was scrapped in Italy in 1950 after the removal of her engines. *El Mansour* was rebuilt during 1946–8, in the course of which her aft pair of lifeboats and mainmast were removed and the latter replaced by a pair of kingposts at the aft end of her superstructure.

Alterations were also made to the front of the bridge deck, her deck openings were closed and the screening on the promenade and boat decks extended. Gross tonnage was now 5,818 and her new passenger capacity sixty-six in first and de-luxe classes, 268 in tourist class and 530 in steerage. She resumed service on 5 September between Port Vendres and Algiers and underwent a further four-month refit during winter 1949–50 prior to transferring to the Marseilles–Algiers route. On 28

October 1963, she was sold to the French Navy and converted into the white-hulled depot ship *Maine* (A 611) for the Pacific Experimental Centre, which was developing the French atomic bomb. A large deckhouse was added behind the bridge and her mainmast removed along with two boilers, reducing speed to 15 knots. She acted as a hotel ship at Mururoa, Tahiti, until January 1974 and on 3 April was taken out to sea and sunk by gunfire from the escort sloop *Doudart De Lagrée*.

Pioneer Belgian high-speed motorships

Few cross-channel ships have caused a greater stir than Belgian Marine's first motor vessel, *Prince Baudouin**, which entered service in 1934. Like most of the preceding Belgian ships she was built by Cockerill, which had fought off competitive bids from other northern European yards but there any similarity ended. Not only was she striking in looks with minimal sheer, single squat funnel and pole masts without rake, she was driven by Sulzer twin twelve-cylinder single-acting diesels with a maximum output of 17,000 bhp and on trials reached 25.25 knots at 16,000 bhp during several 11.5-mile runs off the Scheldt estuary, making her the fastest motorship in the world. Her design was the work of the Marine Administration's technical adviser, who persuaded the Director-General M de Vos to change the contract from a steamship to a motor vessel. This paid off as at sea she consumed around half as much oil as the French steamer *Cote d'Argent*. Gross measurement was 3,300 tons on dimensions of 370.7 x 46 ft on 12 ft draught and she carried 1,400 passengers. In autumn 1937, she was joined by the 25.5-knot *Prins Albert*, which had main engine-driven scavenge pumps allowing around 100 more passengers to be carried in extended second-class accommodation. A third sister, *Prince Philippe*, was under construction when war broke out and despite only one engine having been installed, she escaped to England along with her two sisters when Germany invaded the Low Countries in 1940. After use for troop and evacuation movements, *Prins Albert* and *Prince Philippe* were

converted in 1941 to infantry landing ships, with a single short signal mast between bridge and funnel and carrying eight LCAs. They sailed to Inverary for Combined Operations training and while returning south on 15 July, the latter sank after colliding with the cargo steamer *Empire Wave* north-east of Larne. The same month *Prins Baudouin* left for the Mediterranean via the Cape and on her return was converted for a similar role in 1943. 'Lucky Albert' took part in the Lofoten, Bruneval, Etaples and Dieppe raids as well as the invasions of Sicily and Italy and both ships were at the Normandy landings at Omaha and Sword beaches before returning to the

Mediterranean for the landings in southern France. *Prins Albert* was then fitted with extra ventilation for the landings in Rangoon and Malaysia, remained in the East until February 1946. After extensive refits and with foremast moved aft of the bridge, *Prince Baudouin* returned to service in October 1946 and her sister in July 1947. *Prince Baudouin* was sold in 1964 to accommodate office staff and construction workers at the Zelzate steel works on the Ghent–Terneuzen canal and was broken up in Ghent in winter 1967–8. *Prins Albert* was laid up in Ostend in September 1968 and sold in 1970 for breaking up at Ghent. (*John G Callis*)

Irish Sea developments

The Isle of Man Steam Packet Co returned to Cammell Laird for a third steamer following the new pattern set by *Ben-my-Chree* in 1927. She was also the third of the company's ships to bear the name *Mona's Queen* and was completed during the height of the Great Depression in June 1934. She differed from her Birkenhead-built predecessors in having a raised forecastle and was completed in white livery, her gross tonnage was 2,756 on dimensions of 337.6 x 48.1 ft. Two sets of single-reduction geared turbines gave her a speed of 22 knots. She was taken up immediately after war broke out and used on trooping and refugee duties to Channel and Dutch ports before returning to Dover for Operation Dynamo, the evacuation of Dunkirk. She was one of the first ships to enter the French port on 26 May 1940 and brought back 1,200 men. She sailed again on the 29th loaded with cans of drinking water but hit a mine that broke her back, half a mile short of the harbour entrance. She went down almost immediately with the loss of twenty-four crew members, the majority of whom were engine-room staff.

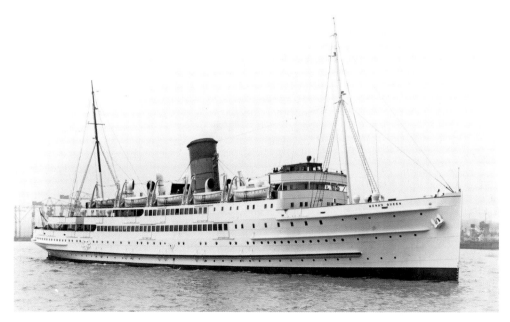

The Great Western Railway's *Great Western* was completed by Cammell Laird, Birkenhead in January 1934 to replace an earlier namesake on the Fishguard–Waterford run. A 1,659-grt vessel measuring 297.5 oa × 40.4 ft driven at 14 knots, she was by two triple-expansion engines. She could accommodate 250 first-class passengers amidships and 200 third-class aft in addition to large numbers of livestock. She acted a troopship in the English Channel between April and August 1944, but otherwise continued on her normal run. She was converted to oil-firing in 1947 and the following year she passed to the London Midland Region of the newly-nationalised British Railways. She stopped carrying passengers in June 1959 and was refitted in Penarth to carry more unit loads. Third-class accommodation was removed and she was remasted. From October 1964, she made special Saturday sailings from Rosslare to Fishguard with cargoes of bacon. Withdrawn in early 1967, she was laid up at Holyhead and after a final stint Heysham–Belfast cargo service stint that spring, went to Tamise in Belgium for breaking up.

The 3,743-grt *Duke of York* was delivered by Harland & Wolff, Belfast in June 1935 and an extra ship for the London, Midland & Scottish Railway's popular Heysham–Belfast run in place of the temporary *Duke of Abercorn*. Dimensionally smaller than the three earlier 'Dukes' at 339.3 × 52.3 ft, she differed in having a raised forecastle, partially glazed promenade deck, bridge (with cabs) one deck higher and no funnel cowls. Internally her saloon-class cabins had twin berths placed sided by side instead of the traditional one above the other and she could carry 240 tourist-class passengers in vastly improved accommodation. She was driven by the standard steam turbines and steam was supplied by mechanically stoked boilers. She had an automatic sprinkler system and four electric cranes for cargo handling. In the Second World War, she took part in the evacuations of St

Valery and Dunkirk and early in 1942 was commissioned as HMS *Duke of Wellington* and converted to an assault landing ship carrying 250 troops and ten small landing craft. She was present at the ill-fated Dieppe raid and the Normandy landings. She decommissioned in 1945 and resuming her original name ran from Harwich on trooping/leave service before returning to Heysham in October 1947. On 1 January 1949, the British Transport Commission transferred her to British Railways' Eastern Region to replace the burnt-out *Prague* on the Harwich–Hook service and the following summer she ran from Southampton to Cherbourg and Guernsey until the end of September, after which she was converted to oil-firing by her builders and her funnels replaced by a large single funnel. She briefly supplemented the Holyhead–Dun Laoghaire service

in 1950, but on 6 May 1953 lost her bows in a collision with the US military transport *Haiti Victory*; several crew members were lost. During repairs she was fitted with a new 90-ft flush-decked bow section with raked stem that increased her length to 346.7 ft and raised gross tonnage to 4,325. Resuming service in February 1954, she acted mainly as a relief and extra summer vessel until sold in July 1963 to Marivic Navigation Inc, of Liberia, a Chandris Group company. Under the temporary name of *York*, alterations were carried out and with a new single mast between bridge and funnel she started cruising out of Venice as *Fantasia* in mid-March 1964, carrying 381 passengers. She was by then owned by International Cruises SA, another Chandris company. *Fantasia* was scrapped in Piraeus in 1976.

New French ships for North Africa and Corsica services

Compagnie Générale Transatlantique's striking 10,172-grt sisters *Ville d'Alger* and *Ville d'Oran** were the largest yet built for its North Africa services. Completed in 1935–6, the former by Chantiers & Ateliers de St Nazaire, and the latter, on long-term demise charter from the French government, by Société Provençale de Constructions Navales, La Ciotat, they introduced a new profile with raked stem and cruiser stern and their hulls, which measured 484 oa × 63.2 ft on draught of 21.8 ft, featured a long combined forecastle and bridge. Main machinery, constructed in St Nazaire, comprised two sets of Parsons single-acting geared steam turbines developing 19,800 shp for 23.5 knots on trial and 21 knots in service. Steam was supplied by four oil-fired Penhöet watertube boilers and they carried around 1,000 passengers in five classes. *Ville d'Alger* made her maiden voyage from Marseilles to Algiers on 25 June 1935 and *Ville d'Oran*'s inaugural took her to Oran on 17 October 1936. Requisitioned in September 1939, the dummy after funnels were removed and *Ville d'Alger* was used as a troop transport and her sister as the armed merchant cruiser (X 5). On 29 April 1940, they both suffered minor propeller damage when bombed by the Luftwaffe at Namsos during the Norwegian campaign and in June helped carry some of the French gold reserves to safety in Casablanca from Brest and Pauillac respectively; they were afterwards laid up in Dakar. They were returned to regular Mediterranean service by the Vichy

government but were laid up in Algiers due to lack of fuel in September 1941. On 6 January 1943, *Ville d'Alger* was seized by the Germans but was returned to CGT in November and laid up at Carate. Her sister had been retaken by the Allies in January and from August was used for trooping under Cunard management. *Ville d'Alger* was used as a floating hotel by the Germans in 1944 but on 20 August was set on fire and scuttled as a blockship at Caronte. Raised in February 1945, she was reconstructed by Ateliers & Chantiers de Provence, Port de Bouc for 156 first- and 422 tourist-class passengers and reentered service on 13 June 1948, sailing from Marseilles to Bone and Philippeville. Following a refit at La Seyne,

her sister resumed her Marseilles–Algiers run on 22 June 1949, carrying up to 180 first- and 376 tourist-class passengers, and was purchased from the government by CGT in 1954. Both were sold in 1966 to Greek owner Aegean Steam Navigation Typaldos Brothers. *Ville d'Alger* was renamed *Poseidon* and *Ville d'Oran* became *Mount Olympos* and later *Olympos*. It was intended to use both on a Marseilles–Piraeus–Haifa run, but only *Poseidon* entered service, on 19 June 1967, while *Olympos* remained laid up at Scaramanga. Typaldos went into liquidation in July 1968 and both went for scrap the following year; *Poseidon* to La Spezia and *Olympos* to Trieste.

The 3,823-grt *Sampiero Corso* was completed for French government account by Chantiers & Ateliers de Provence, Port de Bouc in June 1936 and placed under Compagnie Fraissinet management for Corsica services. A neat single-funnelled steamer, she measured 363 oa × 47.9 ft on 17 ft draught and was propelled by two Parsons double-reduction geared steam turbines giving 15.5 knots in service and 18 knots maximum. She accommodated 194 cabin-class passengers and 650 on deck. Following the outbreak of the Second World War, she was requisitioned by the French navy as a patrol ship (P 8) armed with five 100-mm guns but was taken over by Italy at the end of 1942 and renamed *Canosa*. Seized by German forces at La Spezia on 17 January 1943, she was converted to the flak ship *SG 6* but during the invasion of southern France was scuttled in the entrance to Cassis on 22 June 1944 and the wreck was torpedoed by the submarine HMS *Universal* on 16 November. She was refloated at the end of 1945 and laid up in Toulon. A major reconstruction began in 1949; her short welldeck was enclosed and the central 140-ft section of her hull was replaced with a new section incorporating a fully enclosed and glazed promenade deck. She was towed to Marseilles for

fitting out and finally returned to service in 1951 under the colours and management of Compagnie Générale Transatlantique, which had been granted the Corsican mail contract in the meantime. Her new passenger figures were 113 in first, 115 in third and 596 in fourth classes and her gross tonnage was now

4,041. She sailed from Marseilles and Nice to Ajaccio, Bastia, Ile Rousse and Calvi until 1966, when she was withdrawn. Sold in April 1967 to a Panamanian company associated with Hong-Kong based United China Shipping Co, she was renamed *Fortune Mariner*, and after eighteen months was sold to a local breaker.

Bass Strait ferry

Completed by Alexander Stephen, Linthouse, in January 1935 for Tasmanian Steamers Pty, the joint company set up in 1922 by Union Steamship Co of New Zealand and Huddart, Parker, the 4,286-grt *Taroona* (seashell) measured 354.5 oa × 50.1 ft on 15 ft draught, her two short funnels echoing those of USSNZ's *Rangatira* and *Awatea*. Her hull was initially black but was later changed to USSNZ's olive green with yellow band. Twin-screw geared-turbine machinery developing 6,000 shp enabled her to exceed her normal 16 knots by a couple more knots

if required. Overnight berths were provided for 483 passengers, initially 302 in first and 105 in second classes augmented by thirty-six and forty folding beds respectively, and around fifty cars could be carried in her holds. She arrived in Australia on 28 February, replacing *Nairana*, but was nearly destroyed by fire in Melbourne on 10 May 1936. She emerged from repairs with her hull colour lowered by one strake and in 1937 suffered bottom damage after grounding off Point Cook. In January 1942, she was employed for two months carrying New Zealand troops to Fiji

and then Melbourne after which she was requisitioned by the Australian government and fitted out as a 678-berth troopship with her aft funnel shortened. On her first trip to New Guinea she lay aground on a reef off Port Moresby for several days but was ignored by Japanese bombers. During a post-war refit in February 1946, the aft funnel was removed and part of it was used to increase the height of the forward one while at the same time her hull colour was restored to its original level. After the withdrawal of *Loongana,* she occasional called at other Tasmanian ports but suffered another fire in Melbourne in 1952. Despite Commonwealth Government subsidies, losses continued to mount and her final trip was on 25 September 1959. *Taroona* was replaced by the new Australian National Line car ferry *Princess of Tasmania*. She was bought by Typaldos Brothers, Piraeus, and renamed *Hellas* for a weekly Venice–Brindisi–Piraeus–Istanbul service carrying 150 first-, 125 second- and 150 tourist-class passengers in air-conditioned cabins. She later switched to a Venice–Patras–Piraeus–Heraklion run, but was laid up at Perama in November 1966. Typaldos collapsed in 1968 and she gradually deteriorated until finally towed to Turkey in May 1989 for demolition at Aliaga.

Fast Japanese railway steamers

The short-sea passenger ships *Kongo Maru** and *Koan Maru* were completed by Mitsubishi at Nagasaki for the Japanese Department of Railways in October 1936 and January 1937. Designed for increased occupancy on the Shimonoseki–Pusan service following the annexation of Manchuria, they were the largest in the railway fleet at 7,105/7,079 grt on dimensions of 415 × 57 ft. Resembling Lloyd Triestino's motorship *Victoria* in apperance, they were propelled by two sets of Zoelly single-reduction geared impulse steam turbines driving twin screws and fed with superheated steam by eight coal-fired single-ended boilers. Maximum output was 15,600 shp for a trial speed of just over 23 knots but 12,000 shp was sufficient for 20 knots in service. Air-conditioned Western-style first-class accommodation provided cabin berths for sixty-six passengers, while 367 second class were housed in multi-occupancy cabins and 1,639 third-class passengers in 'futon' dormitories. *Kongo Maru* was damaged in Hakata Bay in 1943, but both survived the Second World War and in 1950 *Kongo Maru* was employed ferrying UN troops between Sasebo and Pusan but grounded near Koshikishima, Goto Island, during a typhoon on 14 October 1951 and broke up. *Koan Maru* was used as a US troopship during the Korean War and in April

1953 she returned the first batch of Japanese civilians to Maizuru from occupied Manchuria, where they had been trapped when the ferry service was suspended at the end of the Second World War. In 1958 she was purchased by Toyo Yusen KK and converted into Japan's first post-war cruise ship, sporting a white hull and blue funnel with broad white band containing

three narrow red bands. After sailing from Tokyo for one season, she was again altered for an Indonesian charter to carry Hadj pilgrims to Jeddah but only sailed in 1959 and 1960. She was then used on Indonesia's inter-island passenger services until broken up in Mihara at the end of 1970.

Second generation Irish Sea motorships

Launched in March 1936 by Harland & Wolff in Belfast, the 3,244-grt *Royal Ulsterman** and *Royal Scotsman* were designed for Burns & Laird Lines' overnight Glasgow–Belfast service. They were developments of the *Ulster Prince* and *Innisfallen* designs with raked stems and a single funnel. Hull measurements were 341.5 oa x 47.7 ft and they were propelled by twin Harland & Wolff/B & W eight-cylinder two-stroke single-acting diesels developing 5,500 bhp for a speed of 18 knots. Passenger accommodation was arranged amidships for 225 in first class and aft for 110 in third class and their eight lifeboats were mounted in gravity davits to provide more deck space. They entered service on 15 June 1936 and made occasional daytime sailings to Ardrossan. During the Second World War, they were requisitioned for trooping in April 1940 and went to Norway, France, West Africa, Tunisia, Gibraltar and Iceland. After service as store carriers, they were both converted in 1942 to infantry landing ships carrying six LCAs for the North African landings, after which they were partly altered for a landing ship HQ role, taking part in the Sicilian and Italian landings and *Royal Scotsman* also visting Bombay in October 1943. Her sister acted as a reserve HQ ship at Juno Beach during the Normandy landings. They returned to normal service in 1946 and continued until October

1967, when they were laid up. *Royal Scotsman* was sold to Ron Hubbard and used for Scientology cruises as *Apollo* while *Royal Ulsterman* was renamed *Cammell Laird* after the shipbuilder that bought her in April 1968. She was used as an accommodation ship at Birkenhead and then at Southampton, while additional work was done on the liner *Queen Elizabeth 2*. In 1970, *Royal Ulsterman* was sold to George Karydas of Greece and as *Sounion* was used mainly on the Brindisi–Corfu–Patras route for Med-

Link Lines Shipping. When on voyage from Cyprus to Haifa, with cruise passengers, she was sunk by a terrorist limpet mine in Beirut on 3 March 1973, but was raised in April and towed back to Greece for demolition at Perama. Her sister ended up in Brownsville, Texas where she was hit by runaway railway wagons on 17 September 1980. Subsequent plans to turn her into a floating restaurant named *Arctic Star* came to nothing and she was scrapped at Brownsville in 1984.

The 4,305-grt motorships *Leinster* and *Munster** were completed by Harland & Wolff, Belfast, in November 1937 and February 1938 for Coast Lines for service with its subsidiary British & Irish Steam Packet Co (1936) Ltd, which had superseded the old B & I S P Co on 1 January 1937. Their three-island design owed much to Belfast Steamship Co's *Ulster Monarch*, but they had a raked stem and a single funnel. Slightly larger dimensionally at 370 oa x 50.2 ft with a 19 ft draught, they were driven at 19 knots by twin Harland & Wolff/B & W ten-cylinder single-acting

diesels developing around 5,200 bhp. They accommodated 1,500 passengers; 425 in first class in single- and twin-berth cabins amidships and over one hundred in third class in two- and four-berth cabins and were the first cross-channel ships to be fitted with radio telephone. Unlike other Irish Sea ships, no provision was made for the carriage of livestock. Their hulls were painted buff with green boot-topping and a narrow white band separated the green from the black top of the funnel. On 19 July 1938, in thick fog off Point Lynas, Anglesey, *Munster* was struck just

forward of the engine-room by the US cargo steamer *West Cohas*, but was repaired only to be sunk by a magnetic mine off the Mersey Bar light vessel on 7 February 1940, fortunately without loss of life. *Leinster* was requisitioned as a hospital ship and based in Iceland for six months, followed by trooping spells in Icelandic and Mediterranean waters. In May 1943, she was converted to the hospital carrier *No 17* with 383 beds and six water ambulances. She supported the Mediterranean landings in North Africa, Sicily and Italy, where she was damaged by a bomb off Anzio, and later shuttled between Bari and Ancona in the Adriatic. After refitting in Belfast, she was transferred within the Coast Lines group to Belfast Steamship Co and in March 1946 placed on the overnight Belfast–Liverpool route as *Ulster Prince*. In September 1966 the Roman numeral *I* was added to free up her name for a new car ferry and she was withdrawn shortly afterwards and sold to Belgian breakers. Resold early in 1967 to Epirotiki Steamship Navigation Co, she sailed to Greece as *Ulster Prince* once more and after a refit was renamed *Adria* in 1968 and *Odysseus* in the following year, thereafter operating cruises around the Aegean. She returned to the UK in February 1976 to serve as an accommodation ship for oil rig construction workers at Loch Kishorn and was finally broken up at Faslane, where she arrived in October 1979.

New design for Isle of Man

The twin-screw turbine *Fenella* and *Tynwald** were the first pair of exact sister ships constructed for Isle of Man Steam Packet Co and the first to have cruiser sterns. Designed for the winter service to Liverpool in addition to summer excursion work, they were both launched on 16 December 1936 by Vickers-Armstrongs, Barrow, and completed the following April and June. Smaller than their predecessors, they measured 2,376 grt on hull dimensions of 327.5 oa × 46 ft and introduced a new profile with flat fronted superstructure and shortened bridge deck ending forward of a horizontal-topped funnel, which echoed the Belfast-built motorships. Internally, they had improved accommodation campared with previous ships before and were driven by two Parsons single-reduction geared turbines fed by three Babcock & Wilcox boilers and developing 8,000 shp for 21 knots. They could be distinguished by *Tynwald* having white painted bulwarks forward whereas *Fenella*'s were black. Both were requisitioned for trooping duties immediately after war broke out in 1939 and later took part in th Dunkirk evacuation, where *Fenella* was bombed alongside the East Mole on her first trip on 28 May 1940 and her engine room destroyed. Her sister carried 8,953 personnel between 28 May and 4 June, more than any other civilian ship. *Fenella* was later raised by the Germans, fitted with a coal-fired steam engine and sailed again as *Reval*. Her eventual fate is unknown but she is believed to have been captured by the Russians in the Baltic. Following a major conversion, *Tynwald* was commissioned as the auxiliary anti-aircraft ship HMS *Tynwald* on 1 October 1941. She had a naval-type bridge and two tall tripod masts and was armed with three twin high angle 4-in guns and two quadruple 2-pounder pom-poms. She escorted convoys around the UK and in 1942 was despatched to the Mediterranean for the North African landings. On 12 November while guarding the monitor HMS *Roberts* off Bougie she was torpedoed and sunk by the Italian submarine *Argo* with the loss of ten crew members.

Advanced North Sea motorships

The twin-screw 3,038-grt *Kronprins Olav* was completed in December 1937 by Elsinore Shipbuilding & Engineering Co for the Det Forenede D/S (United Steamship Co) Copenhagen–Oslo service. She introduced a new streamlined profile with single sloping funnel and was the first passenger ship in the fleet to have her long forecastle merged into the superstructure. Her main particulars were 327.2 oa × 45.5 ft and 16 ft draught and she was driven by a pair of B & W seven-cylinder diesels developing 4,800 bhp for a service speed of 18.5 knots. Berths were provided for 127 first-, ninety-six second- and seventy third-class passengers in addition to 977 deck passengers. Cars could be loaded via a side door and hydraulic lift. Laid up in Copenhagen in the Second World War, she was was taken to Germany in December 1944 and converted to the hospital ship *Frankfurt*. Found lying at Rendsburg at the end of the war, she was restored to her original name and refitted before loan to the UK for Hull–Cuxhaven trooping service. After a further refit she returned to the Copenhagen–Oslo route from June 1946 until 1961, interspersed with odd spells on the Aarhus route. During 1961–4 she ran a seasonal Frederikshavn–Oslo service with occasional spells on her old route and in autumn 1964 made two cruises, one to UK, Irish and northern European ports and the other to Baltic ports. *Kronprins Olav* spent two summers on the Copenhagen–Faroes–Iceland run in 1965 and 1966 and after a final week on the Copenhagen–Oslo service in December 1966 was laid up. In October 1967, she was sold to Fotis Poulides' Traghetti del Tirreno TT and rebuilt in Genoa with new funnel and a single streamlined mast, while new side doors and a stern door increased her car capacity. She operated as *Corsica Express* on Corsica Line's Genoa–Bastia service until sold in 1975 to Libera Navigazione Lauro, which renamed her *Express Ferry Angelina Lauro*. From 1980 she ran as *Capo Falconara* for C&L Espressi and from 1982 for Navaltour Societa di Navigazione, Messina, until sold for demolition in 1986.

Bergen Line ordered in 1937 a larger consort for *Venus* from Cantieri Riuniti dell'Adriatico, Trieste. An Italian shipyard was stipulated by the Norwegian government in exchange for fish exports, although the Elsinore shipyard had provided the lowest quote. The stylish 7,287-grt *Vega* measured 445 oa × 58.3 ft and ran trials on 28–30 April 1938, her twin Sulzer two-stroke single-acting ten-cylinder diesels developing 12,400 bhp for a maximum speed of 21.75 knots; 10,600 bhp was sufficient for 20 knots in service. She was delivered in May and made a maiden cruise to Oslo via Palermo and Algiers, after which she carried King Haakon and members of the Norwegian

parliament on a coastal cruise to Bergen. She entered service on 2 June and made two round trips a week between Bergen and Newcastle, alternating with *Venus* and calling at Stavanger and Haugesund northbound. Although continuing the two-funnelled theme introduced by *Venus*, she was more modern looking in appearance with well-raked stem, masts and funnels, her obvious Italian design owing something to Lloyd Triestino's *Victoria*. Her hull incorporated an extra deck and her superstructure was extended forward of the bridge. Echoing a contemporary trend in sea travel, her aft-placed second class overnight accommodation for 248 passengers exceeded that

supplied for 217 in first class amidships. She was laid up at the start of the Second World War as a result of an excessive demand for additional war risks insurance premiums and was taken by the invading German army on 11 September 1940 but returned to her owners on 16 October. On 18 March the following year, she was seized by the Kriegsmarine and taken to the Baltic for employment as a submarine depot ship and named *Wega*. She assisted in the evacuation of refugees fleeing from the advancing Russian army in East Prussia, but on 4 May 1945 was caught and sunk by RAF Beaufighters in Eckernfjord; a premature end to a fine ship.

Facing increasing competition from new ships belonging to Bergen Line and Swedish Lloyd, Fred Olsen ordered two new ferries from Akers Mek Verksted, Oslo, for its Oslo–Newcastle mail service. Completed six months apart in June and December 1938, *Black Watch* and *Black Prince** were twin-screw motorships of 5,035 grt, their hull dimensions of 385 oa × 53.3 ft – a few feet shorter than Sweden's *Britannia* and *Suecia* but with a greater beam. The elegant design incorporated a long raised forecastle, single funnel and cruiser spoon stern and they were driven by twin nine-cylinder B & W diesels developing 7,000 bhp for a service speed of 18 knots. Their advanced accommodation for 185 first- and sixty-five second-class passengers included plenty of open deck space and the dining saloon, which was served by lifts from the galley below, could be partitioned off with portable bulkheads to cater for different numbers of passengers. *Black Prince* inaugurated an accelerated service from Oslo on 1 July with a call at Kristiansand. The open sea passage from here to the Tyne took twenty-three hours but the overall passage lasted thirty-two hours due to speed restrictions in the Oslofjord. Both ships were laid up in Oslo at the start of the Second World War and were seized by the invading Germans in 1940. The following year they were requisitioned by the Kriegsmarine for use a naval accommodation ships. On 21 December 1942, *Black Prince*, which had been renamed *Lofjord*, was bombed during an Allied air attack on Danzig (Gdansk) and extensively damaged by fire. Her sister *Black Watch* was sunk by aircraft from HMS *Trumpeter* off Harstad on 4 May 1945, while acting as a submarine depot ship. After the war, *Black Prince* was

salvaged by Svitzer minus her engines and towed to the Danish port of Frederikstad. Olsen deemed her unfit for restoration and in May 1947 she was towed to Antwerp, where she was viewed by Norwegian shipowner Sigurd Herlofson with a view to converting her to a fruit carrier. The idea was rejected and she was sold to to be broken up at Burcht.

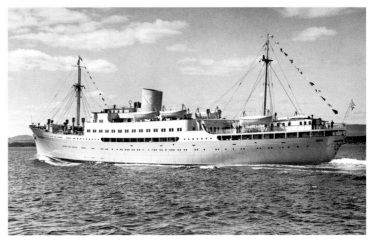

Stoomvaart Maatschappij Zeeland (Zeeland Line) was unique in switching straight from reciprocating machinery to diesel propulsion for two new ferries for its Flushing–Harwich service. Ordered from De Schelde, Flushing in 1937, the 4,135-grt *Koningin Emma** and *Prinses Beatrix* introduced an entirely new profile, with long raised forecastle and cruiser stern while two pairs of kingposts were placed at either end of a low superstructure topped by a single upright mast and 'inverted flower pot' funnel. The low boat arrangement was also unusual as was the light grey hull. Measuring 379.9 oa x 47.2 ft on maximum draught of 14.4 ft, they were driven by twin De Schelde/Sulzer ten-cylinder diesels developing 12,650 bhp for a maximum of 23 knots and 21.5 knots in normal service. Passenger complement was 1,800 persons while twenty-five cars could be carried in the holds. They were completed in June and July 1939 but only sailed for a few months before being laid up on the outbreak of war. In May 1940 they escaped to England and were used in the evacuation of France and for trooping runs to Iceland. In August they were requisitioned by the Admiralty and converted to medium infantry landing ships with new bridge and funnel and carrying six LCAs and two LCMs, the latter in 30-ton davits. After commissioning as HMS *Queen Emma* and HMS *Princess Beatrix,* they had an exciting war, taking part in the Lofoten Raid in March 1941, West Africa and Dieppe raids in August 1942,

North African, Sicilian and Italian landings in 1943, Normandy landings in June 1944 and ended up in the Far East in 1945 where Japanese forces in Malaya surrendered aboard *Queen Emma* at Penang. Released in April 1946, they helped evacuate Dutch civilians from Java before returning to De Schelde for rebuilding in 1947. With new profile and altered accommodation for 1,600 passengers, they reentered the Hook–Harwich service in spring 1948 but

Koningin Emma was chartered to W H Muller for its temporary Rotterdam–Tilbury 'Batavier Line' service between 15 June and 30 September. In 1960 improvements were made to reduce noise levels and *Koningin Emma* was relegated to a reserve vessel. Replaced by new car ferries in 1968, *Prinses Beatrix* was withdrawn in August and her sister in October and after short lay ups, both were broken up at Antwerp.

Unusual Dutch steamer

The 2,687-grt *Batavier III* was completed for Wm Muller's Rotterdam–London service by De Noord, Alblasserdam in June 1939. Unlike previous Batavier Line passenger ships, she had a flush hull and measured 283.5 oa x 43.8 ft on a draught of 16.2 ft. Her main machinery comprised an unusual three-cylinder compound steam engine by Werkspoor fed with steam by two single-ended boilers with a high working pressure. Power output was 3,000 ihp, which provided a service speed of 15 knots. Overnight accommodation was arranged for eighty-eight first-, seventy-one second- and twenty-four third-class passengers and for cargo handling she had a novel system of level luffing cranes arranged three to a mast on revolving turntables. She had been in service for only a few months before war broke out and she was laid up in Rotterdam. Seized by the invading Germans on 27 May 1940, she was initially employed as coastal defence vessel by the Kriegsmarine. From the beginning of January 1941, she acted as a troop transport to Norway under the management of F Laeisz but was mined and sunk with all hands on 15 October 1942 about twenty miles south of Aalborg.

CHAPTER

9

The Second World War and Fleet Reconstruction

The Second World War caused the cessation of all but a few lifeline ferry services in Europe and the majority of ships were again taken up for military duties. The United Kingdom and its allies were fortunate in having the largest and most diverse fleet of such handy vessels, which performed invaluable service as troopships, hospital ships, infantry assault ships, target vessels, anti-aircraft ships and depot ships. Germany used several captured Scandinavian and French vessels for military purposes, some of the latter being initially assigned to Italy but many were later scuttled in the south of France.

Shipyards were busy with war work and only the Southern Railway's *Invicta* was completed as a landing ship during the conflict, while French Railway's unfinished Newhaven–Dieppe steamer *Londres* was completed by the Germans as a fast minelayer. In Japan, two large new railway steamers were both sunk before they could enter commercial service and in Scandinavia two North Sea ferries that had been launched in 1940 were not completed until after the war, by which time European yards had begun to build new ferries to replace those that had been lost.

The United Kingdom's four railway companies were nationalised on 1 January 1948, becoming part of the British Transport Commission which shortly afterwards took delivery of the sister ships *Cambria* and *Hibernia*, the first traditional railway-owned tonnage to be diesel-driven. They turned out to be exceptions and all subsequent railway passenger steamers were turbine-driven as were new French and Canadian ships, although Union Steamship Co of New Zealand continued to favour turbo-electric propulsion. The Coast Lines group together with Belgian and Scandinavian operators continued to build motor ships and diesel manufacturers were busy bringing out new and improved engines with higher outputs per cylinder.

Advances in shipbuilding techniques saw welding begin to replace riveting in hull construction and experiments were made with aluminium to reduce the weight of funnels and superstructure. Light tripod masts in place of the old heavier pole masts were introduced by William Denny & Bros in the British Transport Commission's *Brighton* in 1952 and Compagnie Paquet's Mediterranean ferry *El Djezair* of 1954 was unique in having her engines placed aft.

Note: An asterisk in a caption indicates the vessel shown in the photograph.

Wartime completions

The third *Invicta** for the Dover Strait crossing was ordered by the Southern Railway from Wm Denny & Bros in February 1939 to take over the Golden Arrow service. War intervened and she was not completed until 1 July 1940 and although quickly requisitioned by the Admiralty, remained at anchor off Clynder for nigh on a year painted an overall buff save for black hull and funnel top. After some trooping runs, she was converted to an infantry landing ship and carried six LCA's and 250 armed troops. After she was commissioned in June 1942, *Invicta* took part in the Dieppe raid in August and then joined a number of other SR railway steamers in Force J, landing part of the Canadian 7th Infantry Brigade on Juno Beach on the first day of the Normandy invasion. Decommissioned on 9 October 1945, she undertook a four-month government charter for trooping duties between Calais and Dover and in April 1946 left for a full refit by Vickers-Armstrongs, Walker, where she was converted from coal-fired to oil-burning. She finally entered Golden Arrow service on 15 October, seven years later than originally intended. Stabilisers were finally fitted the following year, having been omitted during her hasty construction. At 4,178 grt, she was the largest traditional packet ship on the English Channel and compared with earlier tonnage had an extra deck, a raised forecastle, larger enclosed superstructure and a shorter funnel. She measured 348.3 oa × 52.2 ft with a draught of 12.8 ft and was driven by two sets of Parsons single-reduction geared turbines fed by two Yarrow three-drum watertube boilers and producing 11,000 shp for 22 knots in service. Passenger capacity was 900 first class and 404 second class and her accommodation was modernised in Southampton in 1962. Her black hull paint was raised to forecastle level forward and in 1967 she adopted the new British Rail colours of blue hull and red funnel with white crossed rail logo. Apart from the odd extra summer sailing to Boulogne, she spent her entire working life on the Dover–Calais run and was finally withdrawn on 8 August 1972 to make way for the new car ferry *Horsa*. While laid up in Newhaven, plans to use her on Greek ferry service between Patras and Brindisi came to nought and she was sold to be broken up at Nieuw Lekkerland, Holland, but was resold and ended her days in a Bruges scrapyard.

In September 1942 and March 1943, Mitsubishi, Nagasaki, delivered the grey-painted *Tenzan Maru* and *Konron Maru** to Japan's Ministry of Railways. Improved and larger versions of *Kongo Maru*, they measured 7,906-grt on dimensions of 443.3 × 59.8 ft, and were powered by twin-impulse turbines developing 16,900 shp. Steam was supplied by five watertube boilers with mechanical stokers and trials speeds were 23.25 and 23.45 knots respectively. On 11 November 1942, while on war service, *Tenzan Maru* collided with and sank the 7,938-grt passenger ship *Kobe Maru* some ninety miles off the Yangtse River estuary and on 5 October 1943 her sister was torpedoed by the US submarine *Wahoo* near Okinoshima in the East Channel of the Korea Strait, while transporting troops from Shimonoseki to Busan. Only seventy-two of the 616 persons aboard were saved and all further night troop sailings were cancelled as a result. *Tenzan Maru* lasted a little longer, but was bombed and sunk by US aircraft on 29 July 1945 near Misaki Light off west Honshu, with the loss of 583 lives. *(Bruce Peter collection)*

In 1939, the Société Nationale des Chemins de Fer Français (SNCF) ordered new steamers from Forges & Chantiers de la Méditerranée, Le Havre, to replace its worn-out *Newhaven* and *Rouen*. Provisional names of *Dieppe* and *Newhaven* were changed to *Londres* and *Vichy* at the start of the Second World War, but the former was seized by the invading Germans, who launched her in December 1941 and sent her to Germany for completion as a minesweeper. She operated as *Lothringen* in the Elbe and Weser estuaries and later in Danish waters but was returned to her builders from Kiel after the war. Her sister, renamed *Arromanches** in honour of the Normandy invasion, was completed in April 1946 and followed into service by *Londres* a year later. They measured 2,434/2,600 grt on dimensions of 308.5 oa × 42.3 ft and were driven by two sets of Parsons single-reduction steam turbines developing 22,000 shp ahead and 12,000 shp astern. Steam was supplied by two oil-fired, superheated Penhöet watertube boilers and speed was 24 knots. Passenger capacity totalled 1,450 persons, equal to a full boat train, and was divided into first and third classes with fourteen private cabins and 402 berths. *Londres* was transferred to the British Transport Commission in May 1955 in place of *Worthing* and sailed with an English crew until the end of 1963, when she was sold to Aegean Steam Navigation Typaldos Bros and left for Piraeus as *Ionion II* in December. She was given a new raked stem and single streamlined mast and, renamed *Sophoklis Venizelos*, operated to both

Rhodes and Crete. She caught fire during a refit on 14 April 1966 and was beached the following day and later broken up. *Arromanches* survived grounding in bad weather just east of Newhaven harbour entrance on 8 July 1964 and the following year was replaced by the car ferry *Falaise* and sold to Petros M Nomikos. Renamed *Leto* and painted white save for Nomikos' blue funnel markings of two narrow bands

enclosing a Maltese cross, she provided a daily service from Piraeus to Tenos and Mykonos. On 25 October 1970, she struck bottom while leaving Tenos in a gale and damaged her rudder and port propeller. She drifted towards Syros and the following day was towed into Ermopoulis, but she never sailed again and was broken up at Elefsis in 1973.

Post-war North Sea motorships

Neutral Sweden could still build ships during the Second World War and Götaverken A/B in Gothenburg was contracted by Swedish Lloyd in 1939 to build a new passenger ship for its North Sea service. The hull was subcontracted to the nearby Lindholmen yard and launched on 10 October 1940. The 6,458-grt *Saga** was completed with an all-white livery (prior publicity had shown her with a black hull) and her hull measured 420.8 oa × 55.3 ft on draught of around 19 ft. She was propelled at 18.5 knots by four eight-cylinder Götaverken diesels geared to a single shaft. She was designed for summer service on the Gothenburg–London route as well as for winter cruising and her partly air-conditioned accommodation provided berths for 160 first-, eighty second- and one hundred third-class passengers with a further sixty portable berths for the summer season. She made her maiden voyage to London on 20 May 1946, the sea passage lasting thirty-five hours, and was the largest ship yet to berth in the Upper Pool at New Fresh Wharf. Her first cruise visited Bergen and Hardangerfjord in spring 1946 and that October she inaugurated a regular pattern of off-season cruises with a month-long

cruise from London to the Canary Islands, Casablanca and the Iberian Peninsula. During the winter, the North Sea service was maintained by the older *Britannia* and *Suecia*. In 1949 her shelter-deck accommodation was changed to single cabins with private facilities. Air competition and increased running costs led to her sale in December 1956 to Compagnie Générale Transatlantique and, renamed *Ville de Bordeaux*, she was placed in service between

Bordeaux and Casablanca. In 1960 she was transferred to her owner's Marseilles or Nice to Corsica services carrying 181/144/66 passengers in first, tourist and fourth classes. Four years later she was sold to Navigation Maritime Bulgare and as *Nessebar* ran from Varna to Marseilles and later to Istanbul and Port Said. Her ownership changed to Balkanship State Passenger Lines in the 1970s and she was finally scrapped at Split, Yugoslavia, in 1976.

Following her launch by her royal namesake at the Elsinore Shipbuilding & Engineering Co on 20 June 1940, the Det Forenede D/S (United Shipping Co) 3,985gt *Kronprins Frederik** was moved to South Harbour, Copenhagen, and stripped of her valuable fittings for safekeeping during the German occupation. On 2 May 1945 she was towed back to Elsinore for completion and made her maiden voyage in June 1946. She measured 375.5 oa × 49.8 ft on a draught of 18.5 ft and was driven by a pair of ten-cylinder B&W diesels developing 8,400 bhp for a service speed of 20.5 knots, sufficient to reduce the 338-mile passage to around nineteen hours. Her stylish design was a development of the earlier *Kronprins Olav* and she could carry 138

first- and 146 second-class passengers whilst provision was made for the carriage of 33 cars in her two holds, the after of which was served by two electric cranes. *Kronprinsesse Ingrid*, an improved sister costing nearly twice as much, was completed at Elsinore in 1948. Her all-welded hull gave a 17-ton saving and she could be distinguished by longer bulwarks on the forecastle and more modern cranes. On 19 April 1953 at Harwich, *Kronprins Frederik* caught fire due to an electrical fault and capsized with much of her accommodation gutted. Raised in August, she was towed to Elsinore where repairs took around eight months. She was transferred to the Newcastle service in 1964 and after a refit in 1965 replaced *Kronprins Olav* on the Copenhagen-

Faroes-Iceland service in 1966. *Kronprinsesse Ingrid* was sold in 1969, briefly passing through other Danish hands as Copenhagen before becoming Costas Spyrou Latsis' *Mimika L* sailing between Piraeus and Rhodes. In 1976 *Kronprins Frederik* passed to Arab Navigators Co as *Patra* for the Red Sea pilgrim trade but *en route* to Suez on 24 December, caught fire about 50 miles north of Jeddah and sank with the loss of 102 lives. *Mimika L* was sold to Dodekanissos Shipping Enterprises in 1976 and Astir Shipping Enterprises two years later, being renamed *Alkyon* (Seagull). From late 1980 until October 1983 she ran for Dimitrios Ventouris and was broken up at Gadani Beach, Pakistan, in 1984.

Second turbo-electric steamer for Cook Strait

Ordered from Vickers-Armstrongs, Barrow-in-Furness, in 1939, the delivery of Union Steamship Co of New Zealand's 6,911-grt turbo-electric inter-island ferry *Hinemoa* was delayed by the Second World War and post-war shortages until December 1946. The first sizeable passenger vessel to be completed in the UK after the end of hostilities, her hull measurements were virtually identical to *Rangatira* at 419.3 and a little over 58 ft in breadth with a draught of 17 ft and she was propelled by two steam turbines connected to two British Thomson-Houston electric motors driving twin screws, with steam supplied by four Yarrow watertube drum boilers. Power output was 13,000 shp, which gave a maximum speed of 22 knots but only around 17 knots was required in service with part of the machinery shut down. A bow rudder was fitted for manoeuvring astern. A one-class ship, she could carry 300 berthed passengers and around 900 on deck, although this number varied seasonally. She replaced the forty-two-year old *Maori* on the Wellington–Lyttelton service, partnering *Rangatira* with *Wahine* held in

reserve. Following the switch to roll-on/roll-off operation with the brand-new *Wahine* and converted *Maori* (1954) in 1966, she was laid up in Wellington on 23 August and was bought the following year by the Hydro-Electric Commission of Tasmania for use as a floating power station/accommodation ship at Bell Bay. She departed as *George H Evans* on 25 October and

arrived in Tasmania five days later. After minimal use due to rains that ended the drought that necessitated the extra power requirement in the first place, she was sold on in 1969 to Hammersley Iron Ore Co for a similar role at Dampier, Western Australia, and was towed there in the spring. Her mission completed, she was towed to Hong Kong in 1971 for demolition.

New Irish Sea tonnage

The Isle of Man Steam Packet Co received its first post-war newbuilding, the 2,485-grt twin-screw *King Orry**, from Cammell Laird, Birkenhead, in April 1946, and this was swiftly followed by a sister, *Mona's Queen*. They were obvious developments of the pre-war *Fenella* pair that had been lost during the conflict but dimensionally were slightly larger at 345.1 oa × 47.2 ft. Two sets of Parsons single-reduction geared steam turbines, fed by three watertube boilers, generated 8,500 shp for 21 knots in service. Passenger capacity was 2,163 and they were designed for year-round operation. Their success led to the building of three more sisters – *Tynwald* in 1947, *Snaefell* in 1948 and *Mona's Isle* in 1951. Finally, a sixth ship, *Manxman*, appeared in 1955, differing externally with her boats mounted in gravity davits and, internally, driven by two Pametrada double-reduction geared turbines running on superheated steam from 350-psi boilers. *Mona's Queen* was sold to the Chandris Group in October 1962 and sailed for Piraeus in mid-November as *Barrow Queen*. She was rebuilt as the 3,158-grt, 350-passenger cruise ship *Carissima* with a deck swimming pool for fortnightly cruises from Venice. She was renamed *Carina* in 1963 and *Fiesta* in 1965 and was was laid up in the mid-1970s and broken up in 1981. *Tynwald* was withdrawn in August 1974 and sold to John Cashmore for demolition in Newport but was resold to Spanish breakers and scrapped at Aviles in 1975. *King Orry* was bought by R Taylor, Bury, in 1975 and berthed at Glasson Dock but broke adrift on 2 January 1976 and ran aground on a sandbank in the River Lune. Refloated three months later, she was towed to Rochester where she lay until broken up by Lynch & Son in 1979. *Snaefell*, which with *Mona's Isle* had closed the Heysham–Douglas service in late August 1974, was broken up in Blyth late in 1978 by the Rochdale Metal Recovery Co and *Mona's Isle*, which ran aground off Fleetwood in June 1955 and at Peel in February 1964 and had reopened the Fleetwood service in 1971, was withdrawn at the end of August 1980 and sold to Dutch breakers but was later resold for eventual demolition in Ghent. After a final season in 1982, *Manxman* sailed to Preston in October and became a restaurant ship in 1983. She was towed back to Liverpool in 1991 and two years later was moved to Hull where a fire damaged her interior. She was taken to the covered drydock of the Pallion yard in Sunderland and despite efforts to preserve her, was dismantled by early 2012.

To replace war losses, the Great Western Railway ordered two ships for its Fishguard–Rosslare overnight service from Cammell Laird, Birkenhead in 1946. *St David* was completed in September 1947 and her sister *St Patrick**, which was intended to sail from Weymouth to the Channel Islands during the summer, the following January. By this time the GWR had been absorbed into the new British Transport Commission, but both ships were officially registered to the Fishguard & Rosslare Railways & Harbours Co and retained their red funnels with black tops. They measured 3,352/3,482 grt on dimensions of 321.3 oa × 50.5 ft and drew 13.25 ft of water. A third deck in the hull, which had combined forecastle and bridge deck together with boat and bridge decks, gave them a compact appearance. Passenger capacity was around 1,300 in two classes with berths provided for 355/295 while 52/27 cars could be carried in the holds. Main machinery comprised two sets of Parsons single-reduction turbines with an output of 8,500 shp, with 70 per cent available for astern power, and the service speed was 19 knots. Three oil-fired Babcock & Wilcox watertube boilers provided steam. *St Patrick* was the first GWR steamer fitted with radar and sailed from Weymouth in summer with occasional excursions from there and Torquay, returning to the Irish Sea as a relief ship in winter. In December 1959, she was transferred to BTC (Southern Region) and operated a winter service from Weymouth with a buff funnel and the following winter was converted to a one-class ship. In October 1963, she moved from Weymouth to the Southampton–Le Havre service, which closed the following May, followed by a short stint on the St Malo service until that too closed in September 1964. She was then converted to a side-loading car ferry, *St David* having been similarly treated and her funnel given white FR letters earlier that year. In new Sealink livery, the 'Paddy' moved to the Dover–Calais and later Folkestone–Boulogne routes, sailing as a two-class ship, while *St David* acted as relief on the Holyhead–Dun Laoghaire service in 1969 before sale to the Chandris Group as *Holyhead* in 1971. Plans to use her for cruising failed and she was broken up near Piraeus in 1979. Meanwhile, her sister had continued to make occasional visits to the Channel Islands and St Malo, the last in May 1971. After a final sailing from Boulogne to Folkestone on 25 September 1971, she was laid up in Newhaven and was sold the following March to Gerasimos S Fetouris for Greece–Italy service as *Thermopylae*. The following year she was resold to Agapitos Bros and renamed *Agapitos 1* for Cyclades service, but was laid up when replaced by the former French ferry *Lisieux* in 1971 and scrapped at Perama in 1980.

Propulsion contrasts on English Channel

The twin-screw turbine *Falaise* was delivered to the Southern Railway by Wm Denny & Bros at Southampton on 14 June 1947. Intended mainly for the St Malo overnight service, she introduced a new profile for the route with a single funnel. She measured 3,710 grt on dimensions of 310.5 oa × 48.1 ft, and her twin Parsons geared turbines, fed with steam at 450 psi by two Foster Wheeler watertube boilers, developed around 8,500 shp for 20.5 knots in service. She was certified to carry 1,527 passengers in two classes with 338 berths and was fitted with stabilisers. During sixteen years on the St Malo run, *Falaise* also made

occasional forays elsewhere, taking the Golden Arrow service in winter 1947–8 and relieving on the Le Havre and Channel Island runs while regular ships were overhauled. She also made spring and autumn cruises with 216 passengers to French ports and in May 1961 offered two 'spring bulb' cruises from Folkestone to the Low Countries. At the end of the 1963 season she was taken in hand by the Vickers-Armstrongs Palmers' yard for conversion to a stern-loading car ferry for a Newhaven–Dieppe roll-on/roll-off service, which she inaugurated on 1 June 1964. Car capacity was 100, 25 of which were on the weather

deck reached by a folding ramp, and passenger numbers were reduced to 700 in one class. Gross tonnage was now 2,416. Replaced by the new *Senlac* in spring 1973, she was moved to Weymouth and opened the first ro-ro service to Jersey in June which was continued throughout the winter on a twice-weekly basis due to demand. From June 1974, the service included Guernsey after completion of the St Peter Port linkspan but engine problems led to her withdrawal on 14 August and replacement by the chartered *Svea Drott*. She failed survey in Holyhead and was broken up at Bilbao that winter.

To replace war losses, the Belgian Marine Administration ordered two new 1,700-passenger motor vessels from Cockerill, Hoboken. Work on *Koning Albert* began in great secrecy during the final period of German occupation and she was launched in June 1946 in the centenary year of the Ostend service. She entered service in January 1948 followed by *Prince Philippe** some six months later. Broadly similar to the pre-war motorships, they differed in having solid bulwarks on the foredeck, a more enclosed superstructure and wider funnel. Gross measurement was 3,700 tons on hull dimensions 373.7 oa × 49.1 ft and they were driven by the same twelve-cylinder Sulzer diesels developing 15,000 bhp for 22 knots in service and a maximum of 25.5 knots. On 16 June 1964, *Koning Albert* badly damaged her bows after colliding with the Norwegian tanker *Prometheus* and her sister suffered substantial damage in Ostend on 30 May 1966 when fire broke out in the seamen's quarters. Prins Philippe became surplus in 1973 and was transferred to the Baltic under the management of Strömma Line Belgium NV, running as *Stromma Rex* between the Swedish port of Norrköping and

Mariehamn in the Åland Islands. Her funnel colour was changed to red with a superimposed white anchor under a black top while her hull belting was painted dark orange. After running for just eight weeks, she caught fire on 2 September following an engine-room explosion and, deemed not worth repairing, was sold for demolition at Ystad. *Koning Albert* acted as a relief

ship in Ostend from 1973 and was put up for sale when her survey became overdue in 1976. She was sold in 1977 to Van Heyghen Frères and broken up at Ghent the following summer. She had been the thirtieth ship built by Cockerill for the Ostend–Dover mail service and fittingly her career lasted almost the same number of years.

New Harwich–Hook steamers

Soon after the Second World War, the London & North Eastern Railway ordered a new steamer from John Brown & Co to replace the lost *Amsterdam*. *Arnhem** was launched at Clydebank on 7 November 1946 and delivered the following May. Larger than the *Vienna* class at 4,891 grt on dimensions of 377.1 oa × 54.4 ft and 15.25 ft draught, and differing in having a raked stem, rounded bridge front and single elliptical funnel, she was otherwise a logical development with an extended upper deck. Originally a one-class ship with four special and 319 single cabins, a third of which had an extra berth if required, she was altered to carry a maximum of 750 passengers in two classes in 1949. Two sets of Parsons single-reduction geared turbines, fed by two watertube boilers, produced 8,000 shp for a speed of 21 knots. A near-sister was ordered to replace the loss of *Prague* by fire and duly appeared as the 5,092-grt *Amsterdam* (bottom) in May 1950. Improvements included an extended boat deck and lifeboats mounted in gravity davits. In spring 1954, *Arnhem* was refitted with improved overnight accommodation for 375 in first class and 200 in second class and given a new window arrangement. With two new car ferries under construction (one for Zeeland), *Arnhem* was withdrawn in April 1968 and sold for breaking up at

Inverkeithing. The new ships arrived in July, but problems with *St George* caused *Amsterdam* to be retained for a while. She was sold to the Chandris group in April 1969 and converted to a cruise ship in Piraeus, emerging in May 1970 as *Fiorita* with superstructure extended fore and aft, new masts and a domed funnel top, plus a swimming pool aft. She inaugurated alternate ten- and eleven-day summer cruises from Venice to Corfu, the Aegean Islands and either Istanbul or Alexandria, returning via Piraeus. Later Haifa and Dubrovnik calls were added. She also made occasional winter cruises, in 1970–1 running from Malaga to Dakar via Tangier and the Canary Islands and in March 1976 visiting the Red Sea. In spring 1978, she began a twelve-month charter to Norway's Aker group as an accommodation ship at Stord shipyard after which she was laid up at Piraeus when a planned programme of short cruises as *Ariane II* was cancelled. In March 1983, she was sold to German owners Sommerland Handels and later to Ef-Em Handels for use as a hotel ship at Kas in south-west Turkey. She was moved to Fethiye in August for an unsuccessful casino venture with Turkish owners and capsized after breaking adrift in a storm on 27 January 1987. Efforts to demolish the wreck were started in summer 2013. (bottom John G Callis)

New Irish Sea motorships

After the Second World War, the British & Irish Steam Packet Co ordered two new ships for its Dublin–Liverpool service. Taking the names of the pre-war pair, *Munster* and *Leinster** were delivered by Harland & Wolff, Belfast, in 1948. Large ships, they had a gross measurement of around 4,100 tons and the dimensions of their three-island type hulls were 366.8 oa x 50.2 ft. Twin Harland & Wolff/B & W ten-cylinder diesels gave a speed of 18 knots in service. Their paint scheme differed from that of their predecessors and comprised a green hull with cream line and a buff superstructure topped by a green funnel separated from the black top by a thin white band. They also reverted to carrying livestock and as a result carried slightly fewer passengers. While awaiting completion of her sister, *Munster* ran for two months on the City of Cork Steam Packet Co's Fishguard service and they began their new service on 5 April. They maintained a regular overnight service between Dublin North Wall and Prince's Dock, Liverpool, until withdrawn in October 1967. In 1968, they were replaced by new car ferries with the same names and briefly carried the suffix *I*. *Munster* was sold in July to George Potamianos' Epirotiki Steamship Navigation of Greece, bore the new name *Theseus* for about a year and became *Orpheus* in 1969. In the same year, *Leinster* also went Greece as *Aphrodite* for Med Sun Lines. Both were altered for Mediterranean cruising and *Orpheus'* more extensive conversion to carry 372 passengers included a new raked stem, filling-in of the forward well, forward extension of her superstructure and new masts and funnel. She cruised between Alaska and Panama in 1970–1 and in 1975 began a twenty-two-year charter to Swan

Hellenic, becoming a firm favourite and making round Britain cruises in 1980–2. *Aphrodite* was broken up at Aliaga, Turkey, in 1987, but her sister sailed briefly for Royal Olympic Cruises before being laid up in 1998. She was broken up at Alang, India, in 2001 after a fifty-two-year career.

A new *Innisfallen* to replace her namesake lost during the Second World War, was completed in June 1948 by Wm Denny & Bros, Dumbarton, for the British & Irish Steam Packet Co. A motorship of 3,706 grt on dimensions of 340 oa x 50.1 ft with a loaded draught of 14.5 ft, she was stabilised and could carry 600 first- and 302 second-class passengers in addition to 800 tons of cargo, some of which was refrigerated for the carriage of dairy products, 433 cattle and eight horses. The cattle deck was later converted to carry around seventy cars. She was propelled by twin twelve-cylinder Denny/Sulzer diesels developing 6,400 bhp for a service speed of 17 knots, which she exceeded by 1 knot on trials. Her outward appearance was typical of the Irish Sea motorships of the time with a single low funnel, in her case painted white a with black top, and she turned out to be the final ship to sail on the Cork–Fishguard route, which was discontinued after she had been laid up in November 1968. She was renamed *Innisfallen I* to free up her original name for a new car ferry building for British & Irish and shortly after was sold to Isthmian Navigation Co of Cyprus, which was an associate of Hellenic Mediterranean Lines. During a refit at Piraeus, she was renamed *Poseidonia* and repainted with a light grey hull and a red funnel with a black top. She entered regular summer ferry service for Libra Maritime Lines, running between Patras and Brindisi, and continued thus until broken up at Brindisi in 1985.

Orders placed with Fairfield Shipbuilding & Engineering, Glasgow in 1939 for two large geared turbine steamers for the London, Midland & Scottish Railway's Holyhead–Dun Laoghaire service were cancelled due to the war. Instead, the 4,972-grt motor vessels *Hibernia** and *Cambria* were completed by Harland & Wolff, Belfast, in April–May 1949 for the new British Transport Commission established in 1948 following railway nationalisation. The only traditional railway passenger ships to be diesel driven, they measured 396 oa x 55.2 ft with 14.8-ft draught and their two B & W eight-cylinder diesel engines produced a combined output of 9,600 bhp for a service speed of 21 knots. They could carry around 2,000 passengers in first and second classes but a propensity to roll led to the fitting of stabilisers in 1951. They maintained overnight services on a year-round basis but also made extra daytime departures during the summer months. During extensive refits in 1964–5, their first-class accommodation was reduced to provide more space for second-class passengers and they emerged in

the new British Rail colours of red funnel with crossed rail logo and monastral blue hulls. Withdrawn in 1976, *Cambria* was sold to Orri Navigation Co of Saudi Arabia and renamed *Al Taif* but sank while at anchor in Suez

Roads in 1981. *Hibernia* was purchased by Agapitos Bros, Piraeus and renamed *Express Apollon* but never sailed as such and rusted away at Drapetsona until broken up in 1980 at Darukhana, India.

New turbine steamers for English Channel

Completed in 1949 for the British Transport Commission's Southern Region, *Maid of Orleans* was the fourteenth and final turbine packet to be built by Denny for the Dover Strait. A vessel of 3,776 grt on dimensions of 341.3 oa x 52 ft with 12.4-ft draught, she was a modernised version of *Canterbury* with a raked stem, more built-up superstructure forward and a shorter and wider funnel. Main propulsion comprised two single-reduction Parsons turbines powered by steam from two Foster Wheeler D type

watertube boilers with a working pressure of 280 psi and on measured mile trials in May 1949 she attained just over 22.5 knots at 10,126 shp. Designed as a day boat for the Folkestone-Boulogne service, she was stabilised and could carry 886 first-class and 736 second-class passengers, with spaces for the latter improved in 1962 and 1966. To counteract deck fume problems, her funnel was raised and a fireman's helmet added during a winter 1958–9 overhaul by Thorneycroft in Southampton. Her normal two return

crossings a day were increased to three in 1964 and the following year she was joined by the Western Region's *St Patrick* in place of *Canterbury*. Consideration was given to converting her to a side-loading car ferry for the Fishguard–Rosslare route in autumn 1965 but the Eastern Region's *Avalon* was chosen instead. On 2 June 1973 she was moved to a summer only one-class service between Dover and Calais and after a final season in 1975 was towed from lay-up in Newhaven to Santander for demolition by Steelnorte S A.

The 2,875-grt *Brighton* was delivered to the Southern Region (British Railways) of the British Transport Commission by Wm Denny & Bros in May 1950. She was the first channel steamer to be fitted with lightweight tripod masts and her hull measurements of 311.8 x 43.5 ft with 11.1 ft draught, made her the largest of all the British-built ships for the Newhaven–Dieppe service. A twin-screw steamer, she was propelled by two Pametrada single-reduction geared turbines fed with steam by two Foster Wheeler watertube boilers. During loaded trials on the Skelmorlie mile she exceeded the contract speed of 24 knots by half a knot with her engines developing around 18,100 shp though failed to make 24 knots during a six-hour trial. Once run in she often exceeded 25 knots in service and on one occasion made three return crossings within twenty-four hours. Her daytime passenger complement was 1,450 persons but she also had two-berth cabins and open saloon berths for night passages. Following the completion of a car ferry ramp in Newhaven in June 1964, she was relegated to relief sailings and 'no passport' trips, making a rare visit to Folkestone in July 1966 for a pilgrim excursion to Boulogne. Her excessive fuel consumption led to her withdrawal after a final Dieppe sailing on 18 September 1967 and she was sold in December to Mr Cowasjee's Jersey Lines and renamed *La Duchesse de Bretagne*. During a three-month refit in Antwerp she was fitted with two quarter ramps at upper deck level to allow her to load up to twenty cars, while at the same time aircraft-type seating and a new bar were installed. On 15 May 1967, with the yellow part of her funnel changed to red and bearing a white anchor, she commenced an ambitious schedule sailing from Torquay and Weymouth to Guernsey, Jersey and St Malo. Her first season was successful but adding Southampton and Plymouth calls in place of Weymouth in 1968 was less so and, taken with her high fuel costs, forced her owner into bankruptcy early in 1969. *La Duchesse de Bretagne* was arrested in Southampton and sold to scrap dealer Harry Pound who towed her to Portsmouth to await a buyer. None materialised and she was resold in April 1970 and towed to Bruges for demolition.

To replace the Société Anonyme de Gérance et d'Armement (SAGA) sisters *Cote d'Argent* and *Cote d'Azur* lost during the Second World War, and for operation by Société Nationale des Chemins de fer Français (SNCF), SAGA ordered a new steamer for the Dover Strait in 1949. Perpetuating the name of the latter, she was launched by Forges & Chantiers de la Méditerranée, Le Havre, on 3 April 1950 and underwent trials on 31 July, attaining over 25.5 knots and reaching 20.5 knots on just one boiler. At 3,998-grt she was the largest of the French channel steamers and had a pleasing sheer to her hull, which measured 365.3 x 50.6 ft and featured a prominent knuckle forward. Considerable use of aluminium was made in the construction of her bridge and superstructure, also in the patent FCM-Valensi 'Strombos'-type funnel, which was narrow in section and aerofoil in shape to keep exhaust gases clear of the decks. Her engine room differed from the two compartment arrangement favoured by the British by having an extra space for the auxiliary diesel generators. She was driven by twin sets of Parsons single-reduction geared turbines supplied with steam by two FCM 47 oil-fired boilers, which provided a maximum output of 22,000 shp and 16,000 shp in normal service. Passenger complement was 690 and 736 in first and second classes respectively and while mainly employed on day service between Calais and Folkestone, she was fitted with 530 overnight berths in twelve private cabins and dormitories. She entered service in August 1950 under the management and colours of SAGA but the following May her funnel colour was changed from white to SNCF's newly adopted buff. Apart from the occasional visit to Dover, *Cote d'Azur* spent her entire career on the Folkestone run and was withdrawn on 30 September 1972 and put up for sale pending the arrival of the new multipurpose car ferry *Chartres*. Bought by SA Monegasque d'Armement & de Navigation the following year, she was briefly renamed *Azur* but arrived in Monaco on 8 July as *Marie F*. Suitable berthing in Monte Carlo could not be found for an intended service to Corsica, Sardinia and Genoa and after an abortive plan to use her as a casino, she was towed away to lay up in the Etang de Berre near Marseilles. She was broken up at Murcia in 1975.

The final pure passenger steamer built for the joint Newhaven–Dieppe service, Société Nationale des Chemins de Fer Français (SNCF)'s 2,946-grt, part-welded *Lisieux*, was a smaller version and from the same yard as *Cote d'Azur*, sharing similar features of an aluminium superstructure and Strombos type funnel. Her two boilers were of the improved FCM 47/60 type for more rapid firing and easier power variation and on trials in spring 1952 she averaged almost 25.5 knots with her twin sets of Parsons single-reduction geared turbines developing 22,000 shp. Overall length of 313.3 ft was some 50 ft less than *Cote d'Azur* but she was 1.5 ft longer and some 2 ft beamier than her running consort *Brighton* but drawing marginally less water at 10.5 ft. Her passenger complement was 1,450 but when overall numbers began to decline five years later, her winter service was suspended from October 1958 and thereafter she only sailed between March and October. The new car ferry service with *Falaise* started on 1 June 1964 but together with *Brighton* she began the 1965 season, but poor occupancy led to her

being withdrawn after making a final crossing on 26 June. She was chartered to Compagnie Générale Transatlantique for twelve weeks and with funnel colour changed from buff to red, sailed five days a week between St Malo and St Helier, Jersey in addition to a weekly return day excursion from Torquay to Guernsey on Wednesdays, returning overnight to St Malo from Weymouth. Heavy losses led to her being laid up and she was sold the following February to Petros M Nomikos who was already operating the former Newhaven steamer *Arromanches*. Refitted in Le Havre with an extended promenade deck aft, she was renamed *Apollon* and given a new all-white livery, save for blue funnel markings. In May 1966, she commenced a daily service from Piraeus to Tinos and Mykonos and quickly proved popular with discerning travellers. Petros Nomikos quit the passenger business in 1975 and *Apollon* was acquired by Agapitos Brothers, who continued to run her on the same service but under their colours of green funnel top and AA emblem. She was finally withdrawn and broken up at Elefsis in 1982.

The 3,543-grt *Normannia* was delivered to the British Transport Commission by Wm Denny & Bros in January 1952 to replace *Hantonia* on the Le Havre station. Dimensionally similar to *Falaise* at 309.2 × 49.6 ft, she lacked a raised forecastle and bridge cabs and had tripod masts and a sloping-topped funnel. Her two Pametrada double-reduction geared turbines were novel in a channel steamer and steam was supplied by two Foster Wheeler boilers, power output being around 8,000 shp for 19.5 knots in service. Her passenger complement totalled 1,400 with berths for 325 persons. She attended the Coronation Naval Review at Spithead in June 1953 and made occasional relief sailings on other routes, notably Harwich–Hook that autumn. From November 1958, she instigated occasional winter visits from Weymouth to the Channel Islands and St Malo and in May 1960 made two weekend cruises from Dover to Antwerp/Ostend and Amsterdam. Shortly before the Le Havre service closed, *Normannia* made her last crossing from the French port on 3 December 1963 and was sent to Hawthorn Leslie, Hebburn, for conversion to a car ferry. Her main and upper decks were replaced by garage space for 111 cars, while gross tonnage was reduced to 2,217 and passenger capacity to 500. She opened a Dover–Boulogne service on 21

April 1964 but sailed from Newhaven on several occasions and on 9 July 1965 inaugurated the Holyhead–Dun Laoghaire ro-ro service in place of the delayed *Holyhead Ferry 1*. She sailed between Dover and Calais on charter to SNCF for six months from April 1973 and then replaced *Falaise* until March 1974 on the Weymouth–Channel Islands service. While shifting berth in Dover on 1 July she was holed and

flooded her engine-room and car deck but returned to the Weymouth station that October for a further nine months. After opening another new service from Dover to Dunkirk West in July 1976, she was put up for sale but still acted as a reserve ship until laid up in Newhaven in May 1978. A potential sale to Red Sea Ferries of Dubai for pilgrim use fell through and she was sold for breaking up at Gijon.

New CP ships for Canadian west coast

The twin-screw turbo-electric sisters *Princess Marguerite** and *Princess Patricia* were completed for the Canadian Pacific Railway by Fairfield Shipbuilding & Engineering Co, Govan, in 1949. With a gross tonnage of 5,911 and hull measurement of 373.8 oa × 58.2 ft with 15.6 ft draught, they were driven by two sets of Parsons steam turbines connected to two British Thomson-Houston electric motors, for a maximum speed of 23 knots. They could carry 2,000 passengers and fifty cars. They left the Clyde left on 6 March and 10 May respectively for their delivery voyages to Victoria, British Columbia and were placed on the 'Triangle Route' between Vancouver, Victoria and Seattle. By 1963, *Princess Marguerite* was only used in the summer months and her sister was converted for summer cruising to Alaska. Three years later the latter was chartered to Princess Cruises for a series of winter cruises from Los Angeles to Acapulco. Canadian Pacific withdrew from the summer service to Seattle in September 1974, but it was resumed the following year when *Princess Marguerite* was bought by the government-owned British Columbia Steamship Co (1975) for operation by the British Columbia Department of Transportation. Both ships were withdrawn in 1979 and *Princess Patricia* was sold in 1985 to Hampstead Holdings and managed by Fox, Morgan & Co, her hull being painted grey. The following year she was chartered by Great American Cruise Lines. In 1987 *Princess Marguerite* was bought by BC Stena Line and used as a summer excursion ship and the following year her sister was sold for scrap and towed by the tug *Baltic Rescuer* to Kaohsiung where she arrived on 8 June to await the attention of Chi Shun Hua Steel Co. *Princess Marguerite*'s active service ended in November 1990 when US legislation banned offshore gambling and she was bought by Mykris Hotels for projected use in the UK port of Bristol. Before she could leave, a dispute over severance pay between Stena and the Canadian Merchant Service Guild led to her arrest and she was eventually towed to India for demolition in 1996.

Canadian Pacific's 6,787-grt *Princess of Nanaimo* was a side-loading car ferry completed by Fairfield Shipbuilding & Engineering Co at Govan in May 1951 for the Vancouver–Nanaimo service. She had an imposing appearance dominated by a large raked funnel and her hull measured 357.9 oa × 62.1 ft. She was propelled by two sets of single-reduction steam turbines that developed 9,000 shp for a service speed of 18 knots. Some 1,500 day passengers were accommodated on three decks and up to 130 cars could be garaged on the main and lower decks. After a final crossing to Nanaimo on the last day of September 1962, she left Victoria on 28 February 1963 for Halifax, Nova Scotia to replace the ageing *Princess Helene* on the Bay of Fundy crossing between Digby, Nova Scotia and St John, New Brunswick. She began operating on 29 April under the new name *Princess of Acadia* and in November 1965 was fitted with a bow thrust during an overhaul at Lauzon in Quebec. Replaced in 1971 by the purpose-built 10,000-grt roll-on, roll-off car ferry *Princess of Acadia*, she reverted to her old name on 3 May and was laid up at the end of the month. Stripped of her passenger accommodation and with car capacity increased to 225 vehicles, she commenced running between St John and St John's, Newfoundland on 14 November under the new name of *Henry Osborne*. On 16 May 1973, she ran aground in St John harbour and due to her age was not considered worth repairing. On 27 November, she was sold for scrap to Union Pipe & Machinery Co of Montreal but was quickly resold and in the New Year was towed from St John to Bilbao for demolition.

North Sea contrasts

Fred Olsen ordered two replacement ships for its Newcastle service from Akers, Oslo but the hull work was subcontracted to John I Thorneycroft & Co's Woolston yard in Southampton. Measuring 4,766/4,776 grt on dimensions of 375 × 53.2 ft with a draught of 17.5 ft, *Blenheim* and *Braemar* were driven by a single eight-cylinder B & W diesel developing 3,750 bhp for 16 knots. Aluminium was used in the construction of the superstructure and wind-tunnel tested funnels and they entered service in February 1951 and May 1953, sailing twice a week on alternate days in winter and three times a week in summer. Overnight berths were provided for around 100 in first class in mainly single cabins, 130 in second in doubles and thirty-six in groups in double, four-berth and six-berth cabins. On 21 May 1968, *Blenheim* caught fire and was abandoned about 220 miles east of Dundee. Towed to Kristiansand with gutted superstructure, she was sold to Uglands Rederi in 1969, who converted her to the 2,404-grt car carrier *Cilaos* at Grimstad. Transferred to Ocean Car Carriers, Singapore in 1974 she was sold through London brokers to Pakistani breakers in 1981 and arrived at Gadani Beach in September. Meanwhile

Braemar continued on her regular run, latterly as the last traditional passenger ship on the North Sea, until replaced in September 1975 by Olsen's car ferry *Borgen*. Sold to Dashwood Finance Co, Manila acting for Peninsular Tourist Shipping Corporation, she was renamed *The Philippine Tourist* and converted to a floating casino off Manila under the management of

Manila Bay Enterprises. In 1978 she was replaced by *Philippine Tourist* (the former Sitmar liner *Fairsky*), renamed *Philippine Tourist 1* and towed to Cebu City. She was returned to Manila in winter 1979–80 after her replacement had burned out and was laid up, but her eventual fate is obscure.

Swedish Lloyd's 7,775-grt *Patricia* was completed on Tyneside by Swan, Hunter & Wigham Richardson in May 1951. An improved *Saga* with a raised forecastle and boat mounted in gravity davits, she measured 454.1 oa × 58.3 ft on a draught of 19 ft but reverted to steam turbines – three Parsons single-reduction units geared to a single screw. Steam was supplied by two Babcock & Wilcox watertube boilers working at 465 psi and output amounted to 8,650 shp for 19 knots in service. Overnight berths were provided for 166 first-, seventy-eight second- and 100 third-class passengers plus seasonal dormitory space for sixty-four. Designed for winter cruising, she made her first voyage from Tilbury to the Mediterranean in September 1951 followed by a twenty-six-day voyage to Istanbul. That winter she made an experimental cruise to Bermuda and for the two following winters was chartered for Caribbean cruising from New York. Declining North Sea traffic in summer 1955 saw her chartered by Hapag Lloyd Travel for two Mediterranean cruises before being laid up in Gothenburg due to the Suez Crisis. Hapag Lloyd bought her in 1957 and converted her to the 249-berth cruise ship Ariadne, extending her forecastle to the superstructure and adding a swimming pool. Sold to McCormick Shipping for Caribbean cruising in 1959, she subsequently passed through several more US owners before being acquired by the Chandris Group in 1973 and renamed *Freeport II*. Refitted in Piraeus, she emerged in 1974 as the 380-passenger

6,725-grt *Bon Vivant* with enlarged superstructure, new single mast above the bridge and a taller funnel and was chartered to Flagship Cruises for Caribbean operation in 1974–5. In summer 1976, she operated fortnightly cruises from Piraeus and from early 1977 was used by Dubai Maritime Corp for a year as a hotel ship in Dubai before being laid up near Piraeus.

In 1979 she was transferred to Gilda Maritime Corp and renamed *Ariane* but after a final season of cruises was again laid up. She was sold to Nios Maritime in 1989 and re-registered to Regent Fortune Corp, Panama in 1995, finally being scrapped at Alang, India as *Empress* at the end of 1997.

Mediterranean melange

After WW2 the French government commissioned two new ships from Swan, Hunter & Wigham Richardson/Wallsend for operation by C N Mixte. The provisional name of the first *El Kantara II* was changed to *President de Cazalet* whilst fitting out and given instead to the second ship which was then deemed superfluous and transferred to the Societé Générale de Transports Maritimes as *Sidi-Bel-Abbes*. Delivered in 1947/48, they measured 5,227gt on dimensions of 402 oa x 54 ft and could carry 899 passengers in total, berths being supplied for 97 in first, 226 in second and 578 in third classes. Two sets of Parsons steam turbines developing 11,000shp and fed with steam by two oil-fired Le Mont water-tube boilers gave a trial speed of 21 knots. *President de Cazalet* entered Marseilles-Algiers service in July 1948 and in October 1949 her conventional funnel was replaced by a narrow Strombos-Valensi aerofoil one. In November 1950 she replaced *El Mansour* on the Port Vendres-Algiers/Oran service and in March 1954 inaugurated a new service from Port Vendres to Algiers via Palma de Majorca. *Sidi-Bel-Abbes* had been given a larger dome-topped funnel displaying her owner's coat of arms in April 1952. On 5 September 1958 *President de Cazalet* was disabled by a terrorist bomb in her boiler room and was towed back to

Marseilles for repairs by the company's *Djebel Dira*. *Sidi-Bel-Abbes* was given a white hull towards the end of her service and in 1963, following a voyage to Jeddah, was sold to Hellenic Mediterranean Lines and renamed *Apollonia* for a seasonal Venice-Ancona-Corfu-Piraeus run. In May 1967 *President de Cazalet* was bare-boat chartered to CGT as *Méditerranée* and the following year was sold to the newly formed Cie Générale Transméditerranéenne. In 1971 she was sold

to Constantine Efthymiadis who ran her as *Arcadi* between Piraeus and Cyprus. In March 1973 she was transferred to Arcadi Shipping but was laid up at Perama in 1974 after Efthymiadis went bankrupt, finally being scrapped locally in 1980. *Apollonia* latterly sailed on a Marseilles-Piraeus-Haifa-Limassol route until laid up at Chalkis in 1980. Sold for scrap in 1988, she sailed as *Precious* to Alang where she arrived on 9 July for demolition by Arya Steel.

The 4,401-grt *Commandant Quéré* was built by J I Thorneycroft, Southampton, in 1948 for the French Ministry of Merchant Marine for the Marseilles–Corsica overnight service. Launched in the colours of Compagnie Fraissinet, she was delivered in the livery of Compagnie Générale Transatlantique, which had taken over the operation of the route in the meantime. She was named after the captain of

the Fraissinet ferry General Bonaparte, who had acquitted himself bravely when she was torpedoed in 1943. *Commandant Quéré*'s design incorporated a long raised forecastle and a poop faired into the superstructure and she was fitted with a Thorneycroft-type funnel for the dispersal of fumes – the only French ship so equipped. Her hull dimensions were 363 oa x 50.2 ft on draught of 17 ft

and her propelling machinery comprised two sets of double-reduction steam turbines developing 5,400 shp for 15.5 knots in service. Accommodation was provided for 204 first-class passengers amidships, 146 in third class forward and 644 fourth class aft. She spent almost the whole of her career on Corsican services and after being replaced by new car ferry services was broken up at Vado Ligure in 1969.

Before the Second World War, Compagnie de Navigation Mixte dropped plans for a 30-knot ferry on financial grounds and instead ordered a more modest but nevertheless speedy ship. Kairouan* was laid down by Forges & Chantiers de la Méditerranée, La Seyne, on 23 June 1940 and launched on 17 January 1942. Construction proceeded slowly, but when almost complete she was scuttled by the retreating Germans on 17 August 1944 in the entrance to the Bay of Toulon, her stern resting on the sunken Italian liner Virgilio. She was raised with great difficulty in 1947 and rebuilt at La Seyne, but while fitting out at La Ciotat a serious fire occurred on 18 November 1949, resulting in delayed completion in June 1950. Designed by Jacques Saugeron, she measured 8,589 grt on dimensions of 486 oa × 60 ft and was the first ship to be driven by two sets of Alsthom turbo-electric machinery developing a maximum of 28,000 shp, with 20,000 shp sufficient for a service speed of 24 knots. Steam was supplied by four La Mont boilers. She originally carried 135 passengers in de luxe and first, 330 in tourist and 923 in fourth classes. Her design incorporated a Maierform bow and prominent knuckle forward as well as a Strombos-Valensi type aerofoil funnel and her three holds were served by four cranes. She entered service without ceremony on 18 August 1950, but condenser trouble necessitated a return to FCM for an engine overhaul. On subsequent trials she made

over 25 knots in a force 7 wind and worrying vibration was cured by changing her propellers in April 1952. In April 1951, Kairouan made a record passage from Marseilles to Algiers in around fifteen hours and thirty minutes at a mean speed of 26 knots. In January 1954, her forecastle was extended to the superstructure to provide more shelter for steerage passengers and her promenade deck extended to the stern. In June 1957, she inaugurated regular cruises with a visit to Greece and over the

next few years visited many of the Mediterranean's historic sites. On 7 January 1961, Kairouan suffered a turbo-alternator explosion and was towed back to Algiers. In July 1969, she was bareboat chartered to Compagnie Générale Transmediterranée, an amalgamation of the Mediterranean ferry fleets of Compagnie Générale Transatlantique and Mixte, and her funnel was repainted red with a black top and white band. She was sold in 1973 for demolition at Vinaroz, Spain.

The final conventional Mediterranean ferries for Compagnie Générale Transatlantique were the sisters Ville de Marseille and Ville de Tunis*, delivered in 1951–2. The former was completed in May 1951 by Forges & Chantiers de la Méditerranée, La Seyne, and the latter in February 1952 by Arsenal de Lorient. Gross tonnages were 9,576 and 9,226 and hull dimensions 465.9 oa × 63.9 ft. Propulsion was by two

sets of Parsons single-reduction geared steam turbines producing an output of 14,500 shp, which gave 23 knots during a twelve-hour trial and 21 knots in service. Steam was supplied by three high-pressure FCM boilers. Both had Strombos type aerofoil funnels and Ville de Marseille was the first French liner to be fitted with Denny Brown stabilisers. Their regular routes were to be from Marseilles to Algiers and

Tunis respectively carrying 148 first-, 364 second- and 468 fourth-class passengers but before completion Ville de Marseille's accommodation was altered to 151/234/143/59 in four classes in addition to 200 deck passengers for transfer to her owner's Bordeaux–Casablanca service in June 1951, for which her speed brought a reduction in passage time to around fifty hours. She was renamed Maroc that December but eventually was found to be a loss maker and was replaced in January 1956 by Ville de Bordeaux, formerly Swedish Lloyd's Saga, and returned to Marseilles–Algiers service under her original name following a refit at La Seyne. Her sister, meanwhile, had remained on the Tunis run but was sold to Helen and Dimitrios Kyriakos of Piraeus in 1967 and after some conversion work was renamed Megalonissos Kriti and placed in overnight service between Piraeus and Crete. Two years later she was renamed City of Athens under K Shipping Enterprises management but with her owners in financial trouble she was laid up. Ville de Marseille was sold to Spanish breakers in 1973 and towed from Marseilles to Bilbao, where she arrived on 12 June. Her sister quietly rotted at Scaramanga until 1980, finally leaving Piraeus for breakers in Barcelona on 14 March 1980, but while in tow she foundered in heavy weather fifty-seven miles east-south-east of Formentera Island on 26 March.

The 7,608-grt *El Djezair*, the second to hold the name in the Compagnie de Navigation Mixte fleet, was the first European passenger ship to have engines placed aft, the idea having been pioneered by Matson Line in the early years of the twentieth century. She was built at La Seyne by Forges & Chantiers de la Méditerranée in 1952 and measured 433.2 oa × 59.3 ft on 19 ft draught. Although striking in looks with a narrow Strombos type funnel, she failed to live up to expectations because her top hamper caused her to roll heavily in bad weather and made her unpopular with the travelling public. Her six Parsons single-reduction steam turbines, which had been salved from her sunken namesake, were fed by two La Mont boilers and developed 12,000 shp for a service speed of 21 knots but she reached a mean speed of 22.75 knots on trials and a maximum of 24 knots for a brief spell. Overnight berths were provided for eighty-eight in first, 240 in tourist and 493 in steerage classes and the crew numbered thirteen officers and 100 seamen. Her three cargo holds, two forward and one amidships, were served by electric cranes and she had a deadweight capacity of 2,119 tons. *El Djezair* was sold to Sovereign Cruises of Cyprus in 1970 and taken to Malta for intended conversion to a cruise ship. Unaltered, she was laid up as *Floriana* in Bilbao until January 1972, when she was bought by Chandris' Piccadilly Steamship Co and towed to Piraeus. Chandris discovered her engines were unsatisfactory and, still unaltered, went to Valencia in summer 1973 for demolition.

In 1952–3, Tirrenia SpA di Navigazione took delivery of five twin-screw motorships named after regions: *Sicilia*, *Calabria** and *Lazio* from Riuniti, Palermo and *Campania Felix* and *Sardegna* from Cantieri Navalmeccanica, Naples. Handsome vessels, they measured 5,200 grt on dimensions of 382.5 oa × 52 ft on 17.3 ft draught and were driven by four Fiat six-cylinder double-acting diesels geared to twin screws and which developed 7,200 bhp, providing a service speed of around 17 knots. Five hundred and sixty passengers were carried in three classes in air-conditioned accommodation. The ships were designed for Naples–Palermo and Civitavecchia–Olbia service, all four engines being used on the former and just two giving 15 knots on the latter. In 1957 the similar but modified sisters *Arborea* and *Caralis* were completed by Navalmeccanica. With bridge and forecastle combined, their gross measurement was 5,485 tons on slightly larger dimensions of 395 oa × 52.5 ft on a draught of 17.8 ft. Their Fiat engines had an extra cylinder to give 18 knots in service and they could carry seventy-five first-, 400 second- and 172 third-class passengers in addition to a number of cars loaded through side doors. They were placed on a Naples–Palermo–Cagliari–Civitavecchia–Cagliari service. The older ships' routes later varied from Naples–Palermo–Tunis to the shorter Palermo–Cagliari, Civitavecchia–Olbia and Naples–Cagliari services as well as Genoa–Port Torres–Leghorn–Bastia–Porto Torres–Genoa. In 1971, *Campania Felix* was broken up in Ortona and in 1973 *Caralis* was sold to Sweet Lines for Philippines service as *Sweet Home*. *Arborea* became the Cyprus-registered *Golden Sun* in 1976 but was laid up in Piraeus in at the end of August 1978 and scrapped in the mid-1980s. Meanwhile, *Sweet Home* had been renamed *Sampaguita* and *Reyna Filipinas* in 1978, then *Reyna Filipina* in 1980, which capsized on 24 November 1981 while laid up off Manila and was later broken up. *Lazio*, which had been converted to a stern-loading car ferry in 1979, was quickly sold to Greece and renamed *Sant Andrea* before further name changes: *Makedomia* in 1984, *Summer Star* 1985, *Corfu Diamond* 1987, *Larnaca Rose* 1989, *Avrasia* 1992 and *Cortina* 1996. She was scrapped as *Avrasia 1* at Aliaga in 1997. The remaining two ships were scrapped at Porto Nogaro in 1988.

Last traditional Irish Sea motorships

The handsome 3,824-grt *Irish Coast** was delivered to Coast Lines by Harland & Wolff, Belfast, in October 1952. Designed as a relief ship for the group's Irish cross-channel services, she followed the pattern set by previous Belfast-built motor vessels. Part welded and measuring 339.6 oa × 51.5 ft on a draught of 15 ft, she was was driven by two Harland & Wolff/B & W single-acting ten-cylinder diesels developing 6,500 bhp for a service speed of 17.5 knots. Stabilised, she berthed 242 passengers in saloon class amidships and a further 146 in steerage aft and also catered for the carriage of 348 head of cattle and eight horses. Chartered to Burns & Laird Line, she replaced *Lairdscastle* on the overnight Glasgow–Dublin service and attended the Coronation Naval Review at Spithead in May 1953. She was joined in December 1957 by near-sister

Scottish Coast (3,817 grt), which in Belfast Steamship Co colours ran on its Liverpool–Belfast service before being initially chartered and then transferred to Burns & Laird Line, whose colours she assumed, in December 1958. *Irish Coast* replaced *Lairds Isle* on the seasonal daylight Ardrossan–Belfast run in 1961 but her five-hour passage only allowed passengers one hour ashore. Her sister took over in July 1965 but otherwise sailed mainly on the Glasgow–Belfast route. Increasing use of air travel and the spread of ro-ro traffic led to their withdrawal and *Irish Coast* was sold to Epirotiki Steamship Navigation Co 'George Potamianos' in August 1968 and renamed *Semiramis II* and *Achilleus* the following year. With superstructure extended forward and redesigned funnel, she was renamed *Apollon II* for Aegean and

Ionian cruising. In 1981 she was sold to Panamanian interests and renamed *Regency* for Caribbean cruising, but later found her way to the Phillipines, where she grounded on 11 October 1989 while laid up off Batangas and broken up in Manila. Meanwhile, *Scottish Coast* had followed her to Greek waters in November 1969, sailing as *Galaxias* for Kavounides' Hellenic Cruises. After operating fly cruises in the Canary Islands, she was sold in 1988 to Global Cruises and registered at Saint John's, Antigua & Barbuda but was laid up in Vancouver. Briefly owned by Golden Cruise Tours, Acapulco, as *Galaxy*, she was acquired in 1989 by Louis Cruises of Limassol and renamed *Princess Amorosa*. A large fin was added to her funnel and she continued to cruise in the Aegean area until scrapped as *Rosa* at Alang in 2003.

Baltic steamers

In 1951, the Scandinavian shipping companies Finland Line, Bore Line and Rederi A/B Svea ordered similar steamships to prepare the Helsinki–Stockhom overnight run for the 1952 Olympic Games in Helsinki. Finland Line's 2,973-grt *Aallotar** was the first to be completed by Elsinore Shipbuilding & Engineering Co, Elsinore, in June 1952, followed by Bore Line's 3,007-grt two-funnelled *Bore III** (*bottom*) from Oskarshamns Varv in December. Svea Line's 3,236-grt *Birger Jarl* was not delivered by Finnboda Varf, Stockholm, until June 1953 and missed the Olympics. *Aallotar* and *Birger Jarl* were 6 ft longer than *Bore III* at 304 ft overall, but all shared the same beam of 46.7 ft and similar draught of around 16 ft. They were driven by two old-fashioned quadruple-expansion engines coupled to a low pressure turbine, output being 3,300 ihp for 14 knots. In winter, they were used on the Turku–Mariehamn–Stockholm run and *Aallotar* was given a larger domed funnel in 1964. In 1969–70 she sailed between Helsinki and Travemünde in summer and undertook several local cruises. She was sold to Bore Line in May 1971 and renamed *Bore II* in September before a Jakob Line charter. Extra cabins were fitted forward early in 1972, but while laid up in Turku she was destroyed by fire on 3 November 1973 and eventually broken up by Helsingin Romuliiki in Helsinki in February 1975, part of her being retained as the work barge *Aksu*. *Birger Jarl* was acquired by Jakob Line in 1973 and rebuilt at Finnboda as *Bore Nord* with a small

ro-ro ramp for trucks aft. In 1974–5 she was chartered to Bore Line for a summer Stockholm–Turku–Visby service and that winter was used as an accommodation ship at Akers shipyard in Stavanger. In 1976 *Bore III* crossed the Atlantic to become Midwest Cruises' *Lowell Thomas Explorer* but her new owners failed before she could make a series of planned Great Lakes cruises and the following year she was bought by Canadian-backed Thoroughfun Corporation and renamed *Royal Clipper*. Shortly before leaving Montreal for Spain, she caught fire on 6 December 1977 and capsized, being eventually scrapped at Port Maitland in 1982. Having returned to Jakob Line's Gulf of Bothnia service in 1977, *Bore Nord* was briefly owned by Bore Line in part payment for *Bore* and passed to Godby Shipping, for which she never sailed under her intended name *Minisea*. The following year she was sold to Caribbean Shipping Co, Panama, which converted her back to the pure passenger ship *Baltic Star*, with new cabins and a prominent saloon aft. She sailed between Stockholm and Mariehamn and in 1982 was re-engined in Frederikshavn with a four-cylinder 2,480-bhp Alpha diesel, which six years later was replaced with a 3,600-bhp MAN unit giving 16 knots. In 2002, she reverted to her original name of *Birger Jarl* when bought by Rederi Allandia A/B of Stockholm and three years later was transferred to Rederi A/B Birger Jarl. With a new modern foremast she is still sailing in her sixtieth year in 2013.

CHAPTER
10

The Final Years

Despite currency restrictions hindering widespread foreign travel in post-war Europe, the market for traditional foot passengers was still large enough to warrant the construction of new ships. The majority of these were destined to be the last of their line as steadily increasing car ownership was leading ferry companies to switch to building specialised car ferries with bow and stern loading doors.

The final traditional passenger ferries appeared in the 1960s – British Rail's *Avalon* of 1963 was the last and largest of all the railway-owned turbine steamers, while Belgium's *Prinses Paola* of 1966 was the last of a long line of motorships built for Dover Strait service.

As an interim measure between conventional passenger ferries and and passenger-carrying car ferries, some companies favoured converting existing tonnage to stern loaders while others opted for side-loading car ferries that retained conventional looks. The latter concept had been developed in Canada and was employed in several ships including DFDS' stylish *England* of 1964, two pairs of Isle of Man sisters – one steam, one diesel – and Spain's *Juan March* and *Antonio Lazaro* series.

Note: An asterisk in a caption indicates the vessel shown in the photograph.

Last traditional North Sea passenger ferry

Completed by Swan, Hunter & Wigham Richardson, Wallsend, in April 1954, the 6,670-grt *Leda** was the last conventional passenger ship built for Bergen Line's service to Newcastle. Sailing twice weekly each way year-round with a call at Stavanger, she measured 436.7 oa × 57.2 ft and was basically an improved *Vega* with a large single funnel and tripod foremast. Aluminium was used in her superstructure to reduce weight and electric cranes replaced kingposts and derricks, while sixty-four cars could be carried in her holds. Diesel propulsion was dropped in favour of two sets of Parsons double-reduction geared steam turbines made by Wallsend Slipway, fed by two oil-fired Babcock & Wilcox boilers, and the power output was 13,000 shp for a service speed of 22 knots. She was the first North Sea passenger vessel to be stabilised and could berth 119 first- and 384 tourist-class passengers. Early in 1954, she made a record passage between Newcastle and Stavanger in sixteen hours and twenty-seven minutes berth to berth. In the mid-1960s, a third crossing was added during peak seasons, but in the early 1970s the winter service was reduced to a weekly departure between September and May. Withdrawn in autumn 1974, she was laid up in Bergen and replaced by the chartered *England*. In 1977 *Leda* was sold to Stord Vaerft to accommodate shipyard staff and in 1979 was resold to Kuwait Livestock Trading & Transport and renamed *Najla*. Conversion to a livestock carrier was shelved and from May 1979 to September 1980,

she served as an accommodation ship at Stornoway. After a brief lay-up in Kristiansand, she was bought in 1981 by Dolphin (Hellas) Shipping, Piraeus, and renamed *Albatros*. At Perama she was converted into the 484-passenger cruise ship *Alegro*. A winter programme in South America failed and she returned to Piraeus. In 1985 she sailed as *Albatross* on a Mediterranean and northern European cruise programme and later that year offered a series of Florida–Brazil cruises for American Star Cruises as *Betsy Ross* but poor demand saw her move instead to a Venice–Piraeus programme. A winter series of

Indian Ocean cruises from Durban in 1988–9 failed and she returned to Venice but for the next two summers was operated as *Amalfi* by Star Lauro. Bought by Stargas in late 1990, she was renamed *Star of Venice* in 1991 for Star Cruise Line but she was damaged by fire and after repairs became a floating police hostel at Genoa and then Pianosa. Her final cruise venture for Mediterranean Cruises in 1998–9 proved disastrous due to her poor condition and she was briefly used as a hotel ship at Ravenna before tow to Aliaga and scrapping in 2002–3.

The Union Steamship Co of New Zealand's 7,480-grt turbo-electric *Maori* was built by Vickers-Armstrongs, Newcastle, to replace *Rangatira* on the eleven-hour Wellington–Lyttelton crossing. Launched on 27 November 1952, she measured 455.5 oa × 63.5 ft and her two sets of steam turbines drove two 5,120 kW electric generators connected to two electric motors, the whole developing 13,000 shp for a potential service speed of 19 knots (21.5 knots on trials), although only 17 knots was required for the overnight run. Berths were supplied for 969 passengers in 395 cabins, the majority two-berth, and some seventy cars could be accommodated in her holds or on deck. Her exterior profile was unique with a large goalpost mast mounted on the forecastle, a tall tripod mast forward of a very large funnel with rounded top and a pair of tall kingposts placed well aft. Her delivery voyage took her via the Panama Canal and she arrived in Wellington on 15 November 1954. On 26 December 1959 she made her one and only visit to Picton to pick up passengers from the grounded *Rangatira*. Continuing growth in car ownership and competition from the new New Zealand railway-owned car ferries on the Picton service persuaded the USSNZ to change to a drive-on/drive-off operation and *Maori* was sent to Hong Kong in April 1963 for conversion to a stern-loading car ferry. The then largest ship to be so treated, part of her interior was gutted to create garage space for around 100 cars, while the after posts were replaced by a tripod mast and a bow thruster installed to enhance manoeuvrability. The changes reduced gross registered tonnage to 7,298 and passenger berths to 790. Replaced by a new *Rangatira*, she was laid up in reserve in Wellington on 27 March 1972 but was reactivated that autumn when her new consort suffered turbine problems. Various plans for her future use were put forward including one by the 'Youth with a Mission' organisation to use her as a

missionary ship named *Agape* (Love) in the Pacific but all came to nothing and she was sold in 1974 to Wiltopps (Asia) of Hong Kong for a proposed Hong Kong–Taiwan service. While *en route* to Hong Kong in tow, she was resold and taken instead to Kaohsiung, where she arrived on 6 March for demolition.

Spanish trio

The 5,195-grt *Playa de Formentor* was delivered to Empresa Nacional Elcano by Union Navale de Levante, Valencia, in February 1955, but after two introductory cruises was bought, together with an incomplete sister, by Compania Trasmediterranea. She entered service (in Elcano colours) from Barcelona to Palma in June 1956 and was renamed *Ciudad de Barcelona* in December. Her sister, which had been launched as *Playa de Palmanova*, joined her as *Ciudad de Burgos* the following February after achieving a maximum of 18.5 knots on trial and the pair offered a daily overnight departure in each direction. They measured 348 oa x 51 ft on a draught of 16.5 ft and were driven by two B & W seven-cylinder diesel engines developing 5,300 bhp for a normal speed of 15 knots for a ten-hour passage. Passenger capacity was 708 and around sixteen cars and two coaches could be carried in a small garage accessed through side doors at the aft end of the main deck. *Ciudad de Burgos* made occasional trips from Barcelona to the Canary Islands and also sailed between Palma and Valencia in 1960, but in December the following year a third sister *Ciudad de Granada** was delivered and after a few voyages on the Palma run replaced the old *Ciudad de Ibiza* on the twice weekly Palma–Valencia service, which was increased to thrice

weekly in summer 1965. After new ships took over the Palma service in 1966–7, *Ciudad de Barcelona* was transferred to the Ibiza and Mahon routes and *Ciudad de Burgos* to the Palma–Alicante service. In 1975 *Ciudad de Granada* was sent to the Canaries for inter-island service and was briefly joined by *Ciudad de Burgos* four years later, after which the latter moved to the Barcelona–Mahon station until scrapped in

Villanueva y Geltru late in 1980. *Ciudad de Barcelona* was withdrawn around the same time and laid up in Palma but after offers from Far East and South African buyers came to nothing she was broken up in 1982. Plans to sell *Ciudad de Granada* for Persian Gulf service also failed and she was sold to Shatley Mercantile, Panama and broken up as *City of Salt* at San Pedro del Pinatar near Murcia in 1984.

Canadian side-loaders

Canadian National Railways took delivery of two new side-loading car ferries in 1955. The 6,419-grt twin-screw *Bluenose** was built by Davie Shipbuilding & Repairing Co, Lauzon, for a new daily round-trip service linking Yarmouth, Nova Scotia, with Bar Harbour, Maine. She measured 345.7 oa x 66 ft on a draught of 16.5 ft and was driven at 18.5 knots by six Fairbanks-Morse twelve-cylinder diesels developing 11,160 bhp. She could accommodate 600 passengers (thirty in cabins) and up to 150 cars on the upper car deck and a mix of truck and trailers on the specially strengthened lower deck. Her all-welded aluminium superstructure was one of the largest in existence at the time and she was fitted with Denny-Brown stabilisers to aid passenger comfort. Her original blue white and red funnel was repainted red with white C N superimposed and hull became pale blue. She was renamed *Marine Bluenose* in 1983, adopting CN's new livery of dark blue hull and funnel, the latter carrying a new logo in white. After twenty-eight years in service, she was withdrawn and reduced to an accommodation hulk at Groton. The larger *William Carson* was a product of Canadian Vickers, Montreal and measured 8,273 grt on overall dimensions of 350.7 x 68 ft and draught of 19.2 ft. Diesel electric machinery provided a service speed of 15 knots and

was based on the icebreaker principle with twin screws aft and a third screw forward for icebreaking and manoeuvring. The three DC propulsion motors received current from six 1,375 kW generators powered by six twelve-cylinder opposed piston Fairbanks-Morse diesel engines with an output of 12,000 bhp. Passenger capacity was 262 and she could carry a mix of fifty-eight cars, six trucks and two buses. She was stabilised and fitted with bow jets

for harbour manoeuvring. Her intended route joined North Sydney, Nova Scotia and Port aux Basques, Newfoundland across the Cabot Strait, but the latter port's facilities were not ready and she sailed to Argentia for the first three years. In 1976 she was transferred to Labrador for the seasonal Lewisport–Happy Valley–Goose Bay run but foundered without loss of life on 2 June 1977, twelve miles off Battle Harbour after hitting a small iceberg.

Belgian trio

The Belgian Marine Administration ordered three new mail ships from Cockerill-Ougree in 1954 in anticipation of an increased in traffic arising from the 1958 World Expo in Brussels. *Roi Leopold III*, *Koningin Elisabeth* and *Reine Astrid** were very similar to the earlier *Koning Albert* pair in overall design but were fitted with tripod masts and a Lascroux type funnel with sloping top and large vents to help disperse fumes clear of the after decks. They measured 3,795 grt and at 373.7 ft oa were the same length as *Koning Albert*, but their beam of 47.5 ft was 1 ft broader. The same twelve-cylinder Sulzer diesels were employed, developing 17,000 bhp for a speed of 23.5 knots. To reduce top weight, aluminium was used in the construction of the funnel, bridge and upper superstructure and *Reine Astrid* was the first Belgian cross-channel ship to be fitted with stabilisers. Maximum passenger complement was around 1,700 in two classes. Delivered in July 1956, autumn 1957 and May 1958 respectively, they formed the mainstay of the Ostend mail route for the next twenty years

and in 1974 adopted RTM's new funnel colours of pale yellow with a blue RTM logo and a thin black top. In 1978 *Roi Leopold III* was sold to Najd Shipping Co, Jeddah and renamed *Najd* (Sea) and *Koningin Elisabeth* to Abha Marine Co, Limassol but the following year she went to Najd Shipping and was renamed *Najd II*. In 1981 their owner was restyled

Najd Trading & Construction Co and *Najd II* was broken up at Eleusis in 1984. Her sister went to Gadani Beach in March 1987 for demolition. In the meantime, *Reine Astrid* had been hulked at Flushing in 1985 and her mid-section converted for use as a passenger terminal in Dover for RTM's new jetfoil service. (*J Mannering*)

Final Irish Sea railway ferries

The 4,797-grt sisters *Duke of Lancaster*, *Duke of Argyll** and *Duke of Rothesay* were completed for the British Transport Commission's Midland Region (British Railways) in 1956 – the first two by Harland & Wolff, Belfast and the last by Wm Denny & Bros, Dumbarton. The last conventional cross-channel steamers to be built for Irish Sea service, they measured 376 oa x 57.4 ft on a draught of 14.7 ft and were fitted with stabilisers. Up to 1,800 passengers were carried in two classes in addition to a number of crane-loaded cars in the two forward holds and 'tween-decks. Propulsion was by two sets of Pametrada double-reduction geared steam

turbines developing 10,750 shp for a speed of 21 knots and steam was supplied by by two Babcock & Wilcox oil-fired watertube boilers. They maintained a year-round overnight service between Heysham and Belfast, but only sailed on Sundays during the summer. *Duke of Lancaster* was designed for off-season cruising with 350 passengers and could be quickly converted for this role. Between June 1958 and 14 September 1966 she visited Norway, Denmark, the Iberian Peninsula and Scotland's western isles, sometimes sailing from Plymouth, and some cruises lasted thirteen days. During winter overhauls in 1964–5, all three had the second-class accommodation improved

and were repainted in the new British Rail livery. In 1965–6, *Duke of Rothesay* performed relief work for a few weeks on the Holyhead–Dun Laoghaire service but early in 1967 was converted to a car ferry by Cammell Laird for the Fishguard–Rosslare route. Her accommodation was modernised and 100 cars could be driven onto her new car deck via side doors. Her sisters were more substantially converted to stern-loaders in winter 1969–70 and the following May inaugurated a new drive-on/drive off service to Belfast, which was discontinued in April 1975. *Duke of Argyll* was sold that October to the A G Yannoulatos-owned Cynthia Navigation and ran as *Neptunia* on a variety of Mediterranean services. *Duke of Rothesay* was mainly used as a reserve ship and was broken up at the end of 1975 by Shipbreaking Industries at Faslane. In 1979 *Duke of Lancaster* was acquired by Empirewise of Liverpool and was permanently beached at Llanerch-y-Mor near Mostyn but projected use as a hotel/leisure centre named *Duke of Llanerch-y-Mor* never materialised and she has continued to deteriorate ever since. In 1987 *Neptunia* was acquired by Scanmed Shipping, Malta and renamed *Corinthia* for Hellenic Mediterranean Lines but was sold East in 1993, becoming Power Sea Transportation's Panamanian-flagged *Faith Power* and *Fairy Princess* the following year. In 1995 she was sold to Galaxy Shipholding of Panama and renamed *Zenith*, but was beached after catching fire off Hong Kong on 19 July and was broken up at Zhongshan in 1996.

Handsome pair for Copenhagen–Oslo service

In March 1955, Det Forenede D/S (United Steamship Co) placed an order with Elsinore Shipbuilding & Engineering Co for a new ship for its overnight Copenhagen–Oslo service. Of advanced design, the 5,061-grt *Prinsesse Margrethe** measured 397 oa × 53 ft on a draught of 16 ft and was completed in May 1957. Her twin eight-cylinder B & W engines were placed well aft, exhausting through the mainmast, and produced 7,300 bhp for a service speed of 20.5

knots. She was the first Danish ship to be fitted with stabilisers and was distinguished by her light and airy open-plan interiors. Overnight berths were supplied for 395 and maximum capacity was for 1,200 persons in addition to thirty-five cars, loaded through a side door. Her success led to the commissioning of a sister, *Kong Olav V*, in 1961 and they settled into a regular routine, departing both capitals at 4.00pm and arriving around 8.00am the following day. It was not

long before lack of garage space became a problem and in 1968 they were replaced by new ro-ro car ferries, *Kong Olav V* becoming *Olav* and then *Taiwan* following her sale to China Navigation Co in 1969 for a Hong Kong–Keelung cruise service, where she proved somewhat lively during the north-east monsoon. *Prinsesse Margrethe* sailed between Esjberg and Newcastle as *Prinsessen* until sold to the Åland Islands-based Rederi A/B Flipper in 1971, which changed the final *c* in her name to an *a*. She sailed between Mariehamn and Stockholm and the following year was transferred to Birka Line, which had acquired her sister, renamed *Baronessan*, after her Far East route had been superseded by air travel. *Prinsessan* was renamed *Prinsen* in 1977 and the following year was sold to Jeddah-based Fayez Trading & Shipping. She sailed in the pilgrim trade between Port Tewfik and Jeddah as *Wid* until broken up by at Alang in 1987. *Baronessan* returned to Eastern waters for a second time early in 1981, initially as Yick Fung's *Min Fung* under Panama flag and then as China Ocean Shipping's *Ji Mei*. Her name was changed to *Nan Hu* when transferred to Fujian Province in 1983 and she retained this under Guangdong Province ownership (Hong Kong & Macao Navigation Co) from 1985. She was finally broken up in 2000.

Last traditional Channel Islands ferries

The 4,174-grt *Caesarea** and *Sarnia* were delivered to the British Transport Commission's Southern Region (British Railways) by J Samuel White & Co, East Cowes, in 1960–1. The last traditional passenger ferries built for the Weymouth–Channel Islands service, they were developments of *Normannia*, with large windows on the upper deck, glazed screening at the forward end of the boat deck, a flying bridge and lifeboats carried in gravity davits. They measured 322 oa × 51 ft on a draught of 17.5 ft, propulsion being by two sets of Pametrada double-reduction turbines developing a maximum of 9,000 shp for 20 knots in service. One-class ships, they were stabilised and carried 1,400 passengers with overnight berths provided for 110 in addition to aircraft type seats which were increased by 146 in 1971. *Sarnia* replaced *Invicta* on the Golden Arrow service from 19 November 1962 to 30 January 1963 and *Caesarea* did likewise in 1966–7. After car ferries were introduced to the Channel Islands, *Caesarea* was transferred to the Dover–Calais route in 1976, switching to Folkestone–Boulogne the following year. *Sarnia* sailed in summer only and in May 1978 was sold to Channel Cruise Lines of Guernsey, renamed *Aquamart* and refitted at Grimsby for 'duty-free'

shopping trips between Ostend and Dunkirk. Four round voyages a day were planned but strong objections by the Belgian tax authorities led to its closure after only a few days. She was bought by Supersave Supermarkets and laid up in London's West India Docks on 4 August but was sold to Grecian Fertility Inc and towed to Greece as *Golden Star* by the Dutch tug *Groenland* the following January, just missing her sister, which was drydocked at Millwall a few days later. After completing her 1980 season, *Caesarea* undertook a week of special

excursions from Dover to Boulogne, her final trip being an RNLI charter from Folkestone on 4 October. Laid up in Newhaven, she sailed for Hong Kong as *Aesarea* on 17 December but her new owner, Superluck Enterprises, appear not to have used her although she was repainted with first a red then yellow funnel and white hull before being scrapped in 1985. *Sarnia*, which had been sold to Hitta Establishment, Jeddah, in 1981 and renamed *Saudi Golden Star*, outlived her by a couple of years before she was demolished at Gadani Beach in 1987.

Zeeland Line's last conventional ferry

The 6,228-grt motor vessel *Koningin Wilhelmina** was the last traditional channel steamer built for Stoomvaart Maatschappij Zeeland (Zeeland Line), but her design was unique because it incorporated a streamlined bridge front, single heavily raked stump mast and long low funnel placed well aft. Launched on 5 June 1959, she was completed by De Merwede, Hardinxveld, early in 1960 and replaced *Mecklenburg* on the daytime Hook–Harwich service on 7 February. Her hull measured 393.7 oa × 56.7 ft and had a raised forecastle merging into the superstructure and a cruiser stern. Main machinery was placed three-quarters aft and comprised twin MAN twelve-cylinder diesels developing 15,600 bhp for a service speed of 21 knots and a maximum of 23 knots. She could carry 1,600 passengers, including 700 in first class, in air-conditioned accommodation and up to forty-five cars loaded through side doors. She was the first Zeeland Line ship to be fitted with stabilisers and also had a bow thruster. The advent of Zeeland's car ferry *Koningin Juliana* in 1968 saw her downgraded to extra summer and relief sailings but her lack of garage space led to long periods of lay up in the 1970s. She was occasionally chartered for the opening of North Sea gas platforms and in 1976 was fitted with an electric bow thruster. Replaced by the car ferry *Prinses Beatrix*, she made her final departure from Parkeston Quay on 28 June 1978 and was laid up in Flushing. On 10 December she was sold to C Ventouris and renamed *Captain Constantinos* for daily service between Piraeus and Syros, Tenos and Mykonos. In 1981 her name was changed to *Panagia Tinou* (Holy Mother of Tinos) and in 1987 she was transferred briefly to A K Ventouris. Later fitted with a bulbous bow, she became the much-loved speed queen of the Aegean and from 1990 sailed under the Ventouris Sea Lines banner. In 1996, she was sold at auction to Minoan Cruises and renamed *Artemis* for day excursions from Crete to Santorini. In April 2001, she was acquired by an Honduran company and sailed as *Temis* to breakers at Alang, India.

Sweden's last steamer

Bore Line's 3,475-grt *Bore** was completed by Oskarshamns Varv, Oskarshamn in April 1960. A handsome two-funnelled ship, the forward funnel a dummy, she measured 327.5 oa × 50 ft on a draught of 16.5 ft. Designed for Stockholm–Helsinki overnight service, she could berth sixty-three first-class and 272 tourist-class passengers with a further 693 carried in deck class and had a garage for sixty-five cars accessed by two small doors on either beam and a larger door on the port side for cars and six trucks. The last steamship to be built in Sweden, she was propelled by two quadruple-expansion reciprocating engines developing 3,050 ihp for a speed of 15 knots. She sailed on both Turku–Mariehamn–Stockholm and Helsinki–Stockholm services and following the formation of Silja Line by Bore, Finland Line and Svea in 1970, her superstructure was extended fore and aft. In October 1977, she was sold to Jakob Lines of Jakobstad, in which Bore held a large share, and renamed *Borea* for a summer Gulf of Bothnia service between Jakobstad and the Swedish port of Skellefteå. Seven years later she was acquired by Ab Helsingfors Steamship Co (manager Henry Nielsen) and was laid up in Stockholm before undertaking various charters including a charter as a hotel ship in Algeria. On her return to Finland in 1984, a charter to Aura Lines for Turku–Stockholm tourist service failed after a few months and she returned to lay near Turku, a rumoured sale to Canada coming to nothing. Early in 1987, she was bought by Rannikkolinjat Oy, Kotka, a company formed by Captain Mikka Partainen and his sister, and re-engined with two 6,489-kW Wärtsilä diesels prior to conversion in winter 1988–9 into the 249-berth cruise ship *Kristina Regina* at the Holming yard in Rauma. Her former car deck was converted to a 250-seat theatre and she began making local cruises in April 1989, later extending her activities to the Baltic, northern Europe, the Mediterranean and the Red Sea. In 1992 she was refitted and re-registered to Kristina Cruises and underwent further renovations in 1999 and 2001. Her non-compliance with new SOLAS regulations in 2010 led to her withdrawal and sale to Oy SS Bore Ab for use as as a hotel/museum ship in Turku under her original name and colours and she opened in October 2010.

Final Italian motorships

The twin-screw ferries *Città di Napoli* and *Città di Nuoro** were built for Tirrenia by Navalmeccanica, Castellamare di Stabia and Riuniti, Ancona in 1961 and 1962 respectively. The largest yet for the company, they measured 5770/5,200 grt on hull dimensions of 395.3 oa × 55.2 ft with an 18 ft draught. Propelled by Fiat two-cylinder diesels developing 12,600 bhp, they had a service speed of 19.5 knots and were designed to carry 315 first-, 642 second- and 227 deck-class passengers in air-conditioned accommodation. They were stabilised to aid passenger comfort and as a result of increased demand for the transport of motor vehicles were equipped with a thirty-six-car garage aft, which was accessed by side doors and ramps. An additional fifteen vehicles could be carried on the promenade deck above. They were designed to serve Sardinia on the 139-mile Civitavecchia–Olbia route, a year-round mail service with a passage time of around seven hours. After a fairly uneventful life, both vessels were broken up at Porto Nogaro in 1988.

New side-loaders for Isle of Man

The Isle of Man Steam Packet Co took delivery of its first car ferry, *Manx Maid**, from Cammell Laird, Birkenhead, in 1962, her entry into service coinciding with a national seamen's strike that saw her laid up for six weeks at Barrow. She differed from most other car ferries in having neither bow, side nor stern doors but instead was fitted with an unusual system of spiral ramps with five access levels aft that allowed her to handle eighty light vehicles at any state of the tide alongside Douglas pier. Her gross measurement was 2,762 tons on hull dimensions of 344 oa × 50 ft and she was propelled by two sets of Pametrada double-reduction geared steam turbines developing 9,500 shp for a service speed of 21 knots. Her passenger complement was 1,400 in two classes and she was the first in the fleet to be fitted with stabilisers. A sister ship, *Ben-my-Chree*, followed in May 1966, with the main external difference that her boat deck was extended round the front of the superstructure and she did not have the traditional triple chime whistle though one was later added. From mid May to the end of June 1966 both sisters were laid up in Barrow during the seamens strike and in winter 1977–8 the 'Ben' was fitted with a steam driven bow thruster and her sister was treated likewise a year later. In 1984 'ISLE OF MAN STEAM PACKET CO' was added to their hulls in large yellow letters but both ships were withdrawn at the end of that season and laid up at Birkenhead prior to the introduction of a full roll-on/roll-off operation with *Mona's Isle*, the former Townsend *Free Enterprise III*. *Ben-my-Chree* was sold to New England Development Co, Cincinnati, for use in Jacksonville, Florida, but nothing materialised and apart from a two-week charter back to the Steam Packet Co for the 1985 TT Races she remained laid up. *Manx Maid* was sold early in 1985 and towed to Avonmouth but a plan to moor her in Bristol never came to fruition and she was towed to Garston in February 1986 and broken up. Her sister was towed to Santander in August 1989 for demolition.

The UK's last traditional railway ferry

The British Transport Commission's 6,584-grt *Avalon**, completed by Alexander Stephen & Sons, Linthouse, in July 1963, was the UK's last and largest conventional passenger ferry. She replaced *Duke of York* on the British Railways' Eastern Region Harwich–Hook of Holland service in September 1963, but because three ships were no longer required year-round, she was designed for off-season cruising. Her all-welded hull measured 404.5 oa x 59.8 ft on a draught of 15.8 ft and featured a very long combined forecastle and bridge deck that dropped down to a short mooring deck aft. Her three-deck superstructure had a curved, streamlined front and was topped by two streamlined masts and a tapered funnel with rounded smoke deflector. Fully air-conditioned accommodation was arranged on four decks for 750 passengers with berths for 331 in first and 287 in second classes and aircraft-type seating for the remainder. A few crane-loaded cars could be carried in the after hold. Her propelling machinery comprised two sets of Pametrada double-reduction turbines fed by a pair of Foster Wheeler watertube boilers and the combined output of 14,500 shp gave a service speed of 21.5 knots. She was fitted with a bow rudder, bow thrust and twin rudders aft, while stabilisers assured passenger comfort. Her spring and autumn cruises, for which she carried 320 in one class, began with a weekend excursion to Amsterdam in April 1964 and over the next few years she visited ports between Scandinavia and Tangier. On 22 August 1966, she stood in for Ellerman's Wilson's unfinished car ferry *Spero* on the Hull–Gothenburg service but after the new car ferries *St George* and *Koningin Juliana* began double sailings in autumn 1967, she was demoted to extra summer and relief work but extended her cruising activities. Displaced by *St Edmund* in late 1974, she was converted to a stern loading car ferry by Swan Hunter on Tyneside.

Reduced to 5,142 grt and carrying 1,200 day passengers and 200 cars plus a few trucks on two decks, she replaced *Caledonian Princess* on the Fishguard–Rosslare service in summer 1975. She alternated between Fishguard and Holyhead and during her final season in 1979 acted as reserve and summer extra at the latter port. Laid up in Barrow, she was sold in November 1980 to Cyprus-registered Seafaith Navigation and made a single voyage as *Valon* to Gadani Beach, where she arrived in January 1981 for demolition.

Elegant Danish side-loader

The 8,221-grt Det Forenede D/S (United Steamship Co) ferry *England** was ordered from the Elsinore shipyard in 1962 in response to rising demand for car travel. A graceful vessel with single streamlined funnel fitted with deflector fins, her design owed much to *Prinsesse Margrethe* with a distinctive observation lounge above the bridge. Although retaining a traditional bow and stern, she was fitted with a car deck for 100 cars accessed by side doors fore and aft. Her easily-driven hull form was developed from the Portuguese liner *Funchal* and she she measured 459.2 oa x 63.5 ft on a draught of 18.2 ft. Twin B & W ten-cylinder diesels developing 14,000 bhp assured a service speed of 21 knots. She carried up to 155 first-class and 244 second-class passengers in light and airy public rooms and was fitted with stabilisers and a sprinkler fire-protection system. She entered service in 1964, bringing new standards to the company's traditional North Sea route and in May 1967 was joined by the similar Italian-built *Winston Churchill*, which adopted the full drive-through principle with bow and stern doors. That winter, *England* made a number of one-class cruises from Copenhagen to the Caribbean, for which she was fitted with a swimming pool, and West Africa. From autumn 1970, she commenced short stints on the Copenhagen–Oslo route and early in 1971 her passenger capacity was increased to 566 in a refit at Aalborg. Replaced by the larger car ferry *Dana Regina* in 1974, she was transferred to the summer only Esbjerg–Torshavn–Newcastle service with sixty-eight new berths and space for an additional twenty cars. There followed a winter charter to Bergen Line and after a final season in 1982 she was laid up in Esbjerg. She was sold in September 1983 to Cunard Line for a two-year contract to shuttle airport construction workers between Cape Town and the Falkland Islands. In 1986 she was bought by the Latsis group and as *America XIII* served for eight months as an accommodation ship in Jeddah. She returned to Piraeus for lay-up and her name was changed to *Emma* in 1987. In 1988 she was again renamed, to *Europa*, after which John Latsis began to convert her into his private yacht. Work was discontinued and as *Europe* she was lost off Aden in April 2001 while in tow to Alang for demolition.

Last conventional River Plate ferries

Completed in October 1964 by Sociedad Espanola de Constr. Naval, Matagorda, the 6,497-grt blue-hulled sisters *Ciudad de Buenos Aires* and *33 Orientales* were the last traditional passenger ferries built for Buenos Aires–Montevideo service. They measured 427.5 oa × 56.7 ft with a shallow 13 ft draught and were propelled by twin ten-cylinder B & W diesels developing 7,800 bhp for a maximum of 18 knots and 15 knots in service, passenger complement being 792 passengers. In 1966 their ownership changed to EFFEA and in 1976–7, *33 Orientales* was used by the military junta to house political prisoners. She cruised to Brazil in 1978 and both ships were sold in 1979: *Ciudad de Buenos Aires* to Yick Fung Shipping & Enterprises, a Panamanian front company for the People's Republic of China, and was renamed *Ming Yi*. This changed to *Gu Lang Yu* when she was transferred to China Ocean Shipping later the same year but in 1984 she was again transferred, first to Fujian Province Shipping, Xiamen and then to Guangdong Province Hong Kong & Macau Navigation which renamed her *Tong Hu*. Ten years later she was re-registered to Guangdong Shantou Navigation, Guangzhou and in 2001 to Shantou Navigation Corporation, Shantou. She was believed to have been moored in Hong Kong in 2004 but her eventual fate is obscure and she was deleted from the Lloyd's

Register book in 2010. Her sister was sold to Atlantis Naviera of Greece and was converted to the 503-passenger cruise ship *City of Rhodos* in 1980. She operated in the Aegean for Cycladic Cruises until 1992 when she was laid up at Eleusis. Two years later she was sold to Vergina Cruises and renamed *Queen Eleni* but did not reenter service until 1996. She changed hands again in 2000, becoming first

Navigation Marathon's Cyprus-registered *Queen Constantina* and then Legend Cruises' *Joywave*. The following year she reverted to *Queen Constantina* and cruised between Lebanon and the Greek Islands, but Navigation Maritime went bankrupt and she was laid up in Limassol. She was sold for scrap and as *Forest* sailed to Alang, India, where she was beached on 27 June.

Last of long line of Belgian packets

Entering service in 1966, Belgian Marine Administration's *Prinses Paola** was the last conventional cross-channel passenger ferry and at 4,356 grt, was also the largest to have sailed on the Dover Strait, eclipsing the Southern Railway's *Invicta* by over 500 tons. The ninth motorship and thirty-second mail ship built for the Ostend–Dover service by the Cockerill yard at Hoboken, she marked the peak of design for this particular type of vessel. She measured 394.2 oa × 52 ft and was the first passenger ship to be propelled by the new Sulzer RD44 turbocharged diesel, in her case two twelve-cylinder units with a normal rating of 15,000 bhp for 22 knots but she was capable of 24 knots if pushed. Her 1,700 passengers, 600 in first-class, enjoyed air-conditioned public rooms and she was fitted with stabilisers to reduce rolling. In 1974 she was repainted in RTM's new Sealink livery, which, as so often in rebranding exercises, did little for her looks. By the early 1980s, car ferries were handing most of the traffic and she only sailed in summer with the occasional bank holiday and special outing in winter. Her hull colour was changed to orange with Townsend Thoresen in large white letters in 1987 and she made her final crossing on 25 September that

year. Early in 1988, she was sold to Sea Venture Cruises and renamed *Tropicana* and sailed to Perama in Greece for alteration to a day cruise ship, which involved extending the boat deck and fitting two large launches in davits abreast the mainmast. She sailed daily out of Miami that summer and in 1990 operated from St Petersburg, Florida on charter to

Sea Escape and then from Freeport, Texas as *Sea Palace* for Freeport Cruise Lines. In 1991 she became Winston Cruise Lines' *Saint Lucie* but reverted to *Tropicana* when acquired by Jubilee of the Bahamas Inc in 1994. After operating for two more years she was laid up in various US east coast ports and in 2006 was sold to Indian breakers at Alang.

Side-loading car ferries for Spanish routes

Compania Trasmediterranea took delivery of two pairs of large ferries in 1966–7: *Juan March** and *Las Palmas de Gran Canaria* from Union Navale de Levante, Valencia, and *Santa Cruz de Teneriffe* and *Ciudad de Compostela* from Sociedad Espanola de Constr Naval, Sestao. They measured 429.2 oa × 63 ft with a draught of 16.3 ft and were propelled by twin B & W two-stroke diesels developing a maximum of 16,000 bhp for a service speed of 21 knots. Manoeuvrability was aided by a KaMeWa bow thruster and controllable-pitch propellers. As built, they had 500 berths and 250 aircraft type seats, a deck swimming pool and a large garage for around 100 cars loaded through side doors. They sailed on their owners Palma, North Africa and Canary Islands services, but their inability to carry trucks counted against them and they were relegated to lesser routes when replaced by new car ferries in the late 1970s. By the early 1980s, they were mainly used as relief ships but *Ciudad de Compostela* inaugurated a new Sete–Palma–Ibiza service in 1982. She acted as a relief ship until 1992, when she was bought by Libton Shipping, Malta, and renamed first *European Star* and then *Saray Star* in 1994 but a galley fire on 13 June *en route* from Piraeus to Venice led to her being abandoned some twenty-eight miles north of Cephalonia and she sank after the fire spread. Her three sisters were sold in 1985: *Juan March* and *Santa Cruz de Teneriffe* went to Cyprus-based Sun Mediterranean Lines and were renamed *Sol Christiania* and *Sol Olympia II* respectively. The latter was destroyed by fire while in drydock at Eleusis on 6 June 1986, her hull being towed to Aliaga in September 1987 for demolition. *Sol Christiania* was renamed *Kypros Star* by Health Shipping, Limassol, in 1986 for Opale Line service between Piraeus and Alexandria. Sold to the Kollakis Group (Chios Breeze Shipping) in 1989 and renamed *Ocean Majesty*, she underwent a lengthy conversion to a 535-berth cruise ship before emerging in 1994 with new Wärtsilä medium-speed diesels and gross tonnage increased to 10,417. She was chartered to Epirotiki as *Olympic* and then *Homeric* before reverting to *Ocean Majesty* in 1995, since when she has operated in the international charter market and is still sailing under Portuguese (Madeira) registry in 2013. The third sister disposed of in 1985 was *Las Palmas de Gran Canaria*, which was returned to her builders for conversion to a cruise ship, her garage being replaced by cabins and public rooms and a three-deck atrium installed. She reentered service in 1988 as the 9,725-grt *Crown del Mar* and operated Caribbean cruises for around 400 passengers on charter to Crown Cruises. She returned to Spain in late 1991 and after a four-year lay up in Barcelona was bought back by Compania Trasmediterranea and towed to Cartagena for a $5 million refit, emerging with a clipper bow and dark blue hull. She operated as *Don Juan* for Royal Hispanic Cruises on weekly summer cruises from Barcelona and was based in the Canaries in winter. In 2000 she became *Riviera 1* and in 2005 *Royal Pacific* but caught fire at Kaohsiung on 29 June and capsized the following day, later being broken up.

Compania Trasmediterranea's 4,912-grt *Antonio Lazaro* and *Vicente Puchol**, completed by Union Navale de Levante, Valencia in 1968, were the only two built of an originally planned series of four. The last traditional passenger ferries to be built in Europe, they measured 350.7 oa × 53.5 ft on 16.7 ft draught and their funnel design echoed that of the *Juan March* series, but they lacked the latter's bow thruster and stabilisers. They mainly ran on the Malaga/Almeria–Melilla services and occasionally on Balearic Islands routes carrying up to 600 passengers, fifty cars and three coaches (loaded through side doors) but lack of ro-ro capacity caused them to be offered for sale in 1983. They were inspected and rejected by Sol Lines of Cyprus in 1984, but in December 1986 *V Puchol* was bought by Attika Cruises and renamed *Arcadia*. An option on her sister was exercised in September 1987, but after becoming *Argo* in 1988 she was quickly sold to Educational Book Exhibits and rebuilt as the sea-going library *Logos II*. She spent the next eighteen years visiting 186 ports in eighty-two countries and was broken up at Aliaga in Turkey in 2008. *Arcadia*'s conversion to a 350-passenger cruise ship was delayed by a fire at Perama in March 1988, but she emerged in 1990

with modernised mast and funnels and a swimmimg pool and was chartered to Star Lauro as *Angelina Lauro* with a dark blue blue hull. She made weekly cruises from Venice to the Aegean in 1990–1, but in 1992 reverted to *Arcadia* and ran Aegean cruises with a white hull and red band, diverting west for two cruises to Expo 92 in Seville from Barcelona and Valencia. From 1997, she sailed for Golden Sun Cruises and in 2001 was chartered for a series of Great Lakes cruises, but was arrested in Montreal. The following year she was renamed *Caribic Star* for short

Caribbean cruises but when these failed she was laid up in the Dominican Republic. In mid-2005, she became C & C Marine's *Coco Explorer 2* but a series of Far East cruises also failed and she passed to Inluck International Cruises of Taiwan in 2006 and two years later to Esteban Tajanlangit, who changed her name to *7107 Islands Cruise* for wreck-diving cruises to Palawan in the Philippines. In May 2009, she was seized by customs in Manila for non-payment of import duties and was laid up.

Final Isle of Man side-loader

The Isle of Man Steam Packet Co's first diesel-driven passenger ship, *Mona's Queen* (V), was completed by Ailsa Shipbuilding Co, Troon, in 1971. A development of *Manx Maid* with similar spiral car-loading arrangement aft, she had a 500-bhp thrust and twin rudders aft as well as the obligatory bow rudder to aid manoeuvring. Her twin ten-cylinder Crossley/Pielstick diesels, mounted well aft and exhausting through the mainmast, drove controllable-pitch propellers and developed a maximum output of 10,000 bhp for 22 knots on trial. She measured 2,998 grt on dimensions of 343 oa × 52 ft and was designed to carry around 100 cars and 1,600 passengers. In 1974 she inaugurated a new car ferry service to Dublin and another to Fleetwood in June 1976, the same month that sister *Lady of Mann** was delivered by the Ailsa yard. Distinguished by four windows below the bridge instead of her sister's three, she had an extra two cylinders that increased output to over 11,500 bhp and maximum speed to 23 knots. The pair operated year-round and in winter 1988–9 *Lady of Mann* was rebuilt with improved accommodation for 1,000 passengers and a second car deck for a further thirty cars, raising her gross tonnage to 3,084. They undertook brief charters elsewhere, *Mona's Queen* in the English Channel (French Post Office and Sealink, 1989) and Holyhead (B & I, 1989 and Sealink, 1990). *Mona's Queen* was laid up in 1994 and sold in December 1995 to to MBRS Lines, Manila, operating as *Mary the Queen* on

Philippines coastal services until broken up at Alang in 2008. After assisting during the busy TT Races period in 1995, *Lady of Mann* sailed in July for Madeira on a three-month charter on PS Line's Funchal–Porto Santo service, which was extended to mid-November. From June 1997 to March 1998 she operated a Liverpool–Dublin service before undertaking a four-month charter in the Azores. This arrangement continued until 2005 with winter lay-ups

in the UK, although she did operate Liverpool–Douglas winter sailings in 2003–4. In September 2005, she was sold to Saos Lines of Samothrace and renamed *Panagia Soumela*. Rebuilt with a stern door aft and with a dark blue hull, she was registered to Dafnes Shipping and sailed between Lavrion and Limnos until broken up at Aliaga in 2011.

Appendix
Distances in nautical miles (approximate)

North Sea

Newcastle–Bergen (direct)	400
Newcastle–Stavanger	350
Newcastle–Kristiansand	370
Hull–Kristiansand	409
Hull–Zeebrugge	207
Grimsby–Rotterdam	198
Gothenburg–Tilbury	577
Copenhagen–Oslo	272
Esbjerg–Newcastle	343
Esbjerg–Harwich	338
Harwich–Hook of Holland	116
Harwich–Rotterdam	117
Harwich–Antwerp	157
Harwich–Flushing	95
Gravesend–Rotterdam	160

English Channel

Dover–Calais	22
Dover–Boulogne	26
Dover–Ostend (high tide/low tide)	61/64
Folkestone–Boulogne	26
Folkestone–Calais	25
Folkestone–Dunkirk	42
Newhaven–Dieppe	64
Southampton–Le Havre	104
Southampton–Caen	114
Southampton–Cherbourg	83
Southampton–Guernsey	103
Southampton–St Malo	150
Weymouth–Guernsey	70
Guernsey–Jersey	28

Irish Sea

Milford–Cork	139
Fishguard–Cork	140
Fishguard–Rosslare	54
Holyhead–Kingstown (Dun Laoghaire)	53
Holyhead–Dublin	58
Holyhead–Greenore	75
Liverpool–Cork	252
Liverpool–Dublin	122
Liverpool–Belfast	136
Douglas–Liverpool	70
Douglas–Fleetwood	58
Douglas–Belfast	80
Douglas–Ardrossan	124
Douglas–Dublin	83
Heysham–Belfast	137

Heysham–Douglas	58
Stranraer–Larne	35
Ardrossan–Belfast	75
Glasgow–Belfast	113
Glasgow–Londonderry	144
Glasgow–Dublin	188

Mediterranean

Malaga–Melilla	114
Almeria–Melilla	96
Alicante–Palma	166
Barcelona–Palma	133
Barcelona–Ibiza	309
Port Vendres–Oran	542
Port Vendres–Algiers	518
Marseilles–Algiers	410
Marseilles–Oran	534
Marseilles–Tunis	472
Marseilles–Ajaccio	185
Nice–Ajaccio	133
Genoa–Porto Torres	214
Genoa–Olbia	256
Livorno–Olbia	201
Civitaveccia–Olbia	139
Naples–Cagliari	263
Naples–Palermo	167
Valletta–Syracuse	84
Brindisi–Port Said	928

Australasia

Melbourne–Launceston	246
Wellington–Picton	58
Wellington–Lyttelton	174

Japan

Aomori–Hakodate	59
Nagasaki–Shanghai	540
Shimonoseki–Pusan	121

The Americas

Vancouver–Victoria	74
Vancouver–Seattle	126
Victoria–Seattle	70
Buenos Aires–Montevideo	129
Boston–Yarmouth NS	237
Bar Harbour–Yarmouth NS	100
Saint John–Digby NS	41
Charlottetown–Pictou	52
Buenos Aires–Montevideo	129

Index